Holding On

Holding On

Family and Fatherhood during Incarceration and Reentry

Tasseli McKay, Megan Comfort, Christine Lindquist, and Anupa Bir

UNIVERSITY OF CALIFORNIA PRESS

University of California Press, one of the most
distinguished university presses in the United States,
enriches lives around the world by advancing scholarship
in the humanities, social sciences, and natural sciences. Its
activities are supported by the UC Press Foundation and
by philanthropic contributions from individuals and
institutions. For more information, visit www.ucpress.edu.

University of California Press
Oakland, California

© 2019 by Research Triangle Institute, d/b/a/ RTI
International

Library of Congress Cataloging-in-Publication Data

Names: McKay, Tasseli, 1978– author. | Comfort, Megan,
 author. | Lindquist, Christine, author. | Bir, Anupa,
 author.
Title: Holding on : family and fatherhood during
 incarceration and reentry / Tasseli McKay, Megan
 Comfort, Christine Lindquist, and Anupa Bir.
Description: Oakland, California : University of
 California Press, [2019] | Includes bibliographical
 references and index. |
Identifiers: LCCN 2018058270 (print) | LCCN 2019000208
 (ebook) | ISBN 9780520973312 (ebook) | ISBN
 9780520305243 (cloth : alk. paper) | ISBN 9780520305250
 (pbk. : alk. paper)
Subjects: LCSH: Male prisoners—Family relationships—
 United States. | Prisoners' families. | Fathers—Effect
 of imprisonment on.
Classification: LCC HV8886.U6 (ebook) | LCC HV8886.U6
 M35 2019 (print) | DDC 362.82/950973—dc23
LC record available at https://lccn.loc.gov/2018058270

Manufactured in the United States of America

28 27 26 25 24 23 22 21 20 19
10 9 8 7 6 5 4 3 2 1

CONTENTS

List of Illustrations vii

Acknowledgments xi

1. Returning Incarcerated Fathers to the Family

   1

2. "Always Having Hope": What We (Didn't) Know about Fatherhood and Incarceration

   20

3. "I Do, but I Don't, Know Where We Are": Couple Relationships during Incarceration and Reentry

   44

4. "None of the Above": Partner Violence and the Limitations of Research

   63

5. "Change Ain't Going to Happen Overnight": Operationalizing Reentry Success

   88

6. "A Breakthrough Type of Thing": Measuring the Impact of Family-Strengthening Programs during Incarceration and Reentry
107

7. On the Horizon: The Social Science of Incarceration and Family Life
129

Appendix 141

References 185

Index 207

ILLUSTRATIONS

FIGURES

1. Multi-site Family Study data collection *18*
2. Father-child coresidence and financial support, before incarceration and after release *25*
3. Factors that promoted father-child coresidence after release *26*
4. Factors that promoted father-child financial support after release *26*
5. Change (and stability) in father-child activities, before incarceration and after release *30*
6. Proportion of men and women who reported that the couple was in an intimate relationship before, during, and after incarceration *48*
7. Relationship happiness (1–10) among study couples during and after incarceration *49*
8. Coresidence among study couples before and after incarceration *49*
9. Relationship exclusivity (no other partners) during and after incarceration *53*

10. Survey reports of abuse victimization in Multi-site Family Study couples before incarceration 72
11. Survey reports of abuse victimization in Multi-site Family Study couples after release 74
12. Proportion of reentering men classified as successful in each domain, by post-release time period 97
13–16. Summary of significant treatment effects across domains and groups 114
17. Trajectories for bonding based on latent growth curve models, by site and group 118
A-1. Understanding what promotes positive parenting after reentry from prison 153

BOX

1. Interviewing Justice-Involved Men and Their Partners about Abuse 67

TABLES

1. Predictors of Success in Multivariate Models, by Domain and Postrelease Time Period 98
A-1. Response Rates, by Wave, Sex, and Group 149
A-2. Characteristics of Reentering Fathers Subsample 152
A-3. Identifying What Kinds of Family Experiences Contribute to Reentry Success 155
A-4. Results from Multiple Regression Model to Identify Predictors of Reentry Success 158
A-5. Characteristics of Reentering Couples Subsample 160
A-6. Predictors of Being Married or Romantically Involved after Release 163

A-7. Characteristics of Analytic Sample for Intimate Partner Violence *164*
A-8. Variables Included in Models *165*
A-9. Characteristics of Reentry Success Analytic Subsample *168*
A-10. Independent Variables Included in Models *170*
A-11. Demographic Characteristics of Male Impact Analysis Sample, by Site and Group *174*
A-12. Demographic Characteristics of Female Impact Analysis Sample, by Site and Group *176*
A-13. Treatment and Comparison Means and Effect Sizes for Bonding, by Site, Sex, and Wave *180*
A-14. Treatment-Comparison Differences in Bonding for Baseline and Change over Time for Couples, by Site, Based on Latent Growth Curve Models *182*

ACKNOWLEDGMENTS

This book was made possible by so many generous and visionary efforts for which the authors are deeply grateful. The stories, insights, and experiences shared with us by participants in the Multi-site Family Study on Incarceration, Parenting and Partnering enabled a new understanding of family life in the context of criminal justice system involvement. We were incredibly fortunate to have had the opportunity to learn from the wisdom and life experiences of individuals and families who had developed this understanding for themselves under profoundly challenging circumstances and often at great cost.

The Multi-site Family Study would not have been possible without the support of the U.S. Department of Health and Human Services, Office of the Assistant Secretary for Planning and Evaluation (ASPE) as well as the Office of Family Assistance (OFA) in the Administration for Children and Families. In particular, this work was enabled by the vision and leadership of Linda Mellgren, Erica Meade, and Jennifer Burnszynski of ASPE and Charisse Johnson of OFA.

In carrying out the study, the four of us were lucky to be joined by a larger team of skilled and committed researchers. The contributions of Justin Landwehr, Erin Kennedy, Danielle Steffey, Stephen Tueller, Derek Ramirez, Kate Krieger, Rose Feinberg, Azot Derecho, and Chris

Carson were invaluable. We were also lucky to be guided by many leading thinkers in this field, including Jacinta Bronte-Tinkew, David Cordray, Justin Dyer, Felix Elwert, Maria Kefalas, Wendy Manning, Howard Markman, Kristin Moore, William Oliver, Jeff Smith, and Alford Young and especially for the ongoing and dedicated involvement of Randal Day, Creasie Finney Hairston, Joe Jones, John Laub, Anne Menard, Christy Visher, and Oliver Williams over many years. The work of creating this book was supported and guided by our leadership at RTI International, including Pam Lattimore, Gary Zarkin, Amy Roussel, Robin Weinick, Meera Viswanathan, and Paul Biemer, to whom we are deeply grateful. We were also lucky to have the editing support of Nathan Yates and Felicity Skidmore and the creativity of Ed Roberts to get us over the finish line.

Finally, we are thankful for the phenomenal energy and vision that Maura Roessner brought to this project as our editor and to all the staff at University of California Press who have contributed to bringing it into print.

CHAPTER ONE

Returning Incarcerated Fathers to the Family

JOEY'S STORY

Under the harsh glare of fluorescent lights, during an interview in prison less than a week before his scheduled release, Joey, a father of four, recalled the precious early days of his youngest child's life. Already "on the run" [his words] at that time for multiple crimes but not yet apprehended, Joey described himself as yearning to bond with his infant daughter. She was not with her mother, whose pregnancy had included a struggle with addiction, but with her maternal grandparents, who had taken her into their home on the outskirts of the city. The grandmother had encouraged Joey's visits, he said, even though they both knew the risks of allowing someone onto the property who had outstanding warrants for his arrest. He described the grandmother's generosity:

> She wasn't supposed to ... but she let me out there. She let me feed and bathe my daughter. And fall asleep with her in my arms and just—she let me be a dad. But there was rules: no guns, no drugs in the house. Which I automatically knew. I'd leave [the guns and drugs] in the city and drive out to the country. Turn off my phone. Throw it in the glove box. Go in the house, and just forget I was who I was.

But Joey had been caught and sentenced to prison. The baby's grandparents cut off all contact with him. He also lost touch with his oldest child. At the time of his interview for our study, with his release date less than a week away, he was intently focused on reconnecting with his other two children, twin daughters who had been three years old when he was incarcerated and had been living with their maternal grandparents in the five years since. When he walked out of the prison gates, Joey would join their household—and see his family in person for the first time in almost exactly sixty months.

Since Joey didn't want his daughters to know he was in prison, they had never visited him in person. Weekly phone calls had been his only mode of communication with the twins since his arrest. But Joey described an ongoing close relationship with the two girls, full of inside jokes and good-natured teasing. Pushing his sleeves up to display muscular arms covered in black-inked tattoos he received while in prison, Joey recounted a recent phone conversation, saying that five years ago, before he went to prison,

> I used to break out the Crayola markers, and I used to let them color in the tattoos and stuff. And [now] they're like, "Daddy?"
> "What?"
> "When you get home, do we get to color in your tattoos?"
> I'm like, "Yeah. Daddy's got a lot more tattoos."
> "Well, we've got a lot more markers."

· · ·

In the United States today, Joey's story is not uncommon. Over half the 2.2 million people in jails and prisons are parents, 2.7 million children have a parent behind bars, and one in every four women has a family member in prison (Lee et al. 2015; Pew Charitable Trusts 2010). Yet these point-in-time estimates drastically understate the reach of the incarceration system, as people cycle in and out of penal institutions. In 2015, for example, over 4.6 million people were supervised under community corrections, often after having been incarcerated (Kaeble and

Glaze 2016). And there is no reliable count of the potentially millions more who, though not currently incarcerated or under community supervision, spend time in a correctional facility during a given year.

These huge numbers have not been matched with commensurate efforts to measure and understand the intricacies of family life during incarceration and reentry. Correctional surveys pose few questions about kinship networks and close relationships. General surveys on family well-being fail to fill the information gap. As leading scholars in the field have noted, "very few of the data sources used to examine the well-being of families include information on incarceration, and those that do are extraordinarily limited in scope" (Wakefield, Lee, and Wildeman 2016). Although important gains in knowledge about the effects of incarceration have been extracted from existing data sources—most notably the Fragile Families and Child Wellbeing data and the National Longitudinal Study of Adolescent to Adult Health—these studies were not designed to understand incarceration as an evolving process that encompasses time before, during, and after imprisonment, nor as involving people who are both prisoners and family members. The result is a fragmented, piecemeal approach to gaining knowledge about incarcerated and formerly incarcerated people's embeddedness in family life and the "repercussive effects" of the criminal justice system on families (Comfort 2007). Calls have been made for more holistic research to capture the complexity and fluidity of family life as it intersects with incarceration and reentry, but these calls have often gone unheeded in quantitative research.

Joey's poignant telling of his story echoes the compartmentalization of family relationships as separate from incarceration in two important ways. First, his desire to leave guns, drugs, and his cell phone behind—and enter a space where he could "just forget who I was" by sinking into the comforting, encompassing role of fatherhood—underscores his own sense of disjuncture between the demands of his criminalized livelihood and the joys and heartbreaks of parenting. Second, his decision not to tell his children he was incarcerated, even at the cost of not being with them in person for five years, further underscores his commitment to keeping separate his identities of father and of prisoner. Perhaps it should not be surprising, therefore, that this compartmentalization carries over into the distinct silos within which society collects the data needed to fully understand Joey's situation: correctional data on Joey in his prisoner status on the one hand, and child welfare systems data on his daughters and the two separate sets of custodial grandparents on the other.

THE MULTI-SITE FAMILY STUDY ON INCARCERATION, PARENTING, AND PARTNERING

Joey does exist as both a father and a prisoner, and his children's lives have been profoundly affected by the criminal justice system, however aware they may be of that fact. In this book, we pull these two sets of experiences together—performing the social science equivalent of Joey's daughters applying their Crayola markers to their father's black-inked prison tattoos to add the color and multidimensionality of family life.

To accomplish this task, our book presents the findings from the largest and most comprehensive study to date of the interplay between imprisonment and family relationships: the Multi-site Family Study on Incarceration, Parenting, and Partnering. This was a groundbreaking study designed specifically to understand families' experiences of incarceration and reentry over time. Funded to document the implementation and impact of a set of federal demonstration programs serving justice-involved fathers with minor children and their female partners, the Multi-site Family Study aimed from the outset to investigate questions about almost two thousand families' experiences of the incarceration of their fathers. Its findings offer an unparalleled opportunity to use a unifying analytic lens to delve deeply into the experiences of incarcerated and reentering fathers, their partners, and their minor children.

The little existing research that considers the family life of prisoners focuses more heavily on incarcerated women as mothers than on incarcerated men as fathers (Rebecca Project for Human Rights 2010; Women's Prison Association 2009; Haney 2010). The Multi-site Family Study's concentration on prisoners' experiences of fatherhood is distinctive. We propose that the separation of research on prisoners and on family well-being has obscured the centrality of men's roles as fathers and partners—and that this separation has helped justify a system that, by removing men from their families, hides the substantial human and other costs to parents, partners, and children. Indeed, the Multi-site Family Study data reveal many justice-involved men to be deeply invested in their roles as fathers, hesitant to subject their partners and children to the financial and emotional burdens of interacting with correctional systems and stymied by the conflicting needs of their families and the requirements of reentry "success." At the same time, mothers with an incarcerated or reentering coparent struggle with their children's desire to see their father and the tolls exacted by prison visiting, the unending and unrecognized costs of maintaining relationships with justice-involved people, and the tremendous work required to keep families stable in the face of sustained hardship.

Our book's in-depth exploration of the issues raised by the massive increase in incarceration in the United States over the last four and a half decades—which has affected millions of families living in socioeconomically marginalized communities across the nation—challenges these false boundaries. The Multi-site Family Study brings valuable new perspectives to issues of widespread importance as the United States moves toward understanding the full harms the country's social experiment with mass incarceration has inflicted and the policy reforms necessary to reduce those harms moving forward.

TWO OVERLAPPING BUT UNCOORDINATED SYSTEMS

The critique of separating people's identities as parents and as prisoners concerns more than data collection. The systems organized around these two identities—the health and human services systems set up to support low-income families and the criminal justice system set up to adjudicate and punish "offenders"—have remarkably few points of interaction. Yet a sizable proportion of families involved with one of the two systems is also involved to some degree with the other. For example, households in which a father has been or is currently incarcerated are more likely to use Medicaid, food stamps, and Temporary Assistance for Needy Families than otherwise similar households who have not experienced a father's incarceration (Sugie 2012; Pruitt Walker 2011). The overlap is to be expected: the same factors that put people at risk of criminal justice involvement (such as living in poverty or having little formal education) also heighten the likelihood of a family's need for government entitlements like food stamps or housing support (Western 2006). Furthermore, involvement with the two systems is synergistic. Incarceration deepens poverty and potentially results in the loss of parental guardianship of children; placement in the foster care system predicts future involvement in the criminal justice system (Western and Pettit 2010; Courtney et al. 2009; Roberts 2002).

Despite this well-documented interconnectedness, people caught up in the criminal justice system are seldom asked about their intimate relationships or parenting status, even when this knowledge could be used to inform decisions to support family ties or leverage family strengths. Likewise, family welfare system records may simply document incarcerated parents as not being present in the household; the scope of case workers' interactions with families seldom includes contact with loved ones who are in jail or prison. Not only do these systems fail to offer integrated support, but they often work against each other. For example, continued accrual of unpaid child support payments while fathers are incarcerated often results in massive arrears that decimate recently released men's earnings, foment acrimony between parents, and cause fathers to avoid seeing their children out of shame or feared confrontation with the children's mother (Pearson 2004; Rodriguez 2016). Likewise, visitation policies and regulations at correctional facilities are often out of sync financially and logistically with the reality of families' lives, which can decrease contact between loved ones, lead to deteriorating relationships, and increase recidivism risk (Bales and Mears 2008; Beckmeyer and Arditti 2014; Christian 2005).

The systems' lack of reference to each other and the consequent absence of shared data replicate the separation between the real-world operations of criminal justice and family in much of the academic and gray literature on these issues—scholars of one area are not expected or even encouraged to think about the other. Researchers who do try to bridge the divide are often stymied by data limitations—with marital status or number of minor children frequently being the sole indicator of family life in correctional data, and yes/no measures of parental incarceration commonly being the sole indicator of criminal justice involvement in family well-being data (Wakefield, Lee, and Wildeman 2016). Ethnographers frequently speak to people's involvement in both the criminal justice and family welfare systems, since their qualitative methodology concentrates on the lived experiences at the crux of the entanglement of the family and the justice system (Sered and Norton-Hawk 2014; Haney 2010; LeBlanc 2003). But quantitative research that combines these two lenses is sorely needed as well, to enable generalization to larger populations of interest, detect causal effects, and provide a foundation for evidence-based policy recommendations.

WHAT EXISTING DATA TELL US ABOUT JUSTICE-INVOLVED FAMILIES

Existing data do provide a foundation of knowledge on the numbers of prisoners with families, despite the data limitations. The Bureau of

Justice Statistics has estimated, through surveys of people in jails and prisons, that over half of incarcerated people are parents of minor children and that the number of incarcerated parents increased 79 percent between 1991 and midyear 2007 (Glaze and Muraschak 2010). In addition to having ties to children, many incarcerated and reentering fathers are in committed intimate relationships, often involving marriage or cohabitation prior to incarceration (Lattimore, Visher, and Steffey 2008). Analyses of a national sample of state prisoners indicated, for example, that 44 percent of men were married or living with an intimate partner at the time of their arrest.[1] A defining feature of mass incarceration is its disproportionate impact on communities of color (Tonry 2011). Recent research estimated that 44 percent of African American women, compared to 12 percent of White women, have a family member currently in prison (Lee et al. 2015). And African American children born in 1990 were estimated to have a 25.1 percent risk of having their fathers imprisoned by the time the children reached age 14, compared with a 3.6 percent risk for White children born the same year (Wildeman 2009).

In addition to providing a sense of the overall numbers of people affected, a burgeoning literature published over the last two decades provides insight into the material costs to families of incarceration. The costs of visitation, phone calls, legal fees, and support of an incarcerated person, for example, impose a serious resource burden on partners and other family members—generating further financial hardship for those whose lives are likely already economically precarious (Arditti 2003; Christian, Mellow, and Thomas 2006; deVuono-Powell et al. 2015; Grinstead et al. 2001; Harris 2016). The loss of direct income from an incarcerated partner or father, as well as the loss of child support payments from a noncustodial father, also reduce a family's economic resources (Schwartz-Soicher, Geller, and Garfinkel 2011). Restrictions on access to public housing support and other government entitlements

---

1. Unpublished analyses based on the 2004 Survey of Inmates in State and Federal Correctional Facilities.

can further decrease a family's resources if the formerly incarcerated person returns to the household (Mele and Miller 2005). The same restrictions can also prevent released prisoners from living with their partners and children, which in turn is associated with diminished formal and informal child support (Geller, Garfinkel, and Western 2011). The financial contributions that individuals with conviction histories make to their family members can be similarly limited, due to decreased job prospects (Holzer, Raphael, and Stoll 2004; Pager 2007; Stoll and Bushway 2008), diminished earnings potential (Western, Kling, and Weiman 2001; Geller, Garfinkel, and Western 2006; Wildeman and Western 2010), and the depreciation during incarceration of skills, information, and work networks (Smith 2007; Rose and Clear 2003).

Existing research also provides some information on the deterioration or dissolution of relationships due to incarceration. Removal of a parent or partner from the household, along with the significant barriers to communication during incarceration, can strain relationships or even lead to sustained or permanent loss of contact (Arditti 2012; Khan et al. 2011). The distance of correctional facilities from residential areas is a primary obstacle to in-person family contact, making incarcerated people housed far from home less likely to receive visitors than those placed closer to their family's residence (Shollenberger 2009; Christian 2005; Hairston, Rollin, and Jo 2004). Family members must also contend with limited visiting hours, lack of visiting-room privacy, and restrictions on movement and physical contact—all of which make the prison atmosphere generally inhospitable (Fishman 1990; Girshick 1996; Comfort et al. 2005; Comfort 2003; Hutton 2016). Indeed, the procedures and protocols for in-prison visiting prioritize security concerns, which are not designed to be "family friendly"; for example, facility policies may permit strip searches of outsiders or keep visitors and prisoners separated by Plexiglas barriers (Aiello and McCorkel 2017; Moran 2013). These conditions can decrease visitation quality, make emotional connection with incarcerated individuals more difficult, and cause family members distress. Finally, families who attempt to maintain contact by phone are likely to confront high costs of receiving collect phone calls from their loved ones. Although the Federal Communications Commission set rate caps for calls originating from jails and prisons, telecommunication companies and some state governments filed a lawsuit against those rules, and correctional calling rates are still considerably more expensive than rates for regular calls (Federal Communications Commission 2017; Kang 2017). These challenges and barriers often result in decreased family contact during incarceration, which may be particularly problematic for the children of incarcerated parents (Poehlmann et al. 2010).

Although some studies demonstrate that in-prison contact can have a negative effect on a relationship that was already troubled before incarceration (La Vigne et al. 2005), maintaining strong family ties during incarceration clearly increases reentering men's chances of securing postrelease employment and decreases the likelihood of recidivism (Berg and Huebner 2011; Duwe and Clark 2013; Bales and Mears 2008; Barrick, Lattimore, and Visher 2014). However, many of the material and interpersonal challenges that make it difficult for men to maintain these ties during incarceration persist after reentry, and reentry often brings new challenges—even in families that did maintain close ties during incarceration (Turney 2015). The strain and disconnection many couples experience when one partner is incarcerated can contribute to distrust and the erosion of partnership bonds, making it difficult for couples to reunite (Herman-Stahl, Kan, and McKay 2008; Massoglia, Remster, and King 2011). Challenges related to residual mental health issues from the trauma of imprisonment may also arise after release (Haney 2003), as well as difficulties relating to the severity of the crime, which may have affected other family members directly or indirectly (Condry 2007); these can all interfere with the functioning of a couple's relationship. Couples may also struggle to establish mutually satisfying coparenting strategies in the wake of one parent's extended absence and the formerly incarcerated partner's daily exposure to a brutally authoritative environment (Nurse 2004; Bartlett and Eriksson 2018;

Fowler et al. 2017). In addition, substance use by one or both partners can loom large, especially if one of the partners used the incarceration period to engage with a treatment program (Cooper et al. 2014). Causal factors that protect against postrelease couple-relationship problems have not yet been identified, but some research suggests that postrelease parenting challenges might be mitigated by high-quality and frequent parent-child contact during incarceration. Such contact has been shown to lower parenting stress, strengthen attachment, and improve child involvement and compliance with child support among noncustodial parents after release (Arditti 2005; Beckmeyer and Arditti 2014; Landreth and Lobaugh 1998; La Vigne et al. 2005; Poehlmann 2005; Song et al. 2018).

Research on incarceration and families is most advanced with regard to the experiences of children of incarcerated parents, with several recent volumes focusing specifically on children (Gordon 2018; Wildeman, Haskins, and Poehlmann-Tynan 2017; Eddy and Poehlmann 2010). Since the U.S. prison population is 93 percent male, children with an incarcerated parent are far more likely to have an incarcerated father than an incarcerated mother. Prior research indicated that children of incarcerated mothers have a high risk of entering the foster care system (Swann and Sylvester 2006; Norman 1995), whereas children with justice-involved fathers typically remain in the care of their mother or a grandparent caregiver (Glaze and Maruschak 2010). Even so, the home environment of children with an incarcerated father can be substantially disrupted; in addition to being less likely to live with both parents, these children move more frequently than their counterparts unaffected by incarceration, and they may be more likely to experience family homelessness (Wildeman 2014; Geller et al. 2009; Johnson and Waldfogel 2004). Although early work suggested that children with an incarcerated mother suffer particularly poor outcomes (Dallaire 2007), paternal incarceration has been associated with maternal neglect and psychological and physical aggression (Turney 2014), which may be related to separately observed associations between paternal incarceration and depression for both fathers and mothers (Turney, Wildeman, and Schnittker 2012; Wildeman, Schnittker, and Turney 2012).

A father's incarceration can also interfere with children's psychosocial development. Children of an incarcerated father may suffer from internalizing disorders, such as anxiety and depression; externalizing disorders, such as aggression and behavioral problems; and other health issues, such as developmental delays and speech difficulties (Wakefield and Wildeman 2013; Aaron and Dallaire 2010; Murray, Farrington, and Sekol 2012; Turney 2014). All these effects are stronger than those associated with other forms of father absenteeism, and they may vary by the gender and age of the child (Parke and Clarke-Stewart 2003; Geller et al. 2012).

Of the unanswered questions about the experiences and trajectories of justice-involved families, many relate to how father-child and couple relationships change over the course of incarceration and reentry and what predicts how reentering men reconnect (or don't) with their partners and children after their release. Whether the documented effects of paternal incarceration on child well-being differ by the father's incarceration or release status and what factors might moderate the effects of paternal incarceration or release on child well-being are also questions that still need to be answered. In addition, the field has not yet developed a strong sense of whether family members' perspectives on incarceration and family life converge or diverge, since studies typically focus on either the incarcerated family member or those on the outside, not the two together.

CONTRIBUTIONS OF THE MULTI-SITE FAMILY STUDY ON INCARCERATION, PARENTING, AND PARTNERING

Data from the Multi-site Family Study on Incarceration, Parenting, and Partnering provide an unprecedented opportunity to delve into these heretofore unanswered questions. The first study of its kind, it followed 1,482 different-sex couples for about eighteen months to three years, beginning during the male partner's incarceration and typically continuing through his reentry into the community. Unique in its couples-based, mixed-methods design, its large scale, and its extended follow-up period, the Multi-site Family Study focuses directly on the nexus of incarceration and family life. Longitudinal interviews with Multi-site Family Study participants collected quantitative information about parenting, child well-being, couple relationship experiences, family stability, and reentry into the community. Quantitative data collection took place from December 2008 through April 2014. These data are now publicly available in the interest of welcoming other scholars to draw upon this unique source for teaching and further analysis.

In addition to the longitudinal surveys, a qualitative substudy was conducted from 2014 through 2015 to better understand family relationships during incarceration and reentry. In-depth interviews were conducted with the subsample of the Multi-site Family Study couples in which the male participant either was nearing release from prison (interviewed twice: both before and after release) or had been released within roughly the prior year (interviewed once: after release). Both members of the study couple were invited to participate in the quantitative and qualitative interviews, but they were interviewed separately.

This book draws upon these rich quantitative and qualitative datasets to provide a multidimensional look at how incarceration affects families and how families grapple with incarceration. Our aim, in part, is to *return* incarcerated fathers to the family—not only in the sense of reentry from prison but also, with the use of empirical data, to understand men as both parents *and* prisoners, as both returning citizens *and* returning partners. A common thread across the chapters that follow is the perspective of incarcerated and returning fathers as full people embedded in family relationships. This approach renders visible what is too often erased by the "subtraction" of people living behind bars from general household surveys. As illustrated with Joey's story at the beginning of this chapter, the Multi-site Family Study data knit together multifaceted identities that are too often divided into data silos, truncated by anonymizing systems, or just tossed in the glove compartment by people struggling to hold their lives together.

OVERVIEW OF CHAPTERS

Chapter 2, "'Always Having Hope': What We (Didn't) Know about Fatherhood and Incarceration," focuses on justice-involved men's relationships with their children. Drawing on the study's quantitative data, we compare various dimensions of father-child relationships before and after an incarceration, identifying factors that shape positive father-child relationships when fathers return to the community. We then use qualitative data to help illuminate how father-child relationships may function in the bleak landscape of men's reentry from prison.

Chapter 3, "'I Do, but I Don't, Know Where We Are': Couple Relationships during Incarceration and Reentry," applies qualitative and quantitative data to illustrate how imprisonment and the return from imprisonment affect intimate relationships. In this chapter, we first examine change in couple relationships from preincarceration to postrelease. We then use qualitative data to explore how incarceration and release may destabilize relationships, and the ways a conviction history may follow a person from the prison gates into efforts to reconstruct family life.

Chapter 4, "'None of the Above': Partner Violence and the Limitations of Research," turns our lens to intimate partner violence (IPV). Challenges in collecting sensitive data safely and confidentially have made couples-based studies of IPV relatively rare. The Multi-site Family Study design was different in that it enabled us not only to gather survey data from both partners about their experiences of relationship violence but also to interpret participants' responses in light of insights from their qualitative interviews as well. This chapter investigates what we learned about IPV that would not be apparent within a single partner's survey reports.

Chapter 5, "'To Be in Jail for Ten Years, Change Ain't Going to Happen Overnight': Operationalizing Reentry Success," expands the two-part definition of *success* typically used in prison reentry studies: that is, avoiding rearrest or a return to prison. We show that additional dimensions of reentry success (for example, family relationships) are relevant as outcomes in themselves and also as factors related to recidivism.

Chapter 6, "'A Breakthrough Type of Thing': Measuring the Impact of Family-Strengthening Programs during Incarceration and Reentry," emphasizes the importance when evaluating relationship-strengthening programs of including the perspective of both members of the couple and of measuring change over an extended period. We discuss how the Multi-site Family Study's impact evaluation used an innovative analytic approach and drew on quantitative and qualitative data to look at the impact of program participation on fathers, mothers, and couples. The study found limited treatment effects in most study sites, with the notable exception of Indiana—where a low-dosage, one-time relationship-skills retreat showed point-in-time treatment effects for individuals and sustained positive effects for couples. In concert with chapters 4 and 5—which discuss the interpretation problems of using data collected from only one partner's perspective or focusing on narrowly defined outcomes—this chapter illuminates the complexities of measurement and evaluation in research. The Multi-site Family Study's approach elicited a multidimensional sense of the experiences of participating families—finding, for example, that members of a couple might have quite different views of the same event or its impact on their family unit. Layering quantitative analytical techniques enabled us to understand the status of individual members of a couple at a given point in time, as well as couples' joint average trajectories over time. Qualitative data provided a window into how it was possible that a short (three-day) intervention could have an impact on the lives of couples weathering years of incarceration.

Chapter 7, "On the Horizon: The Social Science of Incarceration and Family," finishes the volume with a reflection on the unique knowledge gained from a large-scale, mixed-methods study that specifically focused on the family relationships of justice-involved men. By reembedding incarcerated and formerly incarcerated men in their roles as fathers and partners, we make visible the toll that mass incarceration takes on family life. In addition, we highlight how the failure to recognize the centrality of men's roles as fathers and partners has helped justify a system that removes men from their families and hides that system's costs to parents, partners, and children. We conclude with a discussion of the policy relevance of this study's findings for incarceration and reentry and more broadly for contemporary debates on the role of the criminal justice system in a fair and equitable society.

The appendix at the end of the book provides full detail on the data collection processes of the Multi-site Family Study and the techniques we used to analyze those data, which are now publicly available. To facilitate their use by others, the appendix also includes a comprehensive description of the structure of the datasets and additional chapter-specific information on analyses and results.

We close chapter 1 with a brief review of the Multi-site Family Study's methodological approach.

ORIGIN AND METHODOLOGY OF THE MULTI-SITE FAMILY STUDY

In 2006, the federal Administration for Children and Families (ACF), in response to growing public concern about the well-being of children of incarcerated parents, included family-strengthening programs for justice-involved fathers and their partners in its larger Healthy Marriage and Responsible Fatherhood initiative. The initiative's programs typically included some combination of parenting classes, classes on couple relationship skills ("relationship education"), and services to support family economic stability. Their design built on three prior initiatives—Building Strong Families, Supporting Healthy Marriage, and the Community Healthy Marriage Initiative—that had demonstrated modest impacts on couple-relationship quality and stability, though little evidence of hoped-for impacts on child well-being (Bir et al. 2012; Wood et al. 2012; Lundquist et al. 2014). However, none of these prior efforts included a specific focus on strengthening family relationships among incarcerated and reentering men. Recognizing the innovative focus of these programs on families facing an incarceration, ACF worked with the Office of the Assistant Secretary for Planning and Evaluation in the federal Department of Health and Human Services to fund the Multi-site Family Study as a rigorous evaluation of their impact.

The Multi-site Family Study was designed to measure the impact of couples-based services—delivered by ACF-funded family-strengthening programs in prisons in Ohio, Indiana, New York, New Jersey, and Minnesota—on intimate relationships; parenting and coparenting; and postrelease employment, substance use, and recidivism. Couples participating in the prison-based relationship and family-strengthening programs were enrolled in the study, along with an otherwise similar set of nonparticipating couples. Study participants were asked about their own experiences, about their relationships with each other, and about all their minor children. More detailed questions were asked about a single focal child, selected with a formula that favored children coparented with the study partner and closest in age to eight. The decision to use eight years of age to select the focal child was made for two reasons: (1) to enable analysts to compare focal children to one another across the sample and (2) to follow focal children longitudinally during a developmental period over which a similar set of socioemotional adjustment and behavioral outcomes could be measured (in contrast, for example, to the major changes in adjustments and outcomes that occur as infants become toddlers).

In total, 1,991 eligible men and 1,482 of their primary intimate or coparenting partners were enrolled in the study and invited to complete interviews at baseline (when they enrolled) and at nine- and eighteen-month follow-ups. In addition, thirty-four-month follow-up

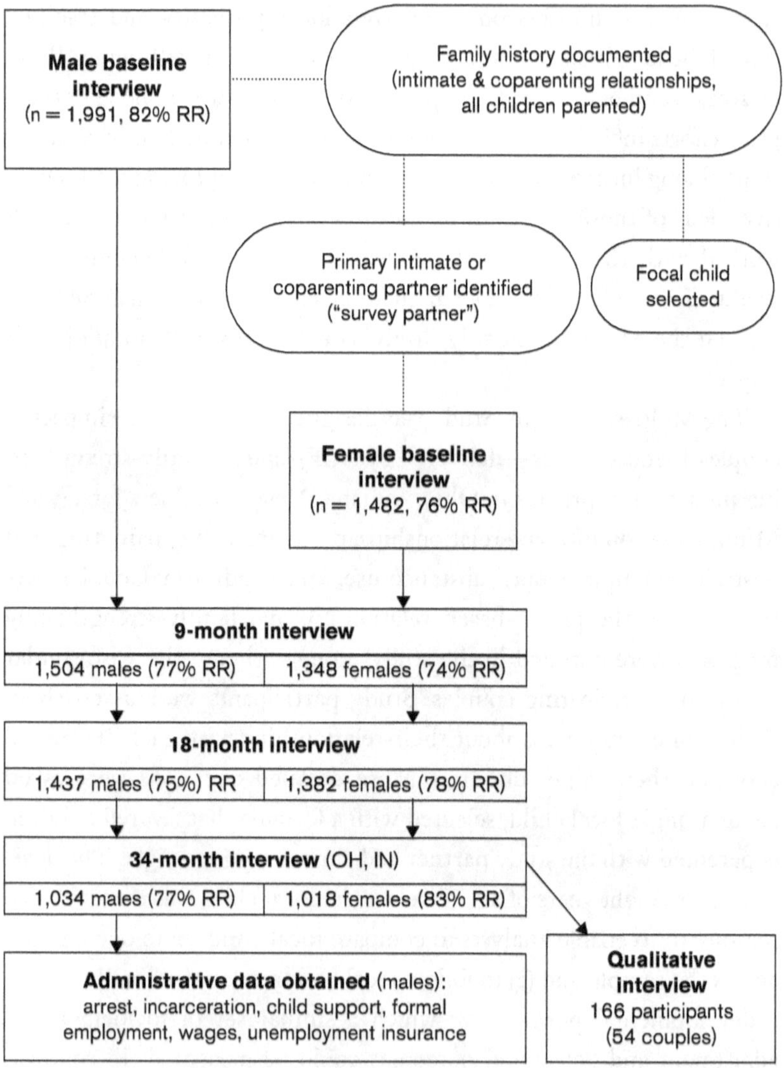

Figure 1. Multi-site Family Study data collection.

interviews were conducted with over 1,000 couples in Ohio and Indiana. The baseline interviews occurred whenever the sites enrolled participants into their programs. Since the timing of enrollment and therefore the study's baseline interview varied by site (anywhere from prison admission to shortly before release), the follow-up interviews sometimes happened while the male partner was still incarcerated and sometimes after his release.

Data were collected from couples in correctional institutions and community environments in five sites and integrated at the couple level across multiple study contacts. Figure 1 shows the data collection focus across study time points and couple members.

In addition to managing the intricacies of these data collection logistics, we had to precisely organize the evaluation to protect study participants who were highly vulnerable—as prisoners, as former prisoners, or as partners of men with incarceration histories. It was critical, therefore, that the study methodology adhere to scrupulous protocols that protected participants' emotional and physical safety behind and beyond bars and maintain the highest standards of data confidentiality—all while also facilitating the kind of rapport needed to encourage participants to provide candid responses and to return for follow-up interviews.

It is fitting that the herculean effort of the Multi-site Family Study brought together members of government, an interdisciplinary team of researchers, and over 3,000 dads and moms navigating the intricacies of parenting and partnering across prison walls. The size and scope of the U.S. correctional system is one of the defining features of the nation's modern-day sociopolitical landscape, and reconnecting the people in that system to their families—whether theoretically, analytically, or in practice—is a heavy lift. This book strives to illuminate promising pathways to move that crucial work forward.

CHAPTER TWO

"Always Having Hope"

What We (Didn't) Know about Fatherhood and Incarceration

Research has documented the challenges of parenting while involved with the criminal justice system. But little is known about what influences parenting after prison or how parenting might shape successful postprison reintegration into family and community. In this chapter, we look for better understanding of these experiences, with analysis of quantitative data from longitudinal surveys and in-depth qualitative interviews. For Multisite Family Study participants, father-child relationships tended to deteriorate during incarceration; how they fared was affected by how much parent-child contact was sustained during the prison term, the quality of fathers' relationships with their coparents, and the children's ages. Analysis of the fathers' qualitative accounts revealed that parenting interactions furnish a sense of day-to-day structure and continuity after release from prison—a potential that chronic unemployment, unstable housing, interpersonal challenges, and the struggle to rebuild a life on the outside might otherwise foreclose. For the fathers in our study, even mundane parenting activities focused their attention beyond their bleak immediate horizons onto the hopes they held for their children.[1]

---

1. This chapter builds on prior work by the authors with analytic contributions from Justin Landwehr, Erin Kennedy, and Julianne Payne (McKay, Feinberg, et al. 2018).

DARREN'S STORY

Darren, a formerly incarcerated father and self-described realist, answered an in-depth interview question about his relationship with his children while he was in prison: "They say absence makes the heart grow fonder—but not like that, you know. Absence makes a great big gap." His stark assessment sets him apart. Among over a thousand families who participated in our study, incarcerated fathers tended to express a rosier view of family life: they were more likely than their partner to perceive that an incarceration had brought them closer together with their partner and children, or at least that it had no effect; they more often identified themselves as being more involved in parenting than their coparent perceived them to be; and they more often characterized the coparenting relationship as a romantic one. Darren was different. Looking at the responses he and his partner gave separately in their first quantitative interviews for the study (when Darren was in prison), we see a consistent picture of a romantically involved, coparenting couple who lived together before the incarceration, were mostly happy with their relationship—although Darren's characterization was less sunny than his partner's—and were strongly committed to remaining together.

It has been several years now since he and his partner completed that first survey. Darren, the realist, out of prison now, commands full attention when he starts talking about "hope" in response to a question about the best thing about parenting in the context of an incarceration:

> Always having hope.... Having a child, you know, you always feel like they're going to love you unconditionally. You look forward to, like, doing the right thing. You look forward to giving that child good, sound advice which is going to help them succeed in the future. Those are the things that really kept me going, you know.

• • •

Unlike many men in our study, whose expectations for life after prison sounded painfully optimistic, Darren's were simple and grounded. But as we talked with him about what kept his spirit and family intact through a long incarceration and a challenging reentry into the community, he repeated that word *hope* twice more. Later in this chapter, we use qualitative and quantitative data from other incarcerated and reentering fathers in the Multi-site Family Study to search out what he meant by that word.

FATHERHOOD, INCARCERATION, AND REENTRY
Prior Research

Having a father in prison is known to have lasting effects on children, including increased risk of infant mortality (Wildeman 2012); increased behavioral issues and mental health problems (Wakefield and Wildeman 2011; Murray, Farrington, and Sekol 2012); and cumulative disadvantage resulting from loss of a father's income (Davis 1992; Grinstead et al. 2001; Wildeman 2009). Yet little is known about the longer-term effects of incarceration experiences on parenting and father-child relationships or how these relationships may evolve as fathers and children reunite during the reentry period. Fathers returning from prison reestablish their parenting involvement in a variety of ways, including spending time with their children, living with them again or for the first time, and providing them with financial support. But a father's resuming contact with children after incarceration, although necessary, is not sufficient to maintain or rebuild a strong father-child relationship (Amato and Gilbreth 1999). Strained relationships can prevent fathers from even resuming contact with their children during reentry; prior research suggests that mothers may assume a gatekeeping role between incarcerated fathers and their children (Smith 2014; Nurse 2004).

Reentering men who do not live with their children after release may face additional barriers to father-child contact (such as geographic distance and transportation costs), which nonresidential fathers in the general population also suffer (Miller 2006; Leite and McKenry 2006). Many factors are known to shape whether a father will live with his children after incarceration. These include whether the father lived with his children before incarceration (many incarcerated fathers report having one or more children who did not live with them before their admission to prison; Johnson and Waldfogel 2002; Mumola 2006); the father's relationship with his coparent; and any new intimate relationships he or the coparent may form (Roy and Dyson 2005).

Financially supporting children after release represents a serious challenge for many fathers returning from prison. In the general population, paternal financial support (via formal child support as well as other means) is strongly related to positive father-child relationships among nonresidential fathers (King 1994; Seltzer 1991). Fathers sometimes distance themselves from parenting if they are unable to fulfill the role of financial provider (Elder, Van Nguyen, and Caspi 1985; Christiansen and Palkovitz 2001). These findings suggest potential challenges for reentering fathers to provide for their children, because typically it is very difficult to secure sufficient employment following incarceration (Western, Kling, and Weiman 2001; Visher, Debus-Sherrill, and Yahner 2011). Indeed, paternal incarceration promotes lasting financial hardship in families, even after a father's release from prison (Johnson 2009; Schwartz-Soicher, Geller, and Garfinkel 2011). Such financial challenges can strain family relationships, including father-child and coparenting relationships (Conger et al. 1994; Wadsworth and Compas 2002).

While reestablishing contact with children and providing financial support are key tasks awaiting reentering fathers upon release, a longer-term consideration for the father-child relationship is the development of high-quality relationships with children. High-quality contact (typically defined as emotional support, warmth, and limit setting) appears even more important to the father-child bond than high frequency of contact (Amato and Gilbreth 1999) and can be present even when the time fathers and children spend together is brief or infrequent (Brown et al. 2007; Taanila et al. 2002). Closeness between fathers and their children becomes increasingly difficult to maintain as children transition into adolescence, a period of generally declining father-child interaction and increased conflict (Larson et al. 1996; Yeung et al. 2001).

Many years of research on father-child relationships in the general population furnish a helpful outline for the kinds of challenges fathers returning from prison are likely to face, but direct research on fathers' efforts at establishing or resuming parenting roles and responsibilities after incarceration is limited. Little is known, for example, about whether or how various aspects of fathers' relationships with their children (such as whether they live in the same household, whether the father financially supports the children, or how much time they spend together) change from pre- to postincarceration. Nor is it known what shapes the extent to which fathers connect with, support, and relate to their children once they return from prison.

Multi-site Family Study Findings

To understand postincarceration parenting experiences and what drives them, our quantitative analysis focused on 772 men (out of a total of 1,991 male Multi-site Family Study participants) who had children and who were released from prison prior to one of the study follow-up interviews. Applying matched-pairs t-tests to compare pre- and postincarceration parenting, we found that reentering fathers and their children experienced prolonged household disruption and deteriorating father-child financial support. Only 50 percent of fathers lived with their focal child after release from prison, compared to 70 percent during the six months before their imprisonment (figure 2). Only 75 percent of fathers provided financial support for their focal child after release, compared to 87 percent during the six months before their imprisonment.

To understand what made some fathers more likely to live with and to financially support their children after release from prison, we ran a pair of multiple regression models using these two outcomes as the dependent variables. The first model (figure 3) showed that a father was more likely to live with his focal child after release if (1) the focal child

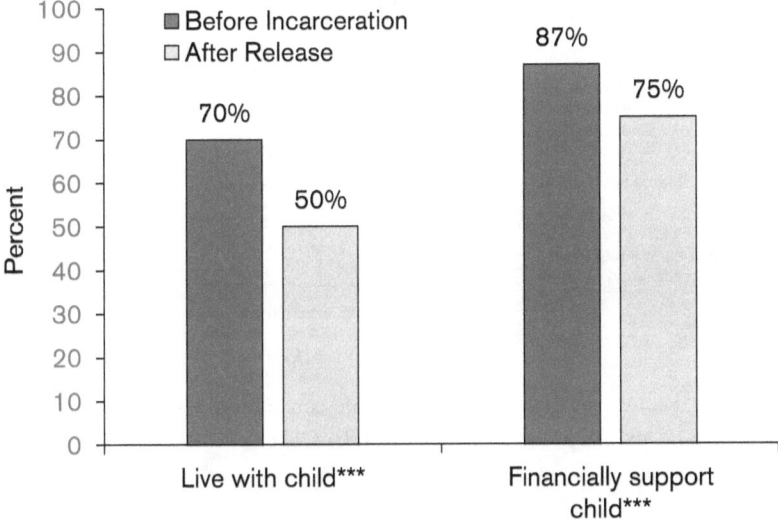

Figure 2. Father-child coresidence and financial support, before incarceration and after release. *** indicates p<.001 for the difference between pre- and postincarceration values. Image credit: Justin Landwehr.

was younger, (2) the father-child contact during the incarceration was more frequent, (3) the father was legally married to his partner or coparent at baseline, and (4) the father was happier in his relationship with his partner or coparent at baseline. The second model (figure 4) showed that a father was more likely to financially support his focal child after release if (1) the focal child was younger, (2) the father-child contact during the incarceration was more frequent, and (3) the father indicated stronger conflict resolution skills in relationship with his partner or coparent.

Next, we applied qualitative analysis techniques to examine in-depth interview data from a subset of 62 Multi-site Family Study parents (including Darren) and their partner or coparent, who were each interviewed shortly before and shortly after the father's release from prison. We queried the ATLAS.ti database of coded interview transcripts to review and analyze passages related to fatherhood and the

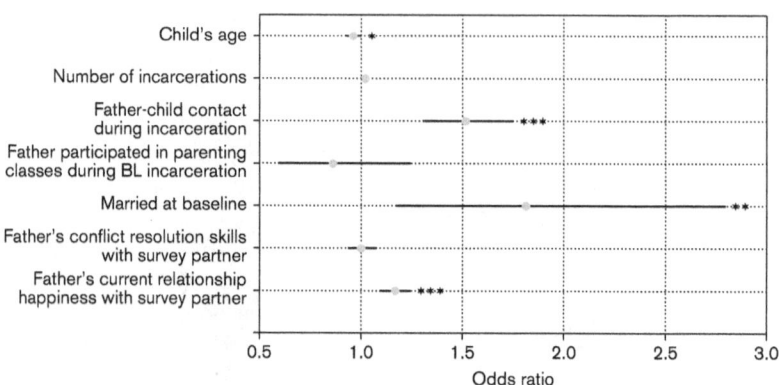

Figure 3. Factors that promoted father-child coresidence after release. ***p<0.001, **p<.01, *p<.05. Image credit: Julia Cohen.

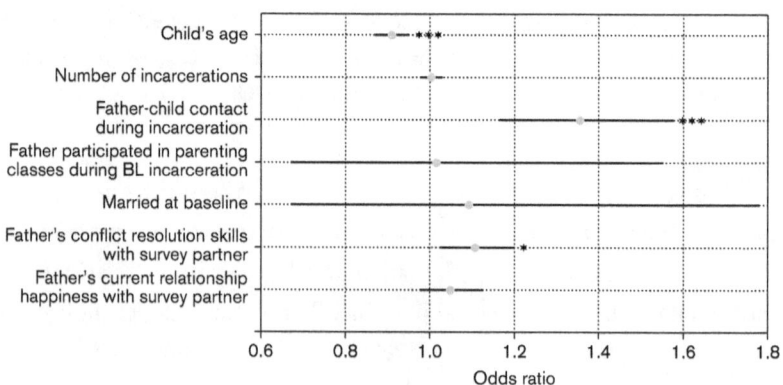

Figure 4. Factors that promoted father-child financial support after release. ***p<0.001, **p<.01, *p<.05. Image credit: Julia Cohen.

return from prison. Echoing the findings from logistic regression, these qualitative analyses indicated that the child's age and the father's relationship with his romantic partner or coparent were profound influences on the father's postprison parenting experiences. While fathers of younger children often recounted joyous reunions with their children, those who had been incarcerated through major developmental phases in their children's lives returned home to find older children had changed in significant ways. Two mothers recounted this problem poignantly: "He is like, 'I came home—she got breasts, butt; she got a period. When I left, she was just a little baby in Pampers'" (see Olivia and Jason's story in chapter 5). "It is kind of like being in a—a dark space.... You know, like being in a coma and waking up and [his son] is 15. And I think that puts a lot of stress between the two of them."

Three major types of challenges were apparent from the in-depth qualitative interviews. First, the interviews revealed how fathers of older children struggled to adjust their parenting to catch up to their children's current developmental stage. Female partners often bemoaned what they saw as fathers reasserting themselves in their older children's lives without sufficiently understanding how the children or their activities had changed as they grew. Interviews with fathers also revealed that, compared to younger children, older children seemed more likely to harbor hard feelings about their fathers' time away: "So, I know I just can't jump back in where I was. I have to pick it up slow and work on our relationships. More so with the oldest. He is the one with the most resentment." Second, fathers found that older children were reluctant to accept the authority of a parent who had long been absent from the household and was still unfamiliar with its routines: "I haven't been there. I can't just tell him to go to sleep.... He is going to look at me like, 'You just came in my life. How are you going to tell me to go to sleep? I don't go to sleep at this time. I go to sleep when I feel like it.' Or 'I go to sleep at this time.'" Third, fathers found that older children struggled to trust them or open up to them after their return. Some older children seemed to doubt that their fathers were home for good: "Oh, you've got to earn their trust again. That was the hardest part right there, earning her trust. Earning my oldest daughter's trust, anyway. My other two, they flock to me because they—you know, they're still little. But my oldest, she think I was going to be back out here on that law ride again. But now she's coming around."

Fathers of older children coped with these three challenges in a variety of ways. For some, a sense of having lost their chances with older children led them to refocus fathering efforts on younger ones. After listing his goals for his relationships with his younger children, one father explained: "I feel that it is too late for the older ones, who don't even know who I am or anything. I am [first name], you know, not Dad." Many others, however, described a slow and patient process of getting to know their older children again:

> I am wanting to catch up, and I am trying to—you know, I am a go-getter: "What you been doing? How you been doing? Who are your friends? Bring your friends over. Let me get to know them."
> "Dad, come on, man!" ...
> They are different people, so you have to get to know them again. Start all over. I got to get to know them first.

These fathers had to find ways of easing into it with their children, while coping with their own impatience and longing for more connection.

The qualitative data suggested that coparents played both supporting and constraining roles in fathers' efforts to reestablish a parenting role during the reentry period. Most mothers in the qualitative study sample reported pouring much time and energy into supporting father-child relationships at reentry. For resident fathers, mothers typically provided housing for the father and children, maintained financial responsibility for the children (and often the father) while the father looked for work, helped to create specific opportunities for father involvement and father-child activities, helped the father to catch up on the children's development and daily routines, and provided him with coaching and encouragement on his interactions with the children. For nonresident fathers, mothers helped create specific opportunities for father-child activities and sometimes offered transportation or other resources to support such activities. Regardless of fathers' residential status, mothers often provided guidance and encouragement for their efforts to reconnect with their children.

However, mothers also sometimes prevented fathers from interacting with their children. When they did not trust that fathers would parent appropriately, mothers tended to temporarily constrain interactions in an effort to protect their children. Both mothers and fathers described how fathers had to win mothers' confidence in their parenting abilities during reentry: "It is like she always tells me she doesn't trust me with my kid but like I have never, ever given her a reason not to trust me with her kid. But like I said, we are working on that. We are starting to—we have got a good line of communication going now. She is starting to let [son's name] come over here and stay on the weekends and stuff." Mothers' qualitative accounts suggested they felt that such efforts at rebuilding trust were likely to pay off eventually. Even mothers critical of or resistant to the father's parenting after his release from prison usually expressed hope that he would someday play a positive role in their children's lives.

Next, we ran another set of multiple regression models to explore influences on three other major dimensions of father-child relationships: father-child relationship quality (as rated by the father), paternal warmth, and frequency of father-child activities. We ran these models separately for residential and nonresidential fathers, based on evidence that the relationship between the explanatory (independent) and outcome (dependent) variables might differ by residential status (Hofferth, Forry, and Peters 2010; Pleck and Hofferth 2008). Results suggested both commonalities and differences. Fathers' baseline marital status, parenting class participation, and number of adult incarcerations did not influence postrelease parenting outcomes in either group. And among both residential and nonresidential fathers, those who parented younger children tended to express more warmth toward their children and to report more frequent father-child activities at reentry than fathers of older children. Fathers who had a happier relationship with their romantic or coparenting partner also tended to rate their relationships with their children more highly. For resident fathers, no other factors we examined played a significant role in shaping their postincarceration parenting. For

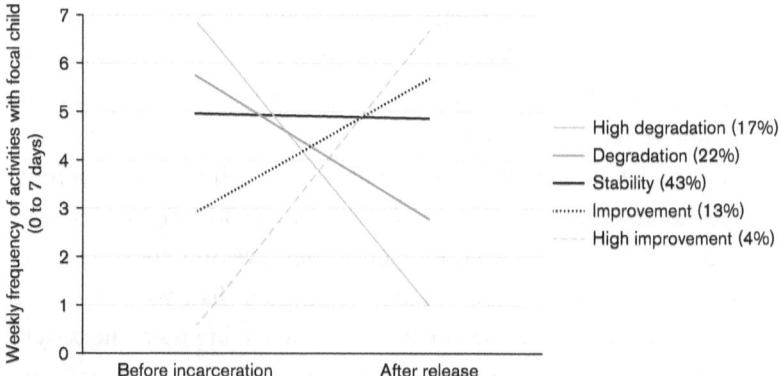

Figure 5. Change (and stability) in father-child activities, before incarceration and after release. Image credit: Justin Landwehr.

nonresident fathers, two additional factors—having had more contact with their children during incarceration and reporting better conflict resolution skills with their partner or coparent—also predicted both the quality of their parent-child relationships and how frequently they engaged their children in activities after release from prison.

Given recent research suggesting that the importance of frequent father-child contact after a separation depends to some extent on the frequency of paternal contact the child was accustomed to before the separation (Poortman 2018), we also examined trajectories of father-child contact from preincarceration to postrelease. Overall, fathers tended to see their children less often after their release from prison than they had before incarceration. Yet several distinct patterns were evident within this overall picture of declining interaction (figure 5). While 39 percent of fathers saw their children less frequently after release than they had during the six months prior to incarceration, 17 percent saw their children more frequently after release. For another 43 percent, frequency of father-child activities was stable across the two time periods.

These different trajectories—steep or modest decline, stability, steep or modest gain—are quantitative shorthand for a different set of stories.

Among the 43 percent of fathers whose survey reports suggested little change in frequency of father-child interactions from pre- to postincarceration—a relatively surprising finding on the face of it—the story may have been one of measurement error related to the difficulty of precisely recalling and quantifying one's typical weekly family interactions over an extended period of time (like the six-month period we asked about). But the lack of reported change in frequency may also have reflected a form of "stability" in a sample of fathers who had been incarcerated six to seven times before and whose relationships with their children had presumably weathered many such transitions into and out of prison. To develop a richer understanding of what these fathers (and also those whose survey reports suggested improvement or deterioration) might have been experiencing, we turned back to the qualitative data.

Diverse parenting trajectories were richly evident in our analysis of the in-depth qualitative interview data. Some fathers, particularly those who no longer lived with their children's mother after returning from prison, struggled to reestablish a parenting routine with their children and had sparse or erratic contact. Other fathers had clearly cultivated a powerful appreciation for and commitment to activities with family and children during their time in prison. Darren was one of those fathers: "I just love just being around, talking to the family and friends, and watching TV, reading. Stuff like that. That stuff that most people call boring, you know. I mean, I love it." Darren's unglamorized account makes it clear that these mundane family activities not only changed in frequency for some fathers; they meant something very different after incarceration than they had before.

PARENTING AND REENTRY SUCCESS
Prior Research

The powerful salience that parenting roles and experiences took on for many Multi-site Family Study fathers (Darren included) raised a further question for us: What influence might these parenting roles and experiences have on the rest of fathers' lives, particularly as they face the immense challenges of reentry from prison? Prior research on reentry "success" focuses on avoidance of criminalized activity (termed *desistance*, which we discuss in more depth in chapter 5). Desistance is closely related to other reentry outcomes, such as finding and keeping employment, avoiding substance abuse, and maintaining stable finances and family relationships (Gill and Wilson 2016; Lindquist, Comfort, et al. 2016). Various studies also suggest that stronger family relationships—particularly parent-child relationships—can help formerly incarcerated people avoid both substance abuse and further criminal justice system involvement after they return from prison (Brunton-Smith and McCarthy 2017; Maldonado 2006; Visher 2011; Visher, Bakken, and Gunter 2013; Visher and Travis 2003).

In general, desistance-related behavioral changes are often precipitated by underlying cognitive changes, including a shift toward identities focused around personal agency and service to others (LeBel, Richie, and Maruna 2015; Simons and Barr 2014; Søgaard et al. 2016). Following this general framework, research with young women suggests that transitioning to parenthood decreases criminalized activity and drug use via changes in identity. Taken together, this body of evidence suggests that the identity and responsibilities associated with parenthood become central (Kreager, Matsueda, and Erosheva 2010)—offering an opportunity to trade a stigmatized or "spoiled" identity (Sharpe 2015) for a more socially affirmed replacement (Giordano, Cernkovich, and Rudolph 2002). Although most prior work focuses on mothers, qualitative research with young fathers points to a similar role for fatherhood identities in the desistance process (Ladlow and Neale 2016). In addition, some qualitative and quantitative research suggests that incarceration itself can change men's identities as fathers (Arditti, Smock, and Parkman 2005; Datchi 2017) and, in turn, potentially influence recidivism or other aspects of reentry success.

Multi-site Family Study Findings

Accounts from Darren and other in-depth-interview participants confirm that family interactions, whatever their quantity, did acquire intensified meaning for fathers during their incarceration. But how these interactions (and the perceptions associated with them) influence fathers' transition from prison back into their families and communities remained unclear.

We went back to the quantitative data to explore how fathers' parenting experiences and roles might influence their reentry experiences more broadly. First, we applied multiple regression to assess the influence of family experiences before and during incarceration on men's reentry "success" (defined holistically as finding employment, avoiding recidivism and substance abuse, maintaining a positive relationship with the romantic or coparenting partner, and providing financial support for the children). We found that fathers who had more contact and interaction with their children during the incarceration, greater parenting responsibilities, and more family support were more likely to succeed in their broader efforts at postprison reintegration.

How significantly parenting-related aspirations had figured in men's minds during incarceration was highlighted when we analyzed the qualitative data. Many fathers described how the experience of incarceration—including the physical separation from their children and the often-painful reflections it prompted—had changed them, bringing their roles and responsibilities as fathers to the fore. This father echoes Darren's sense of how fatherhood changed his decision-making and his orientation to the future:

> Before I got locked up, I didn't think about... what my family looked at me as, or what my daughter looked at me as. [Now] I always think about my family first, and the decisions that I do make always involve them. Because my decision-making—it don't just affect me anymore. It affects me and my family and my daughter. And so now, I just—I actually take the time to think about my answer before I give it.

Perhaps as a result of these changes, parenting-related considerations were often foremost in men's minds during reentry from prison, as they faced the many challenges and decisions that awaited them.

Interactions with children also provided a major source of validation and inspiration for fathers upon reentry. Asked what he enjoyed about being a parent after his release from incarceration, one father answered: "Oh man, just my kids—they are always hugging on me. At their sports, they wave at me. I didn't expect all that when, you know, when I did—I was hard on myself for a long time. I didn't expect to get all the love that I do. Just them loving me is priceless." Other fathers described their love of their children and desire to be good parents as a powerful underlying motivation for their efforts in other areas of their lives. Parenting experiences (and the attempt to fulfill parenting responsibilities) lend meaning and structure to reentering men's daily lives, even as they navigate serious challenges related to employment and reintegration:

> When I do have employment, it is … first and foremost, pay bills … and I got to make [my son] feel better, because I am there and I am asking and I am helping and we are a team … "Nice outfit, man. You look cool, man." You know. "Get up," because I wake him up every day at 6:00, and that is always a good thing. It is a beautiful day. Every morning and every night, I always say good night: "Good night, son. I love you." So … that is what life is. That is why we are here.

Many fathers took pride in both the mundane and the special activities they did with their children after release, describing them at length. They expressed great hope that the presence of a caring and involved father, which many had lacked themselves, might lift their children up and protect them from justice system involvement and other harms. One father summed up this hope in a simple statement: "I am trying to be a good dad and be there. I didn't have my dad there my whole life, but I want that for my daughter. So she is my main priority."

Reentering men's reflections on fatherhood and children suggested that these relationships offer one area in which they can dare to hope their efforts will not end in disappointment, failure, or loss. Yet even these hopes were not set on bedrock. When Darren described the mundane visions for postrelease fatherhood that propelled him, it was excruciatingly clear how tenuous even those simple hopes must have seemed at the time: "Those are the things that really kept me going, you know. Fantasizing, like I say, of pushing your child on the swing and taking them places, like I seen on those commercials."

IMPROVING RESEARCH TO UNDERSTAND FATHERHOOD AND REENTRY
Detailed Survey Data on Family Life and Criminal Justice System Experiences

Lack of data sources with detailed information on family life and equally detailed information on experiences with incarceration and reentry have constrained researchers' efforts to understand parenting and other family experiences in the context of justice system involvement (Wakefield, Lee, and Wildeman 2016). The Multi-site Family Study data make it possible to examine the link between family experiences and reentry success in a more comprehensive manner than ever before. From among many potential aspects of family life that might be expected to influence postrelease success, our logistic regression results isolated the prominence of positive parent-child interactions during incarceration in promoting men's success in multiple life domains after release.

Why might parent-child interactions during incarceration[2] exert more influence than other aspects of parenting or family life on reentry success? Prior empirical and theoretical work (Datchi 2017) taken together with our quantitative findings suggest that parent-child inter-

---

2. This construct was operationalized in our analysis to incorporate respondents' ratings of themselves as parents and of the quality of their relationships with their children during the incarceration; the form, quality, and importance of their contact with their children; and their satisfaction with help they received to stay in contact during the incarceration.

actions during incarceration might enable fathers to maintain forms of positive social bonding and open emotional expression that would otherwise compromise their safety or status in prison. In so doing, fathers might be protected from the incarceration-related psychosocial and identity deterioration that recent research describes as hobbling men's later attempts to reintegrate into family and community (Schnittker 2014).

Prior work with reentering fathers in the Multi-site Family Study and Returning Home samples also shows that fathers' contact with their children during incarceration predicts their postrelease parenting involvement (Lindquist et al. 2015; Visher, Bakken, and Gunter 2013). Postrelease parenting involvement, in turn, is correlated with desistance from substance abuse and criminalized activity and with increased engagement in paid work upon reentry (Visher, Bakken, and Gunter 2013; Visher and Travis 2003). Studies of desistance among justice-involved women suggest that parenting offers an alternate identity that competes successfully with criminalized activity and substance abuse (Edin and Kefalas 2011; Kreager, Matsueda, and Erosheva 2010)—two of the dimensions of reentry success captured in our regression modeling. Survey data alone, however, could not tell us whether something similar might be occurring among the justice-involved men in the Multi-site Family Study sample.

Blending Qualitative and Quantitative Accounts

Qualitative analysis of the in-depth interview data helped expand and confirm findings from our quantitative analysis, showing how important coparenting relationships, father-child contact during the incarceration, and children's ages were in shaping postincarceration parenting and suggesting the salience of fatherhood in postincarceration identity formation and success. But the stories embedded in our qualitative data also exposed a deeper reality the numbers had obscured: the subjectively painful and challenging work of rebuilding relationships between fathers and children after an incarceration and the immense effort and determination both fathers and coparents brought to the task.

The role of the fathers' relationships (and ability to resolve conflicts) with their romantic partners and coparents in supporting or constraining their postincarceration parenting experiences was strongly apparent in both quantitative and qualitative analysis. But it was qualitative data that exposed the difficult, day-to-day work coparents undertook in coordinating, coaching, and facilitating the reintegration of fathers into their children's lives. Earlier research on the "gatekeeping" role of mothers in relationships between incarcerated fathers and their children (Nurse 2004; Smith 2014) generally characterizes gatekeeping as *restraining* father-child relationships. Our mixed-method analysis suggests mothers play a greater role. Although partners and coparents in our study did curtail contact when they perceived fathers as ill-prepared to care for children, they also invested substantial (and scarce) resources to facilitate that contact when they perceived it as healthy and helpful. The strong evidence we present in this chapter for the pivotal role of father-child contact in prison in shaping postincarceration parenting further highlights the importance of the time- and resource-intensive, and sometimes excruciating, efforts mothers and other family members make to support father-child contact during incarceration, often in the face of institutional policies and practices that discourage it (Arditti, Lambert-Shute, and Joest 2003; Hairston and Oliver 2005; Poehlmann et al. 2010).

Finally, an analysis of qualitative data from a subset of the same respondent population who completed our surveys offered insight into the meaning of parenting for incarcerated and reentering men that would have been impossible to glean from numeric data alone. The stories fathers told about parenting while incarcerated and when reentering from prison suggest that an identity as a father, combined with opportunities to interact positively with children during incarceration, confers a sense of self and purpose capable of transcending the separation between prison and community life that walled them off from other sources of meaning, worth, or agency. Their accounts further expressed how, after release, parenting interactions furnished a sense of day-to-day structure and continuity that was otherwise elusive in the context of unemployment, unstable housing, interpersonal challenges, and the struggle to rebuild a life on the outside. These mundane parenting activities offered both mooring and motive, drawing men's focus beyond their bleak immediate horizons onto hopes for their children's lives that often exceeded (or superseded) their hopes for their own.

CONSIDERATIONS FOR FUTURE RESEARCH AND PRACTICE
Supporting Reentering Men's Parenting in Policy and Practice

This analysis of parenting and reentry experiences reveals multiple opportunities for improving parenting supports, strengthening reentry services, and removing policies that work against men's efforts to make good on their parenting commitments and aspirations. It is clear from our analyses that, in the current policy and program environment, father-child relationships are often worse after an incarceration. Reentering fathers as a whole are less likely to live with their children, see them regularly, and support them financially after release than before their incarceration.

Yet within this overall pattern of deterioration lies wide variation. Darren's story, which ends differently than the modal one, is instructive: a strong, grounded (and nonabusive) relationship with his survey partner may have facilitated the maintenance of positive relationships with his children during and after his incarceration. Our quantitative models with the full reentering sample showed that fathers who could communicate and resolve conflicts with their coparent, who had more contact with their children during incarceration, and whose children were younger were better primed for positive parenting upon release. Interventions and policies that take these three risk and protective factors into account hold promise in helping fathers to successfully engage with their children after release.

But this is not enough; institutional and policy barriers measurably affect contact between fathers and children during incarceration (Mowen and Visher 2016) and must also be addressed. Such barriers include harsh parent-child visiting environments in prisons (which could be replaced with child-friendly visitation centers), correctional facility assignment policies that often place prisoners hundreds of miles from their families (which could, instead, take into account the location of a person's home community), and a shortage of affordable public transportation to state prison facilities (which could be addressed by expanding free or subsidized bus service for individuals bringing children to visit their parents). Other forms of father-child communication could also be made more accessible by ensuring enforcement of new Federal Communications Commission (FCC) regulations limiting exorbitant telephone rates for calls from prisons; "eliminating postcard-only rules; allowing children to send photographs or artwork to parents; and making higher speed, lower cost forms of communication such as e-mail and text messaging freely available in prisons (perhaps using existing, secure commercial platforms designed for prison use)" (McKay et al. 2016: 532).

To effectively support incarcerated and reentering men in maintaining or repairing their relationship with the mother of their children, correctional systems must reverse current cost-shifting policies that extract scarce resources from individuals in the community who bring children to visit or help them otherwise maintain contact with an incarcerated family member (Comfort et al. 2016). In addition, parenting programs for justice-involved fathers (e.g., Hayes et al. 2018; Troy et al. 2018) could support these relationships by incorporating an intensive focus on coparenting skills and resources. Parenting education and peer mentoring might also offer a platform to provide fathers of older children with tailored strategies, guidance, and encouragement as they work to rebuild parenting routines and relationships after prison.

Parents in the general population know all too well that developmental changes associated with adolescence can produce conflict and changes in parent-child communication, activities, and parental self-perception with older children (Laursen and Collins 2004; Larson et al. 1996; Shearer, Crouter, and McHale 2005; Steinberg 2001; Yeung et al. 2001)—even without the added hardship of prison-related separation. Research with low-income and justice-involved fathers also suggests that men who have previously struggled with fulfilling expected parenting roles often see the process of making up for prior parenting shortcomings with their older children as too daunting. Younger children, in contrast, offer a "fresh start" (Edin, Nelson, and Paranal 2004). Multi-site Family Study parents' insistence that rebuilding relationships with older children requires much time and patience makes it clear that fathers need support and encouragement to persist through this difficult stage and stay in their older children's lives.

Finally, fathers' stories suggest that father-child relationships offer a unique outlet for aspects of emotional expression and human bonding that could otherwise be inaccessible during (and in the immediate wake of) an incarceration. Whereas quantitative analyses demonstrated that parenting involvement and responsibilities during incarceration influence men's overall reentry success, qualitative data showed that men's self-concepts and their hopes for life after incarceration often center on fathering.

Darren returned repeatedly in his interview to how his relationships with his children during incarceration and his ongoing commitment to being there for them after release helped him to persevere against the other life challenges he faced: "I love my family, you know. And that's—I mean, that really keeps me going.... My goal is to be the best person I can be and stay out here with my family."

Reentry programs would do well to recognize the central place of fatherhood in the self-concepts, goals, and day-to-day activities of the men they serve. Efforts to support incarcerated and reentering men in engaging their vulnerability—for example, efforts aimed at helping men recover from the debilitating experience of incarceration and the lifetime of trauma and violence that often precedes it—might benefit from a concrete focus on fatherhood-related interactions and aspirations. Programs that focus on practical supports (such as employment or housing) might also aim to support fathers in succeeding at the parenting role that motivates their persistence in the face of bleak material circumstances and in which so many of their hopes are vested.

Future Research to Better Understand Parenting, Incarceration, and Reentry from Prison

The unique structure and content of the Multi-site Family Study data offer a new view of the parenting identities and experiences of justice-involved men and how they shape community reintegration after an incarceration. They also reveal certain measurement shortcomings that prevented a richer understanding of these experiences. Qualitative work with this population suggests that the parenting and coparenting relationships incarcerated fathers identify to researchers are both fluid and dynamic, but the survey data we collected from them focused heavily on a single "focal child." To achieve as much comparability as possible among these focal children, who were identified at the very beginning of data collection, we focused on children who were close in age to eight and were coparented with the father's then-current romantic partner. To fully explore the significance of child age and of father-coparent relationship for postrelease parenting outcomes, however, a focus beyond these focal children—one that enables comparisons by household or coparent—is critical. For example, a survey might ask parenting and child well-being questions by household or coparent, with phrases such as "the children you have with Mother A" and "the children you have with Mother B" or "the children you lived with before incarceration" and "the children you didn't live with before incarceration." Such an approach would make visible a greater diversity of parenting relationships, challenges, and strategies; it would also better capture change and stasis in more-challenged parenting relationships over the course of a father's incarceration and release. The insights such an approach would enable could, in turn, be critical to designing better parenting supports, particularly for returning fathers of older children and those who are estranged from their children's mothers.

Obviously, research can only aspire to generate as much insight as the people who have experienced a phenomenon for themselves possess, and our research is no different. But what we have "discovered" here already has thrown the weight and assumed objectivity of research behind the policy advocacy and program development wisdom of many formerly incarcerated individuals and family members. These families have been *forced* to discover for themselves what could possibly enable survival, closeness, even success in the face of repeated, devastating encounters with the criminal justice system. We are left wondering what a realist like Darren, living in a situation most parents would deem impossible, means when he talks about *hope*:

> I have another day to make this better. Every day ain't going to be a rainy day. Every day is not going to be a sunny day. So that's my true outlook on life, you know.... [My kids say,] "You always be in such a good mood." No, I'm not always in such a good mood, but you know, I realize things can be much worse.... It just makes me want to be even a better person, you know. I don't know, I guess somewhat—I guess—what I'm saying is light brings light. You know what I mean?

But do we? The transformative vision of formerly incarcerated individuals and their families—from the Center for Urban Families' father-focused reentry and workforce development programming (designed by a visionary, formerly incarcerated father and community leader in Baltimore) to the recent FCC reforms to end rate-gouging for telephone calls to incarcerated family members (resulting from a grandmother's petition that was joined by thousands of other family members of the incarcerated)—is profoundly, if belatedly, reinforced by our findings. We would do well to consider learning, right now, what else formerly incarcerated individuals and their families are demanding, dreaming, and building up in our communities even before researchers happen to stumble upon similar ideas in our calculations. (And certainly before we presume to think that any of them are impossible.)

CHAPTER THREE

"I Do, but I Don't, Know Where We Are"

Couple Relationships during Incarceration and Reentry

Research on the intimate partnerships of people who have been released from prison tends to focus on how those social attachments influence recidivism. Much less is understood about how reentry affects couples' relationships and how partners experience the shift from incarceration to release. Quantitative data collected from the Multi-site Family Study couples' baseline and first postrelease interviews showed that study couples' relationships tended to dissolve over time and that relationship happiness significantly lowered postrelease. Men were less likely to report that their relationships were exclusive (that they only had one partner) after release from prison than before, although women's reports did not differ over time. Relationship longevity, coparenting, greater relationship happiness at baseline, and engaging in more contact during the incarceration period all predicted couples remaining in the same intimate relationship after the man's release from prison.

Our qualitative data showed that reentry presents new challenges for couples and that obstacles to communicating regularly and openly during incarceration reverberate in relationships when partners return to their communities. Policies and programs could help justice-involved couples strengthen their communication during both incarceration and reentry, potentially reducing conflict, misunderstanding, and loss of contact. Couples' narratives around their relationships also have implications for further research, strongly suggesting that measuring relationship behaviors, rather than asking for relationship categorizations, may be a better way to capture their lived experiences.[1]

DIANE AND JOHNNY'S STORY

Diane and Johnny met in 1994, twenty years before our team interviewed them for the Multi-site Family Study. Over those years, they had two children together, struggled with their respective addictions, and spent long stretches of time apart when Johnny was incarcerated. The love between Diane and Johnny is clearly deep, yet they each struggled to define their relationship as Johnny prepared to return home after eight years in prison. When asked during his in-prison interview who is in his family, Johnny immediately responded: "I have a fiancée, or girlfriend—significant other named [Diane].... We have been together about twenty years, so that to me is pretty serious. But I have been spending most of my time with her incarcerated, because I have been gone; so I don't know how serious we are right now, but from my point of view I think we are serious. I really deeply care about her."

When asked about her relationship status in her first qualitative interview, which took place at the same time as Johnny's in-prison interview, Diane hesitated: "It is unclear.... If you ask [Johnny], we are together. Me, myself, I love him, but I was straight with him and I told him, 'When you get out, you are not going to see me every day.' And I am not even sure if I want to see him. That is crazy, but—I do, but I don't, know where we are."

. . .

Scholarship on postprison relationships tends to focus on the implications of strong or weak family ties for recidivism (Berg and Huebner

---

1. This chapter builds on prior work by the authors with analytic contributions from Kate Krieger, Justin Landwehr, and Erin Kennedy (Comfort et al. 2018).

2011; Mills and Codd 2008; Cid and Martí 2012; Markson et al. 2015). Relatively little is known about the dynamics of partnerships themselves during reentry. For people in intimate relationships, a prison sentence often precipitates dissolution, divorce, and the formation of new partnerships as people struggle to fulfill their emotional, financial, and practical needs in the face of long-term separation (Khan et al. 2011; Massoglia, Remster, and King 2011; Lopoo and Western 2005). Against these odds, however, hundreds of thousands of couples jointly count down to a partner's release date. The months following the exit from prison can be a time of reuniting with a loved one, rediscovering the joys and travails of being together, and renegotiating the practicalities, logistics, and patterns of partnership. Yet as Diane and Johnny highlight, the known struggles and stressors associated with maintaining a relationship when one partner is incarcerated (Fishman 1990; Girshick 1996; Comfort 2008) make it likely that the reentry period will contain its own challenges.

Returning prisoners are highly dependent on family members for material, economic, and emotional support (Bobbitt and Nelson 2004). This dependence can place a heavy burden on partners who want to welcome a loved one home but feel ill-equipped to meet the reentering person's needs (Cooke 2005; Hagan and Coleman 2001). On the one hand, if relationship difficulties that arose during incarceration are unresolved or reentry challenges are not addressed, partnership dynamics can cause tension that hinders postrelease efforts to desist from criminal activity and avoid reincarceration (Bahr et al. 2010; Capaldi, Kim, and Owen 2008; Herrera, Wiersma, and Cleveland 2010; Nurse 2004). On the other hand, supportive interpersonal relationships are an important concomitant of lower recidivism, decreased substance use, and other positive outcomes when men return home from prison (Bobbitt and Nelson 2004; Hagan and Coleman 2001; Shapiro and Schwartz 2001; Hairston 1988; Laub, Nagin, and Sampson 1998; Bales and Mears 2008).

Much remains to be understood about not only how couples navigate reentry but also—as Diane and Johnny's story highlights—how people navigate intimate relationships after prison. In this chapter, we draw on quantitative and qualitative data to examine change over time in reports of relationship status and quality, as well as predictors of couples staying together after the male partner is released from prison. We found that men's and women's reports of their relationship tend to differ, which highlights the importance of collecting data from both members of a dyad when assessing partnerships (a theme that will reappear in subsequent chapters). We conclude this chapter by reflecting on implications for meeting the needs of justice-involved couples, as well as for research that seeks to more accurately understand their relationship.

"WE HAD QUITE A FEW THINGS TO WORK OUT": RELATIONSHIP STATUS AND QUALITY BEFORE, DURING, AND AFTER IMPRISONMENT

Rates of legal marriage are lower among incarcerated men than among men in the general population (Turney 2015; Comfort et al. 2014; Western 2006). But studies consistently find that the majority of male prisoners consider themselves to be in an intimate relationship (Khan et al. 2011; Lattimore and Visher 2009) and that nearly half report having lived with a partner prior to incarceration (Visher and Courtney 2007; Mumola 2000). Most of the couples in the Multi-site Family Study reported being in nonmarried intimate relationships that were exclusive and long-term. Among the 641 study couples on which our analysis of reentry experiences focused, the majority of both men and women had minor children and coparented at least one child together. Men had fairly extensive histories of involvement with the criminal justice system, reporting an average of 6.5 previous incarcerations during adulthood. And many couples described a relationship that had weathered several cycles of incarceration and reentry.

To see what the quantitative data showed about change in couple relationships from preincarceration to postrelease, we used matched-pair

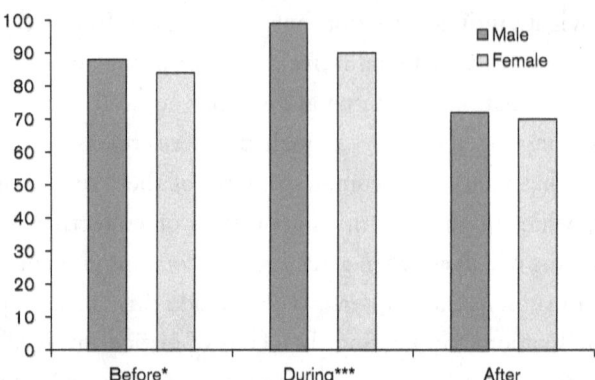

Figure 6. Proportion of men and women who reported that the couple was in an intimate relationship before, during, and after incarceration. *** indicates $p<0.001$ for the difference between male and female partners in a couple, * indicates $p<.05$. Image credit: Justin Landwehr.

t-tests to compare men's and women's reports within study couples at each time point and to compare study participants' relationships with their partner before incarceration and after release. For all three measures we compared—intimate relationship status, relationship happiness, and coresidence—a statistically significant decline (at a critical alpha level of 0.05) was evident over the course of incarceration and release.

Several statistically significant differences were evident between men's and women's characterizations of their *relationship status* (figure 6). Men were significantly more likely than their female partners to consider the couple's relationship intimate both prior to and during incarceration. No within-couple differences were evident in how respondents characterized the relationship after release. Men's and women's ratings of *relationship happiness* (measured on a 1–10 scale) differed within couples as well, but only during the incarceration (figure 7). After release, men's and women's assessments of their happiness were both lower than during incarceration, but not significantly different from one another. With regard to *coresidence*, men were more likely than their partners to report

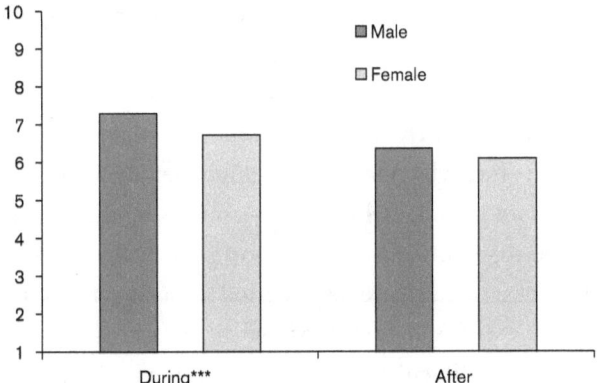

Figure 7. Relationship happiness (1–10) among study couples during and after incarceration. *** indicates $p<0.001$ for the difference between male and female partners in a couple. Image credit: Justin Landwehr.

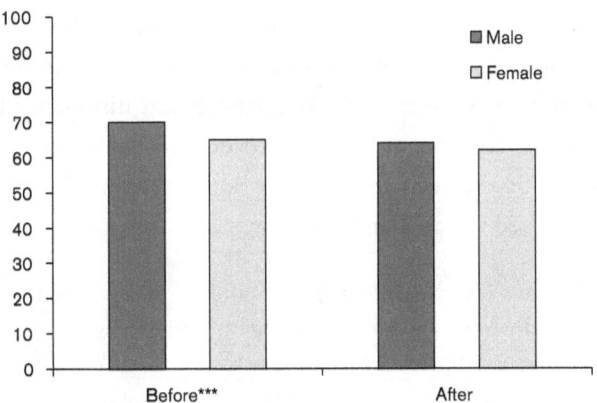

Figure 8. Coresidence among study couples before and after incarceration. *** indicates $p<0.001$ for the difference between male and female partners in a couple. Image credit: Justin Landwehr.

that the couple had lived together prior to incarceration (figure 8). After release, couples' reports did not differ significantly.

Analyses of qualitative data collected with a smaller group of reentering couples shortly before and after the male partner's release provide insights into why relationships might be unhappier or even end after release from prison, including why couples might have decided to no longer live together in the postprison period. Respondents nearly unanimously described the reentry period as posing a new set of challenges that were different from those of the incarceration period. One primary source of difficulty, ironically, was moving beyond the very coping strategies couples had used in the face of their constrained interactions during the male partner's incarceration, such as keeping up a positive front for each other and not telling one another about potentially upsetting incidents that had occurred at home or in the prison. These adaptive patterns served to maintain peace and functioning in relationships when one partner was behind bars; once partners were reunited, the patterns sometimes proved counterproductive. For example, knowing that conversations could be overheard, interrupted, or abruptly ended by correctional officers often led couples to avoid talking about difficult issues during in-prison phone calls or visits. This strategy created a sense of quiet bonding between the partners during the incarceration. It became uncomfortable and distancing for them when they were together at home, however, as couples found it hard to bring up sensitive subjects they had not addressed for a long time. One woman described the challenge this way:

> We had quite a few things to work out [after he was released].... It was, I guess, us really breaking into and telling each other how we really felt during the whole ordeal when a lot of things went unsaid. And a lot of that was on my part. Sometimes I didn't want to upset him anymore or sometimes I felt like when I tried to tell him something, he didn't want to listen.

Not only did reentry carry new challenges, but women frequently arrived at this transition period already worn down from years of managing single parenthood, full work schedules, stretched incomes, and the financial and emotional demands of supporting a prisoner. Whereas incarceration may have represented a crisis for couples that they approached with energy and commitment to "getting through" together, many women's expectations for reentry focused on finally getting a break when their released partner assumed some financial, household, and childcare responsibilities. Disappointment and exhaustion ran high for many women who, instead, now had to cope with the residual effects of imprisonment for their partner: barriers to employment, mental health issues, untreated substance addictions, and the like. For some women, taking care of a needy adult compared unfavorably to living alone, particularly for those who had discovered new capacities to provide for themselves. One woman said that when her partner returned from prison,

> I felt more in control of my life than I ever had and I liked it.... I guess I kind of have this—I don't know how to say it—territorial aspect about things that I feel like are mine.... I did all this. This is all me. This is everything that I wanted to do. And I lived alone for so long and then to have him come in, and I didn't want to think that he could just walk in here and things would be how they were when we were in our immature twenties.

For their part, male partners clearly identified lack of work opportunities for people with conviction histories as a major barrier to getting back on their feet after prison, as well as making them intensely preoccupied and even demoralized. Discussing his search for work in the months since his release, one man summed up his emotional state as "despondent." For some, not having employment led to relationship difficulties; their lack of autonomy and resulting dependency on their partner made them feel restricted and resentful. A man who spent his days at home taking care of his two young sons while his partner worked full time described these feelings:

> [We argue about] her leaving me in the house.... And that's when we get into it bad, because I be telling her like, sometimes I'll be feeling like I'm in

the [prison] cell still.... [I feel like that] when I be locked in, when I get stuck in the house like that. And then I take care of the kids all week.... I feel like I be needing to breathe sometimes. I need me, by myself, sometimes.... But she do that and I be feeling like I'm stuck.

Other men believed they should get a job and achieve stability *before* turning their attention to their relationship: "I honestly don't have nothing bad to say about her and the relationship.... [But] my focus don't be on that right now." In these couples, prioritizing employment and other markers of a "successful" reentry left their relationship in limbo, and they felt uncertain about the whether the partnership had a future: "What I need right now is just to establish myself and get on my feet and get my life started back up and then if we—that way we can work on [our relationship] if that is what we are going to do."

RELATIONSHIP EXCLUSIVITY DURING INCARCERATION AND AFTER RELEASE

Exclusivity is another dimension of couple relationships that can change over time, and perceptions about it can differ within members of the same couple. Figure 9 shows the proportion of men and women who reported that their relationship with their study partner was exclusive during incarceration and after release. Matched-pair t-tests indicated that men were significantly less likely to report their relationships with their study partners as exclusive after their release than during incarceration (at a critical alpha level of 0.05), but women's reports did not differ across the time periods. Within study couples, reports of relationship exclusivity were similar between male and female partners.

In qualitative interviews, few men stated explicitly that they were not exclusive with their partners after their release. But those who did said they desired less serious and committed relationships because they wanted to focus on themselves and enjoy their freedom. Some women described their partners as involved exclusively with them during the

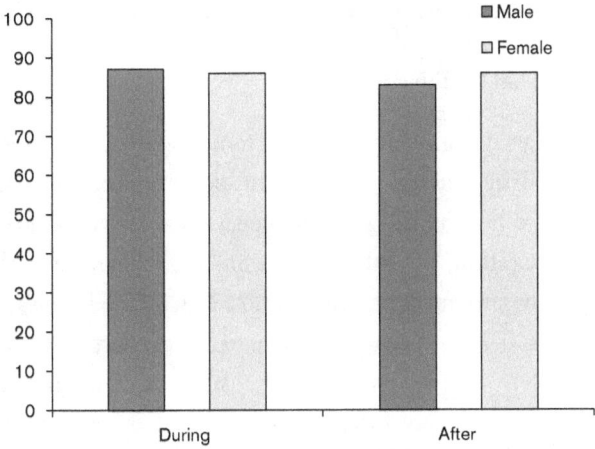

Figure 9. Relationship exclusivity (no other partners) during and after incarceration. Image credit: Justin Landwehr.

incarceration but not after release. One woman explained that she decided to end her relationship with her study partner because once he was released, he was intimate with both her and another woman with whom he had children: "It just got ugly. The situation got ugly because he's a man and he wants to do what he want to do. And then he might sneak with her and then, you know, it just got ugly."

Another woman, who was incarcerated herself shortly before her partner was released from prison, explained that she had remained exclusive with her partner while he was incarcerated and provided emotional and financial support to him. She felt betrayed that he was not doing the same for her:

> Now that he has been released and I [am] reincarcerated, it's not—I don't get the same treatment that I gave him.... I took care of him. Went to see him and kept money on his books, bought his shoes. Anything he needed, he had. And [now] he won't even answer the phone for me. I mean, he wrote me until the day he got out.... I feel like he just did eight years—he has to have sex with somebody.... I was more than faithful. I just don't understand. You know what I mean? And that's—and I don't want to talk to him

and tell him how much I love—I want to know why. Like why are you doing this? ... And maybe he's just—like I said, he's kind of out-of-sight, out-of-mind kind of thing.

Yet men placed high value on their female partner's faithfulness to them, both during their incarceration and after release. Men often questioned whether their female partner was exclusive with them during the incarceration, according to the in-depth interviews. Men and women both suggested that incarceration exacerbated men's anxieties about their partner's fidelity—because of being physically separated, not being able to contact one another easily nor communicate freely, and feeling generally powerless. Women often described their male partner as jealous or suspicious of them, posing questions about their whereabouts and accusing them of having other men in their home. In addition, rumors about women's alleged outside relationships arose easily among incarcerated men and their community contacts, rumors that were hard for women to disprove. One woman described a major challenge to her relationship during her partner's incarceration as "the jail and the word on the street... 'cause when he was in jail and what's going on the outside and someone tells him, and the whole story's misconstrued and mixed up. He used to call me and just flip out about something he heard that I don't even be knowing nothing about." Another woman explained how her partner's distrust of her faithfulness burdened their relationship:

> So when he has doubts about our marriage—every day he heard about people being unfaithful to one another or men cheating with other women and babies' daddy and momma babies and—okay, but [what] all have I ever done to prove to you that I am not wholly vested in this? I don't know what other actions I can take other than the ones that I have taken to prove to you my fidelity to you.... I don't know what else I can do. How dare you trust the things you are hearing versus my actions and my words?

When men spoke about their gratitude to their female partner, many mentioned their partner's sexual fidelity alongside a more general sense of gratitude for their partner sticking with them during incarceration and remaining with them after release: "I been incarcerated for a long time, nine years. But she stuck with me. It has been rough, but she still stuck with me." These statements often included acknowledgement of emotional and practical help that women provided to men in prison: "She gave me everything I needed. She gave me her love and support.... I can't ask for more than that." Men whose partner was willing and able to provide this kind of high-intensity support were often envied by fellow prisoners. As one man whose partner consistently visited and accepted his phone calls explained: "My [incarcerated] buddies, ... they always told me that, man, you got a good woman. You got a good family. You got something beautiful. They would tell me every day—like, man, a lot of these guys in here don't have anybody like that or don't have anybody at all."

"THAT BOND CAN NEVER BE BROKEN": PREDICTORS OF COUPLES STAYING TOGETHER AFTER RELEASE

To better understand factors that predict positive postrelease relationship experiences, we ran a multivariate logistic regression model assessing whether a set of baseline factors predicted the likelihood of couples remaining in an intimate relationship after the male partner's release.[2] The model indicated that couples who remained in an intimate relationship after the release from prison had been together longer, reported greater happiness with their relationship at baseline, were more likely to coparent at least one child together, and had engaged in more contact during the male partner's incarceration than couples whose intimate relationship ended. No significant effects were found for the couple's marital status, baseline communication skills, baseline fidelity attitudes and behaviors, duration of the male partner's incarceration, or his satisfaction

---

2. See the Appendix for a detailed description and list of included variables.

with assistance received for staying in touch with the female partner during his incarceration.

The importance of relationship longevity and of coparenting children in holding postprison relationships together emerged strongly in the qualitative data as well. Respondents often said they had stuck with their relationships through the incarceration because they had "always" been together. This woman's words are typical: "What I think kept us together [is] that I know he loves me and he knows I love him. And we have been together since teenage years. So, that is—that bond can never be broken. So I think we just held on to the fact that we had history together and the love that we have for each other is strong."

Respondents also cited the ideas that a child is best served by having two parents and that raising a child together creates a bond between partners as reasons for maintaining a relationship through incarceration and reentry. When asked what was most important in her decision to stay with her partner, one woman responded succinctly, "Because we have children together." A father spoke in similar terms about his partnership: "Our friendship is more than anything, but we got our daughter. So I am trying to be a good dad and be there for my daughter. She is my main priority and then [my partner], she is my best friend. So that is my family."

With regard to contact during incarceration, respondents spoke frequently of how not being able to stay in touch was detrimental to their relationship. Economic hardship prevented some couples from seeing each other or talking by phone for months or years during the prison term. In their separate interviews, one couple that could not afford to pay for phone calls described developing a sort of personal Morse code to convey information. The incarcerated partner would place a collect call, knowing that his partner on the outside would not accept it. Then, while a message played indicating that the call originated in a correctional facility, they would use the keypad to tell each other how they were doing—for example, by sounding two long beeps as code for "I'm okay." Many couples could not overcome the significant barriers to communication, however. Although they sometimes remained emotionally attached, over time these partners relinquished the idea that they were "together." A woman described completely losing contact with her partner, with whom both she and her daughter wanted to reunite:

> INTERVIEWER: From what you've said, you're not in contact with [your partner]. Is that correct?
>
> RESPONDENT: No. We've been trying to find where he's at.
>
> INTERVIEWER: And when did that contact kind of end?
>
> RESPONDENT: I want to say, I mean, I last contacted him about a year and a half ago. But then this year I sent him a birthday card and... the birthday card came back. His birthday was back in February and the birthday card came back saying that that inmate is no longer there.

This passage exemplifies the looming absence in the qualitative data of outside assistance to help incarcerated men stay in contact with their families. Almost universally, when asked about what services were helpful in their relationships during the incarceration, men and women responded that they had received no support in maintaining family ties. When those ties survived incarceration, respondents gave credit to themselves, their partners, and their extended families for making it happen.

CONSIDERATIONS FOR FUTURE RESEARCH AND PRACTICE
Reentry Needs Its Own Forms of Support

The Multi-site Family Study makes clear that justice-involved couples need support to face the issues that arise in their intimate relationships during reentry from prison. Overall, the men and women in our study faced deteriorating intimate relationships from the time of incarceration to the first postrelease interview. Relationship happiness generally declined, fewer couples reported being in an intimate relationship with one another, and fewer lived together. In the in-depth qualitative interviews, couples described reentry as bringing a unique set of challenges they felt unprepared and ill-equipped to address—particularly when reentry involved revisiting adaptive patterns and strategies the couples had developed during the incarceration period. Policy and programming are sorely needed to address specific reentry issues, such as reopening communication about past events, emotionally processing the impact of the incarceration experience on them and their family, and negotiating familial and household roles in the wake of one person's prolonged absence.

The need for reentry-specific planning and support is underscored by our finding that relationship dynamics within couples changed significantly from preincarceration to postrelease. In keeping with trends discussed in subsequent chapters, men's and women's assessment of their relationship differed from that of their partner and also changed over time, underscoring the importance of collecting data that are both dyadic and longitudinal. Some of the quantitative differences in men's and women's relationship perceptions at baseline disappeared once men reentered the community—at that point, men reported higher relationship happiness, were more likely to report being in an intimate relationship, and were more likely to report that the couple cohabited. In addition, men were less likely to characterize the relationship as exclusive after their release compared to during their incarceration.

That some relationship dynamics observed during incarceration (such as men's tendency to focus exclusively on one partner or their greater relationship optimism relative to their female partner) tended to alter upon reentry suggests that the correctional environment may shape couple communication and interactions in ways that do not readily translate into daily life outside prison. This finding is strengthened by the in-depth qualitative data indicating that men and women had difficulty discussing sensitive subjects with each other during incarceration and felt pressure to smooth over conflict during this vulnerable time. Women also expressed a sense of obligation to fulfill a caretaker role while their partner was in prison. Their desire for a more reciprocal relationship after incarceration sometimes went unmet—as some men became interested in pursuing other relationships or, lacking a job, felt unable to contribute equally to the household. Programs that support open and in-depth communication during incarceration, including prerelease planning for couples and postrelease support services, could help address this need.

The development of support services could build on the observed strengths of the Multi-site Family Study couples who maintained intimate relationships at reentry. Quantitative analysis found that couples who reported being in an intimate relationship at reentry tended to have been in the relationship longer, were more likely to parent children together, and had more contact during the incarceration. Even predictors of strong postrelease relationships (such as family structure and relationship history) that are not amenable to intervention suggest potential targeting strategies. For example, programs might have a greater chance of success supporting couples whose longer relationship or children in common give them an added investment in the long-term survival of the relationship. More malleable predictive factors could be actively supported through program and policy efforts. The in-depth qualitative data make clear that lack of contact during incarceration is a major, and sometimes insurmountable, challenge for couples. Men and women felt correctional facilities did not support them in their efforts to talk on the phone, have in-person visits, and even merely keep track of where an incarcerated loved one was located. Policies and programs that address obstacles to maintaining contact between partners during an incarceration (such as free buses to bring family members to prisons or policy initiatives to reduce exorbitant telephone rates for calls from correctional institutions) could increase the likelihood that couples stay in touch during an incarceration and experience a stronger, healthier relationship after release.

Refining Measurements of Relationship Status and Quality

Our findings suggest new strategies for future research to understand intimate relationships in the context of incarceration. As our data show, assessing couple relationships when such relationships are both highly dynamic and flexibly defined requires measures capable of capturing change within this fluidity. More traditional measurement approaches—for example, asking respondents to report on whether they are in an intimate relationship, whether they have gotten married, whether they have broken up—may be such an imperfect fit for respondents' relationship self-definitions as to introduce measurement "noise." Focusing instead on changes in relationship behaviors and affective responses might better capture the fluid and dynamic nature of family identification. Quantitative measures might elicit this richness by assessing the specific sets of actions and feelings that make up different relationships (How many nights per week do you spend in the same house? How often do you share meals? How often do you experience a conflict?) rather than asking only about predefined, traditional relationship categories (spouse, partner). Such an approach would help make visible a wider diversity of family roles and relationship strategies and enhance the ability of researchers to accurately quantify change and stasis (as well as couple congruence and incongruence) in the more complex and fluid relationships of the real world.

It is also notable that men's and women's reports about their relationships differed quantitatively and qualitatively. This makes intuitive sense, as individuals have their own experiences, expectations, and emotions; yet research too often relies solely on reports from one partner or the other. As the following chapters continue to highlight, Multisite Family Study data provide a nuanced and complex portrait of family life, in large part due to the dyadic interviewing and analysis approach. This strategy not only permits characterizing similarities and differences in men's and women's responses but also helps draw attention to areas where greater discrepancies exist—such as the accounts of intimate partner violence, which will be discussed in chapter 4. Future research should prioritize interviewing both members of couples, even when this adds time and expense, and avoid assuming that one partner's report can speak for both.

Potentially promising areas of future inquiry include delving deeper into how couples and families develop expectations for the reentry period and the specific factors that facilitate or inhibit the realization of those expectations. Within this area of study, a focus on the restrictions applied to people with conviction histories is likely to be fruitful. These include limitations or exclusions placed on housing, voting, employment, government assistance, and other opportunities. All of these might contribute to formerly incarcerated men's difficulties reestablishing themselves in the community and meeting the goals they had set for themselves (and communicated to their partner) during their prison stay.

CONCLUSION

The quantitative and qualitative findings presented in this chapter show a decrease in considering partnerships intimate and less coresidence and relationship happiness for men and women in the reentry period than before and/or during incarceration. They identify being together longer, coparenting children together, having more contact during incarceration, and reporting greater relationship happiness earlier in the relationship as predictors for being in an intimate relationship after release from prison.

Two design limitations merit caution in interpreting these findings, however. First, these couples are not representative of the general population of couples affected by incarceration, because the Multi-site Family Study survey data were collected from a sample of justice-involved men in self-defined committed intimate or coparenting relationships, and our quantitative analyses focus on a subsample of study participants who completed an interview after the male partner's release from prison. Second, although participants in the in-depth qualitative substudy were recruited from within the main survey sample, they are not representative of that sample. For example, the average relationship duration at baseline was ten years for qualitative subsample members, but seven years for the main survey sample. In addition, because time elapsed between completion of the final follow-up survey and recruitment for the in-depth qualitative substudy, the qualitative study would have oversampled participants living under relatively more stable circumstances—because recruitment into the substudy required that couple members be reachable via telephone numbers and addresses that were six to eighteen months old. Thus, the slight differences in perspective afforded by the qualitative data cannot be attributed solely to the method (open- vs. closed-ended interview) but may also reflect the distinct characteristics of the couples participating in the in-depth qualitative substudy. In addition, and perhaps most notably, the findings themselves expose the complexity of attempting to measure relationship status and couple connectedness over time for families in which these constructs can be relatively fluid and adaptable.

The growing body of work on the family relationships of justice-involved people commonly speaks of "the impact of incarceration" on prisoners and their loved ones. The findings presented in this chapter emphasize that scholars in this field must also consider the impact of *reentry* on family life. Although release from prison is intrinsically linked to imprisonment, our findings highlight that the reentry period brings distinct challenges to, and often new directions in, intimate and parenting partnerships. As couples make decisions about continuing their relationship, living together, and being exclusive with one another after an incarceration, they are affected by communication patterns, partnership expectations, employment opportunities, and other factors that may play out differently than they expected during the transition from incarceration to community. These findings strongly suggest that programs and policies tailored specifically to the unique context of partnership after incarceration are an important way to support couples in strengthening their relationship, increasing their happiness and well-being, and perhaps preventing a return to prison.

CHAPTER FOUR

"None of the Above"

Partner Violence and the Limitations of Research

The partners and spouses of incarcerated men have been described as the "front line" of reentry because of how their material and emotional support shapes men's recovery from incarceration and reintegration into the community (Bales and Mears 2008; Bobbitt and Nelson 2004; Hagan and Coleman 2001; Shapiro and Schwartz 2001). This chapter reveals that physical partner violence and controlling behavior are very common in different-sex couples in which the male partner has been involved with the criminal justice system. The findings raise urgent questions about what supports are (and are not) available to intimate-partner violence survivors in American communities, which receive 637,400 individuals returning from prison each year, and nine million returning from jail (Beck 2006; Carson and Golinelli 2013). The findings also demand further reflection from us as researchers, regarding the role and practice of empirical inquiry on intimate partner violence among those who are heavily monitored and surveilled.[1]

---

1. This chapter builds on prior work by the authors with analytic contributions from Justin Landwehr, Derek Ramirez, and Julia Cohen (McKay, Landwehr, et al. 2018; and McKay, Lindquist, et al. 2018).

CHANTELLE'S STORY

Our interview was almost over when Chantelle, sitting on her couch and speaking into the digital recorder, began reflecting on what she feared as she had weathered her now-ex-partner's return home from prison while fielding a steady barrage of questions about their relationship from members of our study team. Unprompted, she said:

> It is so much domestic violence out here, and women are scared. [Now] I ain't trying to get hit, because I am hitting back. Matter of fact, I am hitting to kill, and I don't care who hears it on the recording. You are not going to be hitting me and getting away with it.
>
> I understand that is why you guys want us to be by ourselves when we do this [interview], so that they won't feel, like, intimidated by that man, if he is there or whatever. [Women in the study] need to tell the truth. They need to be honest about it, but they are not going to be honest because they feel like "the man" going to—the police going to knock on the door as you are going out—knock at the door and cuff him out and take him out of there. And I am telling you that is how they—because I felt that way. That is why I was like, "We this and we that."

As if gearing up for a revelation, Chantelle thought back to the accounts she had provided of her relationship experiences with her study partner over several waves of quantitative follow-up surveys before this in-depth qualitative interview. This time, she concluded emphatically: "'None of the above.' That is what I should have put. 'None of the above.'"

After we left the small apartment complex where Chantelle had made a new home for herself—the one she told us she would be proud never to have to share with a partner again—her reflection reverberated. At no point did she choose to tell us directly about personal experiences with abuse. But her forceful and candid account made it very clear that she had opted to answer some of our previous survey questions inaccurately, in hopes of presenting an image of postrelease relationship experiences that would not bring down further punishment on her former partner.

Our impressions from her responses to the follow-up surveys had been of a nonviolent relationship between two sober individuals, whose relationship happiness and satisfaction gradually deteriorated until they ended the relationship. As Chantelle later explained it in our qualitative interview, her partner's postrelease substance abuse and infidelity, and the ugly conflicts that surrounded each, had caused an almost immediate break after his return from prison. They had also left her fiercely resolved not to be deceived, abused, or taken advantage of again by a man. These alternative tellings of the same relationship story (neither of which is complete, and each of which leads to a different "moral") suggest the fundamental challenges of our research endeavor, as well as the untenability of Chantelle's position as a study participant. Carefully triangulating among her study partner, the research team that was asking each partner for truthful reports of their relationship, and a law enforcement presence she assumed was ready to reincarcerate him based on her reports, she concluded that her best available response to our survey questions would have been "None of the above."

. . .

As the moral of that day's story, "None of the above" was a stunning and discomfiting response. It was even more so given the interpersonal suffering (and suggested violence) that Chantelle had narrated—experiences that seemed so important to document and address. We had been careful to craft the follow-up survey questions and quantifiable answer categories in ways we thought would capture exactly the kinds of struggles with substance abuse and partner violence to which she later alluded in her qualitative interview. We had also designed a data collection approach we thought created a secure and comfortable enough environment for respondents like Chantelle to give candid answers (see text box, "Interviewing Justice-Involved Men and Their Partner about Abuse"). This included obtaining a federal Certificate of Confidentiality so we could assure participants during the informed consent process that their answers could never be released for any law enforcement purpose. Our interviewers built rapport with participants while administering the first part of the computer-based survey out loud and then helped them transition to a private self-interviewing mode to answer questions about more sensitive topics (such as the quality of their relationship, their own and their partner's alcohol and substance use, and their own and their partner's use of violence or controlling behavior in the relationship). Interviewers positioned themselves so they could not see the survey during this more sensitive section, and they informed participants that the program would lock the section as soon as they finished it, so interviewers would have no way to learn the responses.

What had seemed to us as researchers to be clear and adequate protections for the sensitive information we asked for was thoroughly unconvincing to Chantelle, however. She explained quite candidly that she and other women in her position could not answer our questions about their postrelease relationships with their partners openly, "because [we] feel like ... the police going to knock on the door as you are going out—knock at the door and cuff him out and take him out of there." Perhaps more stymieing to us was that later, as she reflected at some length on the whole interview experience during our more open-ended conversation, she did not feel even in retrospect that she could have trusted the research process and answered the questions about abuse openly. Rather, she still felt that what she "should have" done was to give no real answer at all.

There was no way for us to know, of course, how many participants had made similar choices to give answers that painted an incomplete or inaccurate picture of their relationship in hopes of avoiding further contact with the law. But we wanted a better understanding of the kinds of experiences that would lead a person like Chantelle to volunteer, forcefully and unprompted, "There is so much domestic violence out here, and women are scared." Toward that end, with access to both qualitative and quantitative data from many other couples, our team set out to better understand experiences and reporting of abuse after one partner returns from prison—how common abuse is; how differently

BOX 1. INTERVIEWING JUSTICE-INVOLVED MEN AND
THEIR PARTNERS ABOUT ABUSE

Private, individual interviews with each couple member: At study enrollment and each study follow-up, participating couples were separately asked the same structured questions about their experiences of abuse. Questions focused on abuse perpetration and victimization with the study partner only. Interviews were conducted in person by field interviewers extensively trained in confidentiality procedures and the protection of human subjects in research with vulnerable populations. The same interviewer was generally not permitted to interview both members of a particular couple and was never permitted to discuss the status or content of one partner's interview with the other partner. Informed consent was obtained before each interview. The section of the interview that included questions about abuse was completed using audio computer-assisted self-interviewing: the interviewer gave the participant a laptop and headphones with which to see and hear each question and set of responses and enter answers directly. This self-administered module was locked as soon as completed, so that the interviewer could not know what answers had been given. Interviews were conducted in private settings and lasted about two hours each.

Behaviorally specific measurement of perpetration and victimization: A condensed version of the Revised Conflict Tactics Scale (CTS2; Straus et al. 1996) was used that shortened the subscale on coercion and omitted subscales on verbal abuse ("verbal aggression"), injury, and negotiation. The CTS2 is the most widely used instrument in survey research on family violence and the instrument against which other intimate partner violence (IPV) measures are typically validated (Reichenheim et al. 2014; Kawakami et al. 2014; Signorelli et al. 2014). Consistent with the CTS2 approach, survey items were constructed to ask first about perpetration and then about victimization for each behavior, to increase reporting of victimization. Survey items elicited information on the number of times each respondent had used a given behavior against his or her survey partner and the number of times he or she was victimized by his or her survey partner in that manner. The reference periods were the six months prior to the male partner's incarceration (for the baseline interview) and the time since the male partner's release (for the postrelease interview or interviews).

Analytic composites representing physical violence and controlling behavior: An adapted summing approach consistent with recommendations of the CTS2 developers (Straus and Douglas 2004) was used to combine behaviorally specific individual-level measures into categories for analysis. *Any physical violence* was defined as one or more incidents in which one partner shoved, hit, slapped, grabbed, threw something at, choked, slammed, kicked, burned, or beat the other; used a knife or gun on the other; or forced the other to have sex by hitting, holding down, or using a weapon. *Frequent physical violence* was defined as six or more incidents of physical violence during a given reference period. *Any controlling behavior* was defined as one or more incidents in which one partner threatened to hurt the other partner or children, family members, or loved ones; tried to keep the other from seeing or talking to friends or family; or tried to keep money from the other, took money from him or her, or made him or her ask for money. *Frequent controlling behavior* was defined as six or more incidents of controlling behavior. *Severe physical or sexual violence* was defined as one or more incidents in which one partner beat, choked, slammed, kicked, burned, or beat the other; used a knife or gun; or forced the other to have sex by hitting, holding down, or using a weapon. To examine violence at the couple level, a composite measure of physical violence was created indicating whether *either* member of the couple reported any physical violence perpetration or victimization with his or her study partner during that period.

two members of the same couple might characterize abuse experiences in their respective reports to researchers; and how and why reports of postrelease abuse might differ from preincarceration reports. In this chapter, we describe prior research in each of these areas, then present findings from our own research with Chantelle, her ex-partner, and 1,481 other couples. Finally, we consider what this body of work means for future efforts to understand and respond to abuse among couples navigating one partner's incarceration and subsequent release.

PREVALENCE OF ABUSE AMONG JUSTICE-INVOLVED MEN AND THEIR PARTNERS
Prior Research

In the general U.S. population, about 3 percent of women and 2 percent of men report experiencing severe physical violence from an intimate partner in the past twelve months.[2] Its impacts, including injury and effects on physical and mental health, are visited more heavily on women (Black et al. 2011). Although rates of abuse perpetration and victimization among justice-involved men and their partners have not been the subject of much recent study, older research in this area suggests relatively high prevalence of preincarceration violence against family members. In one survey-based study, a third of prisoners reported having used physical violence against a partner in the twelve months before incarceration. Another study based on administrative records found that 30 percent had perpetrated some form of family violence before the incarceration (Dutton and Hart 1992). Finally, a study comparing self-reported information from incarcerated and nonincarcerated men found that incarcerated men reported significantly higher

---

2. The National Intimate Partner and Sexual Violence Survey defines "severe physical violence" as including pulling hair, hitting with a fist or something hard, kicking, slamming, trying to hurt by choking or suffocating, beating, burning on purpose, or using a knife or gun. This measure does not include incidents of slapping, pushing, or shoving.

rates of physical and psychological abuse of their partners than the nonincarcerated comparison group (Robertson and Murachver 2007).

Further, many risk factors for abuse victimization or perpetration are highly prevalent among justice-involved men. At the individual level, low income, a history of trauma, alcohol abuse, young age, mental health conditions, and stressful life situations—factors that tend to be disproportionately present among members of justice-involved couples—all correlate with partner violence victimization, revictimization, or both (Cattaneo and Goodman 2005; Golden, Perreira, and Durrance 2013; Jasinski and Kantor 2001; Renner and Slack 2006; Renzetti 2009; Schluter, Abbott, and Bellringer 2008; Slep et al. 2010; White and Chen 2002; Wildeman 2009; Wildeman and Muller 2012). And there is suggestive evidence that distrust of the justice system among those who have had contact with it (whether directly or through their partner) could decrease help-seeking for intimate-partner violence (Hampton, Oliver, and Magarian 2003; Taft et al. 2009) and promote revictimization.

Many of these same individual-level factors have been proposed as influences on partner violence *perpetration* as well: a history of trauma, substance abuse, young age, and mental health conditions, as well as unemployment, low educational attainment, and individual experiences of racism and marginalization (Dutton and Hart 1992; Caetano et al. 2007; Cheng and Lo 2015; Schafer, Caetano, and Cunradi 2004; White et al. 2002). At the interpersonal level, men's adaptation and coping in the prison environment can include hypervigilance, interpersonal distrust, and psychological distancing, all of which might promote interpersonal violence (Hairston and Oliver 2011; Haney 2003; Herman-Stahl, Kan, and McKay 2008). No link between incarceration experiences and family violence has been shown in quantitative analysis, but qualitative research on postrelease parenting among young fathers suggests such a link is plausible (Nurse 2002).

At the individual level, financial and logistical barriers to maintaining communication during incarceration can create feelings of distrust, suspicion, and emotional distance in relationships (Fishman 1990; Girshick 1996; Hairston and Oliver 2011). At the community level, abuse perpetration and victimization may also be shaped by chronic economic disadvantage (Wildeman 2009; Wildeman and Muller 2012; Golden, Perreira, and Durrance 2013; Renzetti 2009) and structural racism (Carson 2014; Wildeman and Muller 2012; Cheng and Lo 2015). Yet despite this extensive body of evidence suggesting the elevation of abuse risk among criminal justice system–involved individuals and their partners, how common these experiences actually are before an incarceration or during one partner's reentry from prison was unknown until the study we report here.

Multi-site Family Study Findings

The first of the three to four quantitative interviews we administered took place while the male partners were incarcerated for a wide variety of violent and nonviolent crimes[3]; the subsequent interviews continued in most cases through their release into the community. At that initial interview, both members of the couple were asked (separately) about physical violence and controlling behavior in their relationship during the six months before the male partner's incarceration. At the first postrelease interview, we asked both members of the couple (again separately) about any physical violence or controlling behavior in the relationship since the male partner's release. At the second postrelease interview, we asked the same questions again (focusing on the time since the last interview).

> 3. Men who were incarcerated on a domestic violence conviction or were subject to a restraining order against their intimate partner were excluded from the study in most sites (due to exclusion criteria in the family programs this study was evaluating). Those incarcerated for crimes against persons (e.g., robbery, homicide, assault) were *less* likely than those incarcerated for other types of offenses (e.g., drug, property, or public order offenses) to report using physical violence against their study partner prior to their incarceration ($p<.01$).

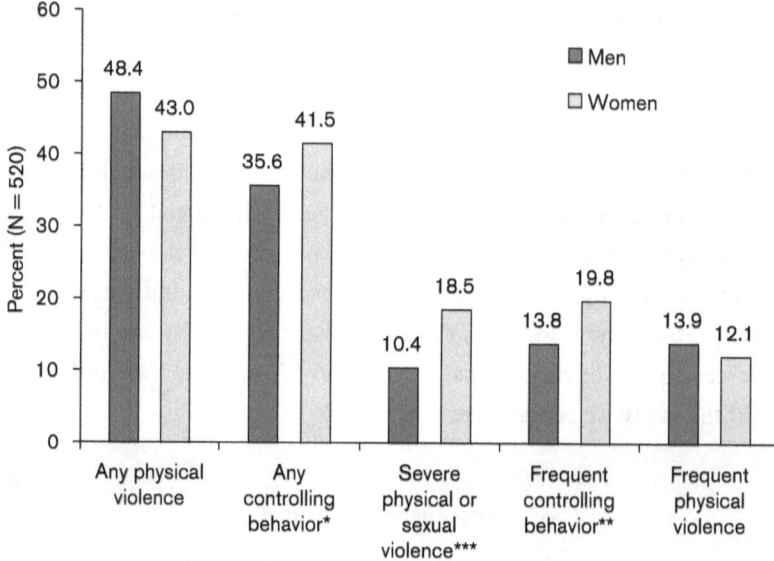

Figure 10. Survey reports of abuse victimization in Multi-site Family Study couples before incarceration. Asterisks indicate that differences between male and female partners within couples were statistically significant at the $p<0.05$ level (*), the $p<.01$ level (**), or the $p<.001$ level (***). Image credit: Justin Landwehr.

Well over 40 percent of men and women reported experiencing physical violence from their study partners during the six months before the incarceration, and over a third reported they were subject to controlling behavior by their partners (figure 10).

Using matched-pairs t-tests, we found that women were more likely than their male partners to be victims of any preincarceration controlling behavior, frequent preincarceration controlling behavior, and severe physical or sexual violence in the relationship. In many couples, participants reported the use of physical violence by both partners, but its effects differed by gender. In couples in which both partners used physical violence against one another, women were significantly less likely to feel safe (67 percent indicating they "always" or "often" felt safe compared to 78 percent of men).

COMPARING REPORTS OF ABUSE BEFORE AND AFTER INCARCERATION
Prior Research

Qualitative researchers have long suggested an elevated risk for abuse in couples reuniting after one partner's incarceration (Fishman 1990; Bobbitt, Campbell, and Tate 2006). Focus group research conducted separately with reentering men and with female partners of reentering men has showed that many expect abuse victimization or perpetration in the context of reentry challenges and stressors—including jealousy and accusations of infidelity; conflicts over roles and authority, coparenting difficulties, and financial pressures; as well as partners' feelings of helplessness and anger. Some reentering men said they would feel justified in using violence against a partner during the reentry process if she were to challenge his authority in the family or reveal that she had been unfaithful during his incarceration (Hairston and Oliver 2005; Oliver and Hairston 2008).

Little quantitative research on the prevalence of abuse among released prisoners and their partner exists, but one study used administrative data from a state correctional agency and local law enforcement agencies to assess postrelease relationship abuse perpetration among 1,137 men released from state prison between 2004 and 2009 (Freeland Braun 2012). The author found that 25 percent perpetrated physical abuse against a partner between the time of their release and the end of the study follow-up period (averaging seven months).

Multi-site Family Study Findings

In our study sample, abuse remained widespread after the male partner's release from prison. Approximately a quarter of men and women reported physical violence victimization by their study partner between the male partner's release from incarceration and the first postrelease follow-up interview (a median time of six months). Reports of physical violence

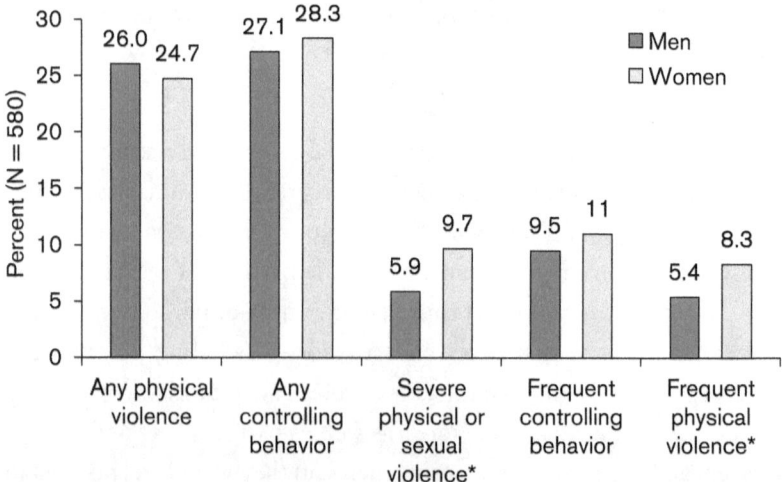

Figure 11. Survey reports of abuse victimization in Multi-site Family Study couples after release. Asterisks indicate that differences between male and female partners within couples were statistically significant at the $p<0.05$ level (*), the $p<.01$ level (**), or the $p<.001$ level (***). Image credit: Justin Landwehr.

victimization did decline from preincarceration to postrelease, however. After the male partner's release, 50 percent of couples reported no physical violence in their relationships, compared to only 30 percent of couples who reported violence-free relationships before the incarceration.

Matched-pairs *t*-tests indicated that within couples, women are more likely than their male partners to report severe physical or sexual violence victimization or frequent physical violence victimization in the relationship after the partner's release (figure 11).

COMPARING ABUSE REPORTS FROM BOTH PARTNERS
Prior Research

Research on abuse experiences often elicits information from study participants on both victimization and perpetration—but research seeking to understand these experiences through direct reports from both members of a couple is scarce. Three studies using couples-based survey methods found that members of different-sex couples provided starkly incongruent accounts of abuse experiences within the couple: for example, one partner often reported violence within the relationship when the other reported none. A national study of different-sex cohabiting couples found that about 50 percent more couples disagreed than agreed on the presence of abuse in their relationships, as measured by an adapted Conflict Tactics Scale similar to that used in the Multi-site Family Study (Schafer, Caetano, and Clark 2002). Similarly, a study of young adults found that among couples in which one partner reported any abuse, the other partner gave the same report less than one-third of the time (Berger et al. 2012).

A study of blue-collar adult couples found widespread disagreement for different forms of abuse and injury—with men likely to contradict their partner's reports of abuse victimization, and both men and women likely to disagree with their partner regarding whether they caused any injury (Cunradi, Bersamin, and Ames 2009). Disagreement within the couple regarding male-on-female abuse became more likely as severity of the reported abuse increased (Cunradi, Bersamin, and Ames 2009). In all three studies, within-couple differences in abuse reporting typically involved a female partner reporting abuse when her male partner did not (Schafer, Caetano, and Clark 2002). In two of the studies, this held true regardless of whether the violence reported was perpetrated by the male or female partner. In one, comparisons between men's reports of victimization and perpetration and those of their partner suggested that men might be underreporting perpetration but not victimization (Cunradi, Bersamin, and Ames 2009). In a fourth study, which enrolled men in residential substance abuse treatment and their female partner in the community, partners' agreement with one another regarding one form of abuse (sexual aggression in the relationship) was no greater than expected by chance alone (Freeman, Schumacher, and Coffey 2015).

Prior research also suggests that within-couple abuse reporting differences could be related to gender differences in memory (with women remembering more than men; Armstrong et al. 2001), social desirability effects, cognitive dissonance, or fear of punishment (Medina et al. 2004). In addition, reporting differences were found to be more common among couples of color (Medina et al. 2004). However, the literature contains no prior quantitative study on disagreement in abuse reporting among men and women who are involved with the criminal justice system or subject to ongoing monitoring and surveillance after a release from prison (Hairston and Oliver 2011).

Multi-site Family Study Findings

First, we examined differences in abuse reporting within Multi-site Family Study couples. Matched-pair *t*-tests showed that members of the same couple often provided different accounts of abuse in their relationships, particularly when it came to frequent or severe physical and sexual violence (with the partner of someone who reported frequent or severe physical or sexual victimization in the relationship often not reporting such perpetration). In addition, men whose partner reported frequent controlling-behavior victimization often did not themselves report frequent controlling-behavior perpetration (whereas women's reports of their own controlling behavior tended to better match their partner's accounts of victimization).

Next, we explored how common it was for Multi-site Family Study couples to disagree about abuse within their relationships and whether disagreement varied by the form or severity of abuse. Among couples who reported any physical violence or controlling behavior in their relationships before the incarceration, 67 percent disagreed on some aspect of their experiences. Disagreement became more common with increasing severity of abuse and was particularly likely regarding severe physical or sexual violence.

In couples whose reports of severe physical or sexual violence in their relationship did not align, the female partner was significantly more likely to be the victim and to be the one who disclosed abuse in her survey reports. Women who reported severe physical or sexual violence victimization but whose partners did not acknowledge perpetration reported lower relationship happiness, commitment, and communication; higher levels of post-traumatic stress disorder (PTSD) and binge drinking; and stronger disapproval of the use of violence in relationships. They also felt less safe.[4]

MAKING SENSE OF CHANGE AND DISCREPANCY IN ABUSE REPORTS

More often than not, study couples gave discrepant reports of abuse in their relationships. Indeed, our expectation of such differences was one of our strongest motives for undertaking a couples-based study, despite the significant additional resources and risks involved. But in general, we expected any differences between couple members might be related to relatively minor differences in perspective, misperception, or recall of their family experiences: for example, one parent saying he spent more time with the children than the other partner saw him spend, or even one partner reporting a joking shove that the other did not remember or did not consider relevant to the survey question.[5] In sharp contrast, men's and women's reports of abuse were most likely to disagree with one another regarding an experience that should have been highly

---

4. Although our analyses looked for what was distinct about either member of these couples, the only statistically significant differences we identified were among women; no statistically significant differences were evident among men.

5. Survey questions did not ask participants to distinguish the intent or context of instances of physical violence but simply asked them to report the behavior itself. This approach does not permit researchers to differentiate physical behaviors undertaken in a joking or affectionate context from those undertaken in the context of conflict or intent to harm or control.

salient and memorable: severe physical or sexual violence. Rather than a matter of interpretation or of salience, then, these patterns of discrepancy appeared to be a matter of how high the stakes were.

We also embarked on the study with expectations, based on a rich body of other qualitative data, that many couples experienced a time of heightened abuse when one partner returned from prison. We were surprised to find that rates of postincarceration abuse in our sample, while staggeringly high, were actually lower than reports of abuse before the incarceration. Interpreting this apparent decline in the context of prior research, combined with our own findings on discrepant within-couple reporting, we had to consider three distinct possibilities: (1) individuals might decide to stop using violence after the incarceration, (2) something might prompt individuals to end abusive relationships, or (3) individuals might become less willing to report experiences of abuse to researchers after the male partner's return from prison.

Abstinence from Abuse

No prior research has examined how or why individuals might come to abstain from abuse during the reentry period. To explore this phenomenon in our data, we used multiple regression to compare the experiences of a set of couples in which neither partner reported any physical violence perpetration or victimization at the first postrelease follow-up to the experiences of all the other couples.[6] Several individual and interpersonal factors set the nonviolent couples apart. They had been together as a couple longer; the male partners scored higher than other men in our study on healthy relationship beliefs; and the women scored higher than other women in our study on conflict resolution and were subject to less jealousy and possessiveness from their partner. In addi-

---

6. We speculated that perfect agreement from both partners on the total absence of both male-to-female and female-to-male violence suggested that their reports were more likely to represent a "true" violence-free relationship than that of couples in which just one partner reported a violence-free relationship.

tion, at the time of their first postrelease interview, these couples had been back together in the community for a shorter period than the other couples—giving them less exposure time for abuse to occur.

Separation-Instigated Violence or Violence-Instigated Separation?

Regarding the possibility that individuals might end abusive relationships at reentry, general population research indicates that abuse is a significant predictor of relationship dissolution (Shortt et al. 2006; Zlotnick, Johnson, and Kohn 2006). Conversely, data from divorcing couples indicates that the experiences surrounding dissolution of a relationship can also precipitate a first instance of violence in a previously nonviolent relationship (often referred to as *separation-instigated violence*); other literature suggests that existing violence can escalate during relationship separation as an abusive partner attempts to retain control (Kelly and Johnson 2008).

Two-sample t-tests showed that respondents whose relationships had ended during the postrelease follow-up period reported higher rates of several forms of abuse than those still romantically involved with their study partner. These included any controlling behavior, frequent controlling behavior, frequent physical violence, and severe physical or sexual violence. Among the 256 respondents who reported in the postrelease follow-up that they had separated from their study partner since the last interview, 10 percent of men and 28 percent of women named physical partner violence as one of the reasons the relationship had ended.

To assess whether abuse made couples more likely to separate or, conversely, whether relationship separation influenced the likelihood of abuse (as in Kelly and Johnson's [2008] theory of separation-instigated violence), we constructed cross-lagged autoregressive models using all available waves of men's and women's survey data to assess whether reporting abuse at one wave made it more likely that a respondent would no longer be in a relationship with the study partner at the next wave, or vice versa. Reporting abuse before the incarceration did not affect the likelihood that couples would be in a committed romantic relationship after the male partner's release. Nor did relationship status at one interview wave influence abuse reporting at the next. However, men's reported abuse victimization at the first postrelease interview did influence their reported relationship status at the second postrelease interview: men who reported victimization at their postrelease interview were 1.4 times less likely to be in a romantic relationship with their study partner the next time they were interviewed.

No comparable effect was present for women in the quantitative data.[7] In our in-depth qualitative interview data, however, many women described ending the relationship with their partner due to abuse—even though abuse was not a topic we asked about directly. For example:

> INTERVIEWER: Were there other issues that caused problems in your relationship?
> FEMALE STUDY PARTICIPANT: That was just about it. Just the abuse. But nothing else I could think of other than him going to jail all the time. That is basically it. That is what did it. Because we was in love.

A few women described the decision to separate from an abusive partner without mentioning his incarceration, but many noted that incarceration had created a specific opportunity to end an abusive relationship. In one woman's words: "I seen it as a way out.... He went to jail so I could be free. I don't have to be scared no more and I don't have to worry about nothing no more."

For others, when their partner was in the community, pressure from the abusive partner to stay in the relationship combined with their own

---

7. The result for women has somewhat less statistical power to detect an effect because there were more men than women in the analytic samples for the prerelease interview wave (574 men and 552 women) and for the first postrelease interview wave (632 men and 590 women). For the second postrelease interview wave, there were more women than men (418 women and 390 men).

pain and ambivalence was too much to overcome. Episodes of incarceration sometimes tipped this balance:

> It's different if they're incarcerated and if they're not. Because if they're incarcerated you don't have to deal with the emotional part because you can cut that world off. But if they're out, it's totally different because they have the access of communication and being able to follow, being able to find you, being able to beg and plead, and you've got to be very strong-willed. I mean, I wasn't strong-willed for a long time. And then [when] I knew it was going to be a longer incarceration, I knew it was my time [to leave]. But on the outside, if they are not incarcerated, I—gosh, I wouldn't know what to do because I was so weak at those times and felt sorry. "Well, I don't have no place to go." And "Please let me back in." And I always did.

Still, it was not as if the abusive partner's incarceration simply lifted the weight from these women's shoulders. When asked more about how she felt when her ex-partner was incarcerated, the participant who had moments ago declared, "He went to jail so I could be free," related:

> I had mixed emotions. I felt safe, I felt hurt again, and I felt abandonment. I felt lost, like I was just—all these feelings at once. I cried, I cried, I cried. I didn't want to live no more ... like what is the use of me living? But I thought about it. I was like, "I got kids. Snap out of it and get yourself together! You got to take care of your kids, regardless of what." I was depressed, I would say. I was depressed because he was gone, but a little happy that I didn't have to go through the domestic violence. But me missing him and everything like that, I still did. I still did regardless.

These in-depth reports make it clear that, despite nonsignificant quantitative findings in our regression models, abuse did lead some women in our study to end their relationship with their study partner at various points over the course of those partners' incarceration and reentry. Their accounts further emphasize how challenging it was to make, and stick by, such decisions: that the line between staying and leaving was often tenuous and that leaving did not spare women from many of the other hardships associated with a partner's (and coparent's) incarceration.

For all that these qualitative results clarified, however, they also raised further questions. Something was still escaping our notice. Our qualitative data indicated that incarceration was an opportunity for some women to end relationships with abusive partners—a finding reinforced by survey reports among women whose relationships had ended as of the postrelease interview (28 percent of whom cited physical violence in the relationship as a reason for ending it). In both qualitative and quantitative analyses, parallel findings for men were either weak or absent. Yet our relatively well-powered cross-lagged autoregression had shown a link between abuse victimization and relationship status for men but *not* women (as our qualitative data would have suggested), as well as between the first postrelease interview and the next postrelease wave but *not* from preincarceration to postrelease (which is what our qualitative data suggested). These apparently contradictory findings needed further investigation.

Willingness to Disclose Abuse

Research on abuse, like any stigmatized behavior or experience, is always subject to inaccurate reporting. Such inaccuracies are difficult to measure by definition, but comparing couple members' survey reports of an experience they both shared offers a window into these issues (Freeman, Schumacher, and Coffey 2015). Our within-couple comparisons of abuse reporting indicated that our study couples' accounts differed more often than they aligned. To explore whether changes in respondents' willingness to disclose these experiences to researchers could have shaped other study findings (including the observed decrease in abuse reports from preincarceration to postrelease), we examined the qualitative data on participants' perceptions of these disclosures.

Although the qualitative interviews did not include an explicit focus on study participants' reporting to probation and parole, their statements indicated that the period after men's release from prison was dominated, and structured, by high-stakes monitoring and reporting responsibilities. As one man stated:

> I feel like I learn something, and now I got this [parole officer] on my back saying, "Well, make sure you come see me, or you are going to jail. If you don't come see me twice a month you are going to jail." I don't have a vehicle. I got to get people to bring me here. Not only am I coming here, you are interfering with me trying to go to school, you are interfering with me trying to get a job.

Another expressed the constant, uneasy awareness that many others alluded to when discussing probation and parole monitoring: "All you would have to do is call my PO [parole officer] and make up something, and they send you back to prison. Now I get took away from my family, my children, everybody who care about me."

Women, too, conveyed acute awareness that their partner's life (and often their own) was being monitored by the criminal justice system after his release from prison. Some felt this kind of monitoring was coming from our study as well. One woman explained how carefully she considered her responses to our questions about behaviors that could have caused her partner to be reincarcerated if his parole officer had been notified:

> That is why I didn't put on there that [my partner] was drinking. Because I thought it was going to violate him. I didn't put it on there. Didn't think that the arguing that me and [my partner] was doing—I didn't put it on there because I didn't want you to say that, "Well, he is this," and then the test came out a certain way. I didn't know how you all was grading this test.

These comments, which came from a female study participant who had ended an unhealthy relationship with her study partner soon after his release from prison, suggest that respondents did not necessarily distinguish "reporting" to study staff from "reporting" to formal authorities. They raise the possibility, in turn, that women's pronounced reluctance to disclose their partners' illegal or problematic behaviors during the postrelease period could have kept our study from being able to meaningfully assess whether their disclosures of abuse at one postrelease survey wave influenced their reported relationship status at the next (the two time points when such an effect was observed for men).

CONSIDERATIONS FOR FUTURE RESEARCH AND PRACTICE
Supporting Safety through Adjudication, Incarceration, and Reentry

Prior studies suggested but had not quantitatively assessed elevated rates of abuse at the time of a partner's return from prison (Bobbitt, Campbell, and Tate 2011; Fishman 1990; Hairston and Oliver 2005). In our study, 10 percent of men and 19 percent of women reported severe physical or sexual violence victimization by their study partner during the six months prior to the male partner's incarceration; after the incarceration, 6 percent of men and 10 percent of women reported severe physical or sexual violence victimization (during a median period of six months postrelease). In contrast, roughly 2 percent of U.S. men and women in the general population report experiencing severe physical violence from *any* intimate partner over a twelve-month reference period (Breiding, Chen, and Black 2014).

Our research lends strength to prior assertions that addressing abuse is critical to a safe and successful reentry for formerly incarcerated persons and their partners (Bobbitt, Campbell, and Tate 2011). It also suggests that individuals experiencing abuse may choose to end their relationship following the male partner's release from prison, and it highlights the importance of creating opportunities to do so in a safe and supported manner. Expanding reentry case management—which typically begins six to twelve months prior to release and is often focused on those considered at high risk for recidivism, morbidity, or mortality during reentry (e.g., those with serious mental illness or HIV)—shows promise for creating such opportunities. It could also be helpful for community-based transitions clinics—which provide culturally competent peer support, health care, and health coverage enrollment assistance to newly released individuals—to add a focus on abuse prevention. In addition, case managers and peer navigators already working with prerelease or newly released individuals, their partner, and other members of the household to which they are returning could usefully offer abuse screening, basic universal education on relationship safety and available community resources, and a coordinated ("warm handoff") referral for those who disclose abuse. Further, our findings show that partners of released men who might need help to end or maintain their safety in an abusive relationship are juggling multiple threats beyond the relationship itself—including the threat that their disclosure might send their partner back to prison. It is crucial to create opportunities for women to disclose abuse to service providers or other truly trusted individuals in the community or to access alternative forms of safety-related support without making a direct disclosure.

Our findings also call attention to a previously undiscussed need for abuse prevention programming *before* an impending incarceration, as couples weather one partner's adjudication or await his incarceration. Funding community-based domestic violence or crisis response programs to conduct tailored outreach to justice-involved individuals and their family and to staff satellite offices at Family Justice Centers and other community locations frequented by families in contact with the criminal justice system could also be valuable. Pretrial family outreach, used in a few jurisdictions to connect family members of arrestees with resources and support, could also be expanded to include abuse screening, universal education, and a warm-handoff referral.

Studying Abuse and Abuse Disclosure among Justice-Involved Couples

Unlike prior studies of abuse among justice-involved individuals and their partners, ours afforded the ability to trace experiences over time, to compare individuals' disclosures with those of their partners, and to review in-depth qualitative data that illuminated the patterns we observed in quantitative analyses. First and foremost, this combination of methods revealed widespread, serious safety concerns in couples navigating pre- and postincarceration relationships that merit immediate attention. At the same time, these methods exposed great complexity and ambivalence in participants' relationships to one another, to the forced separation of an incarceration, and to our own research.

Our study's extensive assurances of neutrality and confidentiality did not prevent study participants from making many strategic choices about what they told us, and when and how. Comparing participants' accounts through time, across interview formats, and against those of their partner, as we did in this analysis, made those choices more apparent. The stories we wove in the analytic process were shaped not only by our choices of analytic focus and approach but also by thousands of storytelling choices made by our study participants over the several years of their participation. Chantelle's conclusion—"'None of the above.' That is what I should have put. 'None of the above.'"—revealed participants' sharp awareness of the constraints within which this story-craft occurred. Chantelle weighed a set of complex and high-stakes factors in drawing her conclusion: on one hand, interviewers' assurances of confidentiality, the implicit request for truthfulness, and perhaps the desire for some form of help or understanding; on the other, the knowledge that even a small misstep would send her partner back to prison and the expectation that any information she offered was likely to be used in ways far beyond her control.

In Chantelle's retrospection, then, simply picking a response that better captured the reality of her relationship was not an option. Given that the topic was her partner's (implied) addiction and (implied) abusiveness, the complexity of risks she measured in giving her original survey answers and measured again in reflecting back on them during her qualitative interview was evident—and the vulnerability of her position, chilling. In researching these experiences and deriving recommendations for practice (including screening for abuse), it is easy to join Chantelle in exhorting women "to tell the truth" about these experiences. It is all too unsettling to hear, "They are not going to be honest because they feel like ... the police going to knock on the door as you are going out."

Victims' decision-making about whether and when to disclose abuse to authorities or service providers is the subject of much research (e.g., Demers et al. 2017; Spangaro et al. 2016). But victims' (and perpetrators') decisions about whether, when, and how to disclose such facts to *researchers* remain very little understood—despite the critical, ongoing role of study participants' answers in shaping our empirical understanding of the reality of abuse. Our research strategies were intended to get us closer to that reality by triangulating across modes, methods, and reporters. Instead, these methods deprived us of the illusion that we had captured reality. This work succeeded in revealing not the "truth," but rather the profound constraints on truth-telling reentering men and their partners are subject to—constraints that became inextricably woven into the story crafted through our research. Future research with such families must do better at considering and addressing these constraints on truth-telling, particularly if the aim is to inform and support victim safety, rather than to contribute yet another source of threat.

CHAPTER FIVE

"Change Ain't Going to Happen Overnight"

Operationalizing Reentry Success

The tendency to view prisoners from a corrections-focused lens that largely overlooks their identities as parents and intimate or coparenting partners, as we noted earlier, has resulted in a narrow metric for assessing whether they are "successful" after release: that is, whether they avoid rearrest or reincarceration. In this chapter we use, instead, a multidimensional approach to describe the reentry experiences of over 1,000 men released from incarceration over the course of the Multi-site Family Study. Using a traditional recidivism indicator based on official corrections records, we found that the vast majority of the men would be considered successful. Yet self-reported quantitative interview data on other important aspects of their lives told a more complicated story, identifying areas where many struggled. In general, these men were more successful in avoiding illegal drug use, having a positive couple relationship, and financially supporting their children than in gaining employment or avoiding criminal justice system involvement. Importantly, family contact during incarceration and in-prison services (including employment, education, and substance abuse treatment programs) predicted more successful reentry.

This multidimensional approach to understanding reentry success introduces complexity in discerning patterns and interpreting findings, as reentering individuals do not fit neatly into categories of "successful" and "not successful." But it enables a more comprehensive picture of what happens to people—and families—after the end of an incarceration. Our findings show areas where formerly incarcerated men need additional support, time periods when intervention may be most beneficial, and specific policies and practices that show promise as ways to promote success across several important areas of people's lives as they reenter the community after prison.[1]

OLIVIA AND JASON'S STORY

Olivia was eight and a half months pregnant at the time of her interview, going stir crazy after several weeks of bed rest due to preterm labor. Jason, her partner and the father of the baby, had been released from prison about a year earlier after serving a ten-year term. Although they were living in New York City, Jason had spent most of his sentence in a prison in Ohio. Olivia was currently working as a certified nurse's assistant, but for years during Jason's incarceration she had been making $7 an hour at Popeye's Chicken. As a mother also supporting two children, her visits to the Ohio penitentiary had been few and far between. Both of them acknowledged that the lack of contact had strained their relationship, causing tensions that included Jason's belief that Olivia was seeing someone else and Olivia's that Jason had struck up a romance with an Ohio-based pen pal who visited him regularly in prison.

Nonetheless, the bond between the two of them ran deep: Olivia had met Jason through his sister, with whom she had been in foster care. Olivia's first pregnancy was with another partner but she and Jason had become involved soon thereafter, and when Jason was asked how many children he had, he firmly stated: "I have two children. One is not biologically mine, but I've been with his mother since he was six months,

---

1. This chapter builds on prior work by the authors with analytic contributions from Stephen Tueller and Danielle Steffey (Lindquist, Steffey, Tueller, Feinberg, et al. 2016).

so that's my child." In her interview, Olivia noted that in fact the emotional toll of Jason's incarceration had been hardest on their son—because he had been parented by Jason for around seven years and was old enough to understand the loss of his father figure, whereas their daughter had been a toddler and over time had lost any memories of being with her dad. Both parents identified the enormous difference a decade makes in the lives of children as a challenge for Jason's return to the household. When Jason left, Olivia noted that their daughter "was a little baby in Pampers"; when he returned, she was a "strong-minded" teenager with "breasts, butt—she has a period," and she saw her mother as the sole authority figure in her life. Jason said of their son: "I came home, and everything is different. My son is my size.... I left, he didn't have no front teeth. I come back, he got a girlfriend. He think he smooth."

With their third child on the way, the family was struggling to find their footing. Olivia and the children were living together, and although Jason spent extended periods of time with them each day, he had a separate residence not far away. Both of them sidestepped our question about this arrangement, alluding to issues of convenience and leaving the possibility hanging that Jason was not permitted to share the family residence—perhaps due to parole conditions or to interdictions of formerly incarcerated people living in Section 8 housing. Jason was in an OSHA training program but had not been employed since his release. His lack of income frustrated him because he strongly believed that the man should be the breadwinner in a family. He attributed his lack of income to his resolution not to return to criminalized activity: "If I was doing the wrong thing, I'd probably have a car right now, a pocket full of money." According to him, his former contacts in the drug economy took him shopping and gave him money to support him: "That's how I'm living now.... I get money every week." He joked that this left him awkwardly perched between two worlds: "I ain't merged good with society yet. I ain't picked up on the little nuances.... When I left, I was the man—grrr! I was a monster! Now I'm Bill Huxtable."

From Olivia's perspective, it made sense that Jason found it hard to adapt: "He had a routine for ten years.... To be in jail for ten years, change ain't going to happen overnight." When asked about changes she had observed in him since he had been incarcerated, she responded immediately: "Mentally, it messed him up," and she talked about his quickness to anger, his hypervigilance, and his tendency to talk to himself. She was helping him apply for SSI and wanted to "get him a therapist so that he can talk to somebody"; she also had managed to get him signed up for Medicaid and obtain a social security card and ID card. It angered her that these tasks fell to her. She expressed frustration that the parole system does not provide such services for Jason: "They wouldn't even help him get Medicaid. I had to do that. But if you know the system, it's designed for you to do a 365 circle and end up back in jail. That's why they don't help you." Despite all these challenges, Olivia and Jason expressed excitement about the future with the baby on the way and plans to get married. Jason was solemn when he said, "This is the woman that stood by me when I was incarcerated for so long. You know, I owe a debt to her.... And my debt is that I owe her the rest of my life, because she stood by me for ten years."

DEFINING AND UNDERSTANDING "SUCCESSFUL" REENTRY AMONG FORMERLY INCARCERATED PERSONS
Prior Research

Not surprisingly, given the tendency to view incarcerated individuals nearly exclusively as "prisoners" whose relevance is defined by their interaction with the criminal justice system, much prior research on what happens after release focuses on avoiding recidivism—commonly understood as a return to criminal justice system involvement through arrest or reincarceration. This approach considers formerly incarcerated persons such as Jason to be successful in reentry, as long as they avoid a new arrest or incarceration within a certain period after their release. Recidivism is an important metric, because many justice-involved individuals do, indeed, experience rearrest and reincarceration after a release from prison despite practically universal hopes of avoiding it. For criminal justice system stakeholders, whether individuals return to the system or not is considered very important from both cost and public safety perspectives.

Previous research clearly shows that avoiding rearrest or reincarceration is a significant challenge for reentering individuals. The most recent and commonly used data from the Bureau of Justice Statistics, which examined patterns across thirty states, found that the vast majority (83 percent) of individuals released from prison were rearrested at least once during the nine years after their release (Alper, Durose, and Markman 2018). The importance of recidivism, especially regarding the need to uncover factors that help reentering individuals avoid a new arrest or incarceration, is clear.

At the same time, recidivism is a very limited and often flawed metric. It conflates criminal justice system surveillance and decision-making (e.g., police activity and supervision efforts) with individual behavior and does not account for social context, such as neighborhoods of concentrated disadvantage (Butts and Schiraldi 2018). Considering alternative measures and using a desistance framework that incorporates other measures of how people are reintegrated into a community after an incarceration are therefore important (Butts and Schiraldi 2018). Further, a number of other dimensions of reentry experiences have costs and benefits for families, communities, and society as well.

Avoiding drug use and being employed are two such outcomes. While these outcomes tend to be less of a focus in reentry research than avoiding recidivism, several previous reentry studies have explored them. Drug addiction is one of the most challenging barriers to successful reentry. An overwhelming proportion of those involved with the criminal justice system have substance abuse problems. Based on a comprehensive review of 11 federal correctional reports and more than 650 articles, the National Center on Addiction and Substance

Abuse at Columbia University estimated that almost two-thirds (65 percent) of incarcerated individuals have a diagnosable alcohol or other drug use disorder (Center on Addiction and Substance Abuse 2010)—a prevalence seven times higher than in the general population (Karberg and James 2005).

Securing employment also poses challenges for many reentering individuals. Described as "a centerpiece of the reentry process," finding a job has often been identified by incarcerated men as their number one reentry priority (e.g., Solomon et al. 2004). Certainly, self-sufficiency after imprisonment requires a stable income. But the positive effects of employment can extend beyond the individual to the broader community. These include daily structure and positive social connections for former prisoners, increased income and financial stability for their family, a broader community tax base, and lower overall criminalized activity (Solomon et al. 2004). Employment is a particular challenge, however—in part because prisoners typically have lower educational attainment than the general population (Harlow 2003). They are also disproportionately released to communities with high unemployment and limited job opportunities (Solomon et al. 2004). Data collected for the Multi-site Evaluation of the Serious and Violent Offender Reentry Initiative found that almost all participants worked prior to incarceration (90 percent), but the majority worked low-wage, low-skilled jobs, and many supplemented their incomes with money from criminalized activities (Lattimore and Visher 2009). Individuals with a criminal record also face discrimination in the labor market, particularly if they are Black (Bushway 2004; Pager 2007).

Beyond avoiding recidivism and substance abuse and finding employment—all critical to a successful transition back to community life—several other dimensions of reentry are important to returning prisoners, reflecting the strength of their identities as parents and intimate partners. As we describe in chapters 2 and 3, positive family functioning and the fulfillment of family responsibilities are key priorities for many reentering individuals. The in-depth qualitative data discussed in chapter 2 show that men's self-concepts and their hopes for life after incarceration often center on fathering. Although reentry is generally recognized as taking place in the context of family relationships (healthy or unhealthy), very few studies have examined these personal dimensions of the reentry experience. Interviews with incarcerated individuals before and after release confirm that partners and other family members often serve as sources of housing, emotional support, financial resources, and overall stability during the reentry period (Visher et al. 2004). Studies with former prisoners have found that those with close ties to family members, including spouses or intimate partners, report higher optimism, confidence, financial and emotional support, and intent to desist from future criminalized activity than those without such ties (Burnett 2004; Naser and Visher 2006; Nelson, Dees, and Allen 2011). Providing financial support for children is a closely related dimension of reentry success for reentering parents; it may reflect positive family engagement and internalization of a parental role, and it may also serve as motivation for postrelease employment (Edin, Nelson, and Paranal 2004). Taken together, this body of research highlights the importance to reentry success of assuming (or reassuming) meaningful family roles after release. Yet many studies and policies have neglected the fact that reentering individuals are embedded in family relationships that often constitute a large part of their identity.

Further, very few studies have attempted to identify predictors of reentry success that can be influenced by policy. The small amount of research that has examined predictors of various reentry outcomes has tended to focus on static factors, such as history of involvement with the criminal justice system, and demographic characteristics, such as age. This limits the policy relevance of many of these works. Research to identify malleable factors that influence the likelihood of reentry success is sorely needed.

Finally, reentry is an ongoing process with no definitive end point, yet it is rarely viewed as such in research or reentry programming.

Reentering prisoners may also be more or less successful at certain time points after release, but prior research has rarely been able to assess "success" periodically and thus identify the time periods when intervention is needed the most.

Multi-site Family Study Findings

The methodological approach we describe in this chapter diverges from previous reentry research by (1) introducing a multidimensional definition of reentry success, (2) comparing factors that affect postrelease trajectories across domains, and (3) offering a quantitative perspective on how these factors influence one another during the reentry period. Our study looked at reentry success among 1,017 men in the Multi-site Family Study who were released from incarceration at some point during the follow-up period and participated in at least one postrelease interview. Exploring both traditional and multidimensional measures of reentry success, we found that discerning and interpreting patterns using a multidimensional conceptualization of reentry success, although introducing substantial research complexity, provided a more nuanced understanding of men's postrelease lives.

First, we examined men's reentry success using a single, official measure: whether they had been reincarcerated in a state prison during a certain period of time based on administrative prison records. These analyses indicated that official records of reincarceration paint only a partial picture of men's experiences after release. Simply using administrative-records data provided by the state departments of correction in the five states where the study was conducted, we found that most men were successful in avoiding a new incarceration in state prison. Only 11 percent of the men were reincarcerated in state prison within twelve months of their release, and only 21 percent were reincarcerated in state prison within twenty-four months. Among men who were reincarcerated, the average time from release to the first reincarceration was just under one year (341 days).

We also found that not many factors significantly predicted the likelihood of reincarceration in state prison among our sample. When we ran multivariate regression models to identify characteristics associated with reincarceration within twelve or twenty-four months, we found very few significant associations. Men who were older at study enrollment and at the time of their first arrest were more likely to be successful in avoiding reincarceration at both time periods. Men with more extensive histories of criminal justice system involvement (e.g., more previous arrests) were less likely to avoid reincarceration at both time periods. Men who had more in-person contact with family members during their incarceration and less problematic alcohol or drug use prior to their incarceration were more likely to avoid reincarceration within twenty-four months of release.

Next, we examined reentry success using a more holistic measure based on men's own reports during their study interviews. This work yielded a somewhat deeper, although still not completely clear, understanding of postrelease experiences. We examined success in the five areas of life (domains) shown in figure 12. Reentering men were more successful in some domains than others. They were more likely to be successful after release in having a positive intimate/coparenting relationship (domain 4), financially supporting their focal child (domain 5), and avoiding illicit drug use (domain 2) than they were in obtaining employment (domain 3) or avoiding rearrest or reincarceration in jail or prison (domain 1).

Third, men appeared to "gain their footing" over time with regard to securing employment and providing financial support to their focal child. However, the odds of success in a positive intimate/coparenting relationship and avoiding illicit drug use deteriorated slightly over time—and deteriorated much more dramatically with regard to avoiding rearrest or reincarceration. When we examined how many men were classified as successful at each postrelease time period in all five domains, the pattern of deteriorating success as the postrelease period lengthened was inconsistent (see "Multidomain success" bars in figure 12).

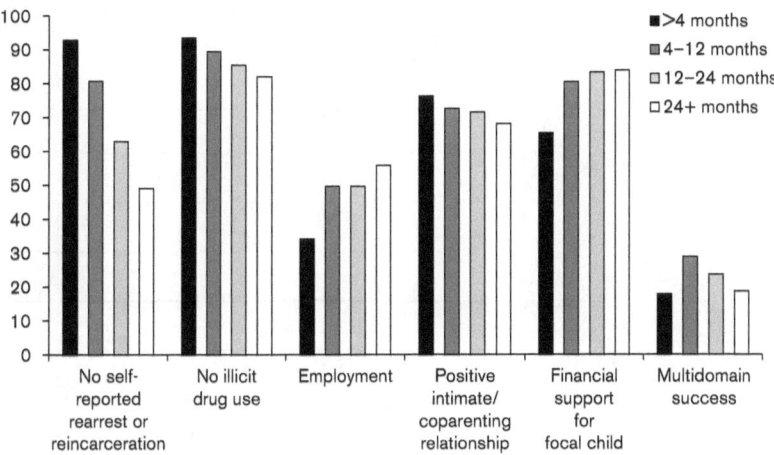

Figure 12. Proportion of reentering men classified as successful in each domain, by post-release time period. Image credit: Danielle Steffey.

Whereas men appeared to make strides four to twelve months postrelease (compared to the period immediately after their release), in the two subsequent time periods decreasing proportions of men experienced multidomain success.

To identify predictors of reentry success in the five domains shown in figure 12, we ran a series of multivariate regression models (see table 1 for a summary of findings). As with the earlier multivariate regression models to identify characteristics associated with reincarceration in state prison based on official correctional records, men's histories of criminal justice system involvement (in this case, the number of previous arrests) was negatively associated with self-reported avoidance of rearrest or reincarceration. That is, men with more prior arrests were less likely to avoid self-reported rearrest or reincarceration during the first three postrelease time periods. Other factors assessed at the baseline interview that were associated with avoiding self-reported rearrest and reincarceration at one or more postrelease time periods included receiving employment services prior to release, being older at first arrest, having at least a high school diploma or GED, having been

TABLE I
Predictors of Success in Multivariate Models, by Domain and Postrelease Time Period

	No self-reported rearrest or reincarceration				No illicit drug use				Postrelease employment				Positive intimate/ coparenting relationship				Financial support for focal child				Multidomain success			
	1	2	3	4	1	2	3	4	1	2	3	4	1	2	3	4	1	2	3	4	1	2	3	4
Prerelease employment services			+								+												+++	
Prerelease education services									+	++			+						−			++	−	
Prerelease substance abuse services									++															
Prerelease family services									−													+++		
In-person contact with family during incarceration										+				+++	+	+	++	+++	+	+				
Age (older)															+	+								+
Race = white (vs. nonwhite)							−	−−		+														
Hispanic (Hispanic vs. non-Hispanic)														+										
Married												+					−							
Higher number of children											+	+								−				

Time period^a

Variable																
Greater number of previous arrests	-	-	--					-					-	--		
Older age at first arrest	+	+		+								-				
Higher number of years incarcerated												---	-			+
Has at least a HS diploma/GED		+				+	+									+
Employed prior to incarceration		+			+++	+++	++	+					++	++	++	
Fewer problems with alcohol/drug use prior to incarceration	-	+		+								-		+		
Higher locus of control			++													
No physical health limitations			+	++	++++++	+						+	+		+	
Good mental health		+		+								+	++			
Fewer learning problems	-			-	+											--

[a] TIME period: 1 = less than four months postrelease, 2 = 4–12 months postrelease, 3 = 12–24 months postrelease, 4 = more than 24 months postrelease.

+++/++/+ Statistically significant positive association at the .001/.01/.05 level.

---/--/- Statistically significant negative association at the .001/.01/.05 level.

Note: All models also controlled for site and treatment/comparison group status. Blank cells indicate nonsignificant associations.

employed prior to incarceration, and having good mental health at the time of the baseline interview.

When looking at success in terms of avoiding illicit drug use (domain 2), we found that the men who tended to do better were older at first arrest, reported fewer problems with alcohol and drug use prior to incarceration, and had a stronger sense of agency ("locus of control"), no physical health limitations, and good mental health. White men, those who had more previous arrests, and those with fewer learning problems were less likely to avoid illicit drug use. All of these associations were significant at only one or two postrelease time periods.

Postrelease employment—a critical component of reentry success for many reentering individuals—was more likely for men who received employment, education, or substance abuse services prior to release, had more family contact while incarcerated, had at least a high school diploma or GED, were employed prior to incarceration, had no physical health limitations, and had fewer learning problems. In addition, White men and men with more children were more likely to find employment. Factors negatively associated with postrelease employment were the number of prior arrests and having received family services (e.g., parenting classes, healthy relationship education, couples' counseling, or batterer intervention classes) prior to release.

Success in intimate or coparenting relationships was more likely for men who received education services prior to release, had more in-person contact with their families during incarceration, were older, and had more children. Men who received any family services prior to release were less likely to be successful in this domain, suggesting that perhaps receipt of such services was independently linked to prior family-related problems that might have also affected postrelease intimate and coparenting relationships.

For the final domain in which we measured success (financial support for the focal child, domain 5), we found that men who were more successful had more in-person contact with their family during incarceration, no physical health limitations, and more positive mental health. Several factors were negatively associated with success in this domain. Men who received family services prior to release, had more children, were older when first arrested, had been incarcerated for a longer time, and had fewer problems with alcohol or drug use prior to incarceration were less likely to provide financial support for their focal children at one or more postrelease time periods.

When examining multidomain success (the right-hand column of table 1), we found several factors to be significant. Men were more likely to be successful across all five domains at one or more postrelease time periods if they had received employment services prior to release, had at least a high school diploma or GED, were employed prior to incarceration, had fewer alcohol and drug problems prior to incarceration, or had no physical health limitations. Mixed results were found for education services and, inconsistent with the domain-specific findings, men who received family services prior to release were more likely to be successful across all domains four to twelve months after release. Older men were more likely to be successful across all domains twenty-four months or longer after release. Men with more prior arrests, who were younger at first arrest, and who had fewer learning problems were less likely to be successful across all domains in at least one postrelease time period.

CONSIDERATIONS FOR FUTURE RESEARCH AND PRACTICE
Looking at More Than Recidivism Rates to Understand the Whole Story

The findings presented here help broaden our understanding of successful reentry. Reincarceration in state prison is, indisputably, an important outcome, as it is critical to reentering individuals and their family and often the focus of cost-benefit analyses by correctional systems and policy makers. However, it is a flawed measure (Butts and Schiraldi 2018) that cannot lead to full understanding of the process of community reintegration. Our analysis explored reentry success across five domains that are meaningful to reentering individuals, their family, and society—employment, avoiding recidivism (based on both self-reported and administrative records data), abstaining from illicit drug use, positive intimate or coparenting relationships, and financial support for children. The latter two dimensions of family relationship experiences are much more rarely considered in reentry studies. This exercise was important for developing a multidimensional understanding of individuals' postrelease lives. Had we only examined official reimprisonment rates, we would have concluded that our sample was largely successful, as fairly low proportions of men had been reincarcerated within twelve or twenty-four months after release. However, self-reported survey data (which included self-reported arrests and incarcerations in jail or prison) revealed a less promising picture of recidivism. These data also showed that many study participants struggled in other domains, particularly employment.

Examining Success across Domains to Identify Areas for Intervention

Our analytic approach uncovered specific life domains and time points when reentering men appear to be struggling, and it identified factors that made success in each domain more or less likely. As such, the findings enable us to identify areas for intervention on factors amenable to change. Clearly, additional supports are needed to help reentering individuals find employment and avoid recidivism, two areas where men appeared to have the most difficulty (based on the self-reported measure of recidivism that was more inclusive than the measure based on administrative data alone). The need for support in these areas is not surprising, given men's long histories of involvement with the criminal justice system and the barriers to gainful employment faced by people with criminal records (especially people of color) (Bushway 2004; Pager 2007). Many men in our study also had limited educational attainment and faced a host of other barriers that made it particularly difficult to obtain employment in a competitive job market.

The relative lack of success in employment suggests the need for more supports to help reentering prisoners compete. Our findings identified some good places to start. For example, the men who found jobs were more likely to have at least a high school diploma or GED, to have been employed prior to incarceration, and to have no physical health limitations or learning problems. Also, getting employment, education, and substance abuse treatment services while incarcerated increased the odds of finding a job after release. Therefore, finding ways to increase access to these services during incarceration, helping men complete high school (and postsecondary) coursework, and addressing physical health limitations could all be promising areas for intervention.

Although our study did not identify other in-prison services that reduce the likelihood of recidivism, other research identifies programs that deter engagement in criminalized activity after release; these could be promoted and evaluated. For example, cognitive behavioral interventions have consistently proved effective in reducing recidivism (Pearson et al. 2002; Wilson, Bouffard, and MacKenzie 2005; Lipsey, Landenberger, and Wilson 2007).

Targeting Predictors of Reentry Success That Are Amenable to Change

Echoing findings from chapters 2 and 3, the analyses described in this chapter highlight that family contact during incarceration is important for reentry success. Men who had more in-person contact with family members during their incarceration were more likely to be successful after their release—more likely to get jobs, to have positive intimate/coparenting relationships, to avoid reincarceration, and, among fathers, to financially support their children after release. The findings discussed in chapter 2 show that family contact during incarceration facilitate postrelease parenting relationship quality (e.g., father-child coresidence, frequency of engagement for nonresidential fathers), while chapter 3 demonstrates the role of family contact during incarceration in promoting postrelease intimate relationship stability and exclusivity. Taken together, these findings strongly indicate that policies and programs designed to encourage and facilitate family contact during incarceration could help men avoid further criminal justice system involvement, promote better intimate or coparenting relationships, and promote fathers' support of their children after release.

Employment, education, and substance abuse treatment services in prison should also be promoted to bolster the chances of success after release. Men who receive these services during their incarceration are more likely to get jobs after release. Given the difficulty returning prisoners face in securing employment, the positive effect from such services is very promising for future interventions. Increasing access to such services may generate a substantial return on investment for policy makers if participants can obtain legitimate employment when they get out of prison. In addition, participating in employment services during incarceration is associated with cross-domain success and less recidivism (based on the self-reported measure). Our data were insufficient to clarify whether this is a direct effect of the services or an indirect effect through increased employment.

Our models also suggest that additional education and mental and physical health services could promote successful reentry. The positive influence of education (having at least a high school diploma or GED), as well as good mental and physical health, on reentry success suggests several additional priority areas for prerelease programming. Increasing access to basic education programs, supporting prisoners in obtaining education credentials, addressing unmet mental health needs, and helping manage physical health conditions could all be important investments for postrelease success. Educational attainment and health are factors amenable to change through appropriate intervention—unlike characteristics associated with reentry success such as age, criminal history, number of children, preincarceration employment, and problematic alcohol and drug use. Services that address educational and health needs could facilitate incarcerated fathers' postrelease employment, financial support for children, and desistance from criminalized activity.

Providing Long-Term, Integrated Supports after Release

Our findings also show that support services well after the immediate transition back into the community are needed. Although many reentry initiatives that provide a menu of services both before and immediately after release have been implemented during the past several decades, practitioners continue to struggle to ensure postrelease services for the long term and to connect reentering individuals with the services available in their communities. Some reentry studies have documented a decline in service use among former prisoners as postrelease time passes, even though self-reported needs for services remain constant or even increase with time (Lattimore and Visher 2009). Among Multi-site Family Study participants, although some men became more successful over time in certain domains (such as getting jobs and providing financial support to the focal child), the odds of success appeared to deteriorate slightly over time for intimate or coparenting relationship quality and illicit drug use and to deteriorate dramatically over time for recidivism. For these domains, fewer men were classified as successful with each postrelease period explored—a pattern that highlights the need to identify and promote service delivery models that ensure continued support services well after the release from prison. More program development work on integrated service delivery models is particularly needed. Our analyses show that some individual program components (e.g., employment, education, and substance abuse treatment services) can make a difference in men's likelihood of reentry success in individual domains. But more research is needed to figure out how to combine these separate elements into holistic programming that would meet the myriad needs of reentering individuals. Identifying program models that effectively support multidomain success could help to promote true public safety as well as the quality of life of returning prisoners and their family—outcomes that we have sometimes failed to recognize as deeply intertwined.

The Value and the Challenges of a Multidimensional Approach

Our multidimensional approach to reentry success generated a number of important insights that would not have been evident had we relied on recidivism as the only indicator of success. However, even with this approach, patterns (e.g., over time, across outcome domains) can be difficult to discern, causing a level of complexity in interpreting the findings that may be uncomfortable for some researchers. As evident from Olivia and Jason's story at the beginning of the chapter, the lingering effects of incarceration are pervasive, and reentry experiences may be widely different across domains within the same person's life (for example, Jason was struggling to get a job and support his family, yet was apparently successful in avoiding criminalized activity and preserving strong relationships with his partner and children) and over time (as Olivia and Jason transitioned back into domestic life and the birth of the third child approached). The criminal justice system might count Jason a success simply because he had managed to avoid arrest and reincarceration while apparently receiving few formal supports along the way—but the actual picture is more complex. Determining what supports might promote successful reentry can be particularly complicated with a multidimensional approach, because some factors that predict success in certain domains are not associated with success in others. This mixed pattern can frustrate researchers wanting to make clear policy and programming recommendations. But embracing the complexity of this reality will enable researchers to generate a deeper—and ultimately more fruitful—understanding of men's reentry experiences, the aspects of their lives that can most benefit from additional supports (and the appropriate timing of these supports), and factors that are most helpful along the way.

CHAPTER SIX

"A Breakthrough Type of Thing"

Measuring the Impact of Family-Strengthening Programs during Incarceration and Reentry

The Multi-site Family Study was designed to develop a deeper understanding of the experiences of families impacted by incarceration, including the kinds of informal and formal supports that benefit families the most. In this chapter, we explore the impact of couples-based relationship education in four sites that received federal funding to implement demonstration programs (Indiana, Ohio, New Jersey, and New York). As in chapters 2 through 5, we used a mixed-methods approach. Two complementary quantitative techniques examine the impact of programming on couples and also assess men's and women's individual experiences (which, as we learned in chapter 4, can diverge). In-depth, qualitative data explore the meaning of programming to participants, enabling deeper understanding of the quantitative findings.

The quantitative results showed positive treatment effects for couples-based healthy-relationship retreats in one of the four sites (Indiana). Effects were generally stronger for men than for women, and a pattern of positive findings was evident at each point in time. Couples-based analyses using latent growth curve modeling showed that couples who received the healthy-relationship retreats in this site had more positive trajectories over time; that is, their relationship quality deteriorated less than that of comparison couples who did not participate in the retreats. Qualitative data illustrated that in the Indiana program, implementation context (not just program content) was important. Services were delivered in the context of special prison housing units for individuals participating in a variety of character- and faith-based programs. In in-depth interviews, participants cited specific contextual details of the healthy-relationship retreat as highly memorable and meaningful. Taken together, these analyses illustrate the value gained from a mixed-methods approach and, once again, the complexity of understanding the full impact of formal supports on different aspects of families' lives.[1]

ANDRE AND ANISA'S STORY

Andre and Anisa had been together on and off for about five years when Andre went to prison. She had visited him every week during the year he spent there. Partway through his incarceration, they participated together in a weekend healthy-relationship retreat at the state correctional facility in Indiana where he was assigned. Anisa explained that the program focused on skills for dealing with transition: "It shows you how to deal with relationships and arguing and the 'person in transition.' I think they said they do it for military families and stuff. So, yeah, just like the transition of coming back home and how to handle a situation if it escalates—an argument and stuff like that." Andre observed that the context of the program felt special to his partner: it was delivered in a couple-centered setting; it was fully catered, and partners like Anisa were put up in a hotel for the weekend. He also noted that the curriculum content included "a lot of good stuff," particularly for committed couples with children ("if you're a real couple and you all serious"). "It's stuff you can use. They have little exercises

---

1. This chapter builds on prior work by the authors with analytic contributions from Danielle Steffey and Stephen Tueller (Lindquist et al. 2018).

on—we practiced with each other on how to talk ... and to stop arguing, you say this. You know, little techniques and stuff. Some good stuff in there."

Soon after Andre's release, he and Anisa conceived a child together—her third, his first. Her voice was warm as she described how excited he was about becoming a father, and their appreciation for one another as parents was clear. Andre admired Anisa for the futures he saw her making possible for the children; she noted how his impeccable involvement in his son's life was driven by a commitment to be there in a way his own father (who served twenty years in prison) could not: "He's a good dad. And he's always in his life. I always—so, I don't have to do anything really. He buys everything. Takes him to haircuts. Do everything. So, he's a good daddy.... He's very responsible for his kids and stuff, so he, you know, he takes initiative and pick up, drop off, you know. All of that stuff." Their romantic relationship didn't last, however. They both explained emphatically that they're "better as friends"; she said she got tired of the interpersonal drama that surrounded his involvement with multiple women, and he conveyed that he was more focused on work and parenting than on being in a committed romantic partnership.

Yet at the time of our study interview, their day-to-day lives were still intertwined and highly collaborative. They lived in separate households about two blocks away from one another. Anisa explained, "We're family. Like, you know, if he needs me or, you know what I'm saying, I need him." Now their shared life revolved around raising the children, and both seemed proud of what they had accomplished: Anisa's oldest daughter was about to leave for college; all three children had done well in school; and the couple had recently secured a scholarship to send their youngest child to a private school. Describing the consistency and mutual effort required to keep their family life running, Anisa reflected: "That's probably why he hasn't gotten in any more trouble or went back to jail or anything, 'cause, yeah, he's pretty consistent with being a father—you know, grounded."

ISSUES IN EVALUATING FAMILY-STRENGTHENING PROGRAMS DELIVERED TO COUPLES

Incarceration has far-reaching negative consequences for families, as highlighted in chapters 2 through 5. The families in the Multi-site Family Study found that incarceration impacted them in a myriad of ways, including deteriorating relationships after release between fathers and children, as well as between intimate partners. These families also consistently reported few formal supports to help them remain connected during incarceration. Although the families who stayed in contact during incarceration did better after release in many important domains (as shown in chapters 2, 3, and 5), nearly all participants in the in-depth qualitative interviews indicated they had received no support from the correctional facility in maintaining family ties during the male partner's incarceration. Clearly, new policies and programs designed to facilitate family contact during incarceration are needed to address deteriorating family ties and their associated consequences.

Simply facilitating contact is an important first step in supporting families during incarceration. But given the challenges families experience during an incarceration, more intensive, skills-building efforts (e.g., communication and conflict resolution skills) for incarcerated individuals and their family members could have an even greater impact on family relationships. As shown in chapters 2 and 3, better relationships between intimate or coparenting partners are associated with a number of positive outcomes, both during incarceration and after release.

Our findings, and those of others, imply that programs to preserve and strengthen intimate and coparenting relationships merit increased attention. Previous research suggests that supporting family relationships during incarceration could facilitate family reunification and lower recidivism after incarceration. Various forms of support have shown promise in preliminary intervention studies—including family-friendly visitation accommodations, group parenting and relationship education classes, and assistance in maintaining contact with family members during incarceration (MacDonald and Kelly 1980; Minnesota Department of Corrections 2011; Eddy, Martinez, and Burraston 2013; Dunn and Arbuckle 2002).

Yet figuring out what approaches are effective is extremely complex. Evaluating the impact of family-strengthening programming on *individuals* involves similar challenges to those that confront evaluations of other types of corrections-based programming. The primary obstacles include limited options for comparison group selection, low-quality administrative data on actual program dosage, and difficulty collecting data from individuals after release (including the high cost and often high attrition).

Assessing the impact of family-strengthening programming on *couples*, however, which was the goal of our impact study, poses unique additional methodological challenges for evaluators. As shown in chapter 4, members of a couple may provide quite different accounts of what is happening in their relationship, particularly when it comes to stigmatized behaviors such as partner abuse. This difference is one of the strongest arguments in favor of taking a couples-based approach when examining relationship quality and other indicators of family functioning. But it is virtually impossible to ensure complete data from both members of a couple at each measurement point in a longitudinal study—leading to missing data that raise serious analytic problems. These issues are exacerbated when one member of the couple is incarcerated; in such cases, even collecting baseline data from both partners (particularly the partner on the outside) is extremely difficult. Further, in addition to the typical challenges of successfully recruiting and locating a difficult-to-reach population for follow-up interviews, couples-based studies face an extra obstacle: when a relationship ends, a study participant may be reluctant to participate in a follow-up interview that will ask detailed questions about the former partner.

These factors result in substantial missing data in couples-based longitudinal studies, and traditional analytic approaches limit use of the data that are available. Such analyses, for example, may exclude couples with data missing for one member, impute the missing partner's data in an attempt to use the data that are available (Wood et al. 2012), or report on the effects of programming for men and women separately (based on whatever data are available), without attempting to assess impacts on couples as a unit.

Another limitation of existing couples-based evaluations, as well as with individual-based evaluations, is the tendency to focus exclusively on "point-in-time" impacts of programming, comparing treatment and control groups at specific follow-up periods after programming (e.g., six months after enrollment, twelve months after enrollment). This approach can make it difficult to draw conclusions about the overall impact of the programming, particularly when the findings are inconsistent from one time point to another. Finally, the near-exclusive reliance on quantitative data limits our understanding of how programs affect certain outcomes (or not) from the perspectives of the participants themselves.

COMPARISON OF QUANTITATIVE FINDINGS FROM INDIVIDUAL- AND COUPLE-LEVEL ANALYSES

The Multi-site Family Study impact evaluation was designed to overcome many of the limitations apparent in previous evaluations of couples-based programming. We used two quantitative statistical techniques to assess the impact of couples-based programming on men, women, and couples. Comparisons of weighted means tested for statistically significant differences between treatment and comparison groups (with tests for men and women separately at each follow-up wave, by site) on the outcomes of interest. Latent growth curve modeling (LGM) compared how outcomes changed over time for treatment group couples and comparison couples in each site. In addition to assessing impact through these quantitative techniques, we incorporated in-depth qualitative data to generate a more nuanced understanding of how participants themselves perceived the program's impacts.

Four sites were included in the impact analyses: the Indiana Department of Correction, the RIDGE Project (Ohio), the New Jersey Department of Corrections, and the Osborne Association (New York). The Indiana program served men residing in character- and faith-based residential units within the state prisons targeted by the program. This evaluation was designed to determine the impact of a one-time healthy-relationship retreat delivered during a weekend at the prison, which both members of the couple attended. The Ohio program served fathers in committed relationships who were incarcerated in one of the state prisons targeted by the program. This evaluation was designed to determine the impact of a twelve-week relationship-education course delivered at the prison to incarcerated men and couples. Partners of incarcerated men were invited to participate but did not have to attend. The New Jersey program served fathers who were in committed intimate or coparenting relationships, had a history of chemical dependency, and were serving out their full sentences at one of the state prisons targeted by the program. This evaluation assessed the impact of the overall program delivered to couples—which included relationship, parenting, and domestic violence education; substance use treatment; and reentry case management. The program spanned six to nine months prerelease and six months postrelease. The New York program served fathers in committed relationships who were incarcerated in one of the state prisons served by the program. This evaluation was designed to assess the impact of a one-time healthy-relationship seminar delivered to couples during a weekend at the prison. Both members of the couple attended the seminar.

The results of the quantitative analyses generally suggested that in most sites, couples-based programming had limited effects on outcomes in the three domains on which we focused: intimate relationship quality, parenting and coparenting quality, and employment, drug use, and recidivism.[2] Sustained, positive effects emerged in one of the four sites

---

2. See the Appendix for detailed descriptions of the outcomes explored within each domain.

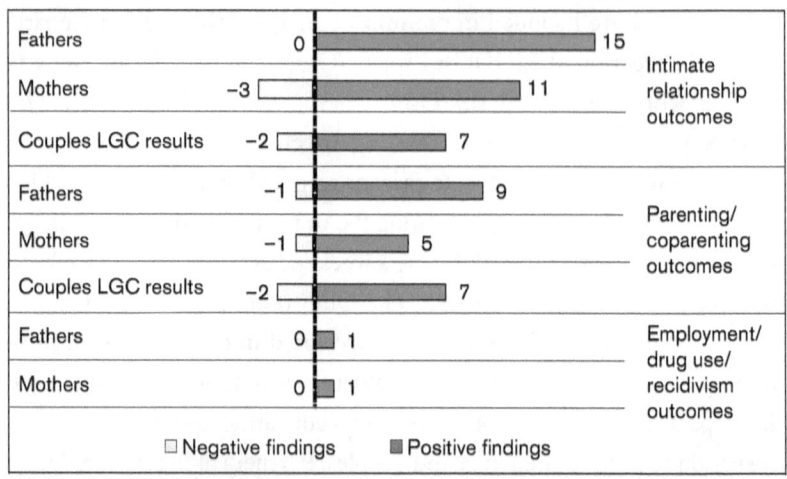

Figure 13. Treatment effects, Indiana.

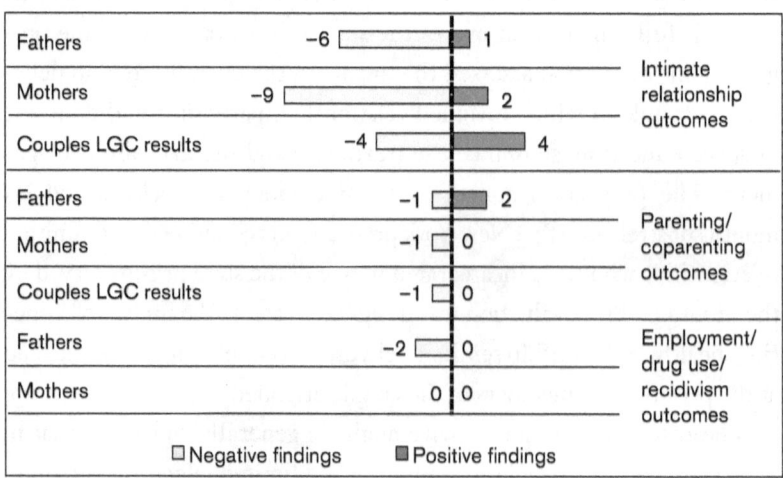

Figure 14. Treatment effects, Ohio.

Figures 13–16. Summary of significant treatment effects across domains, by site. Images credit: Danielle Steffey.

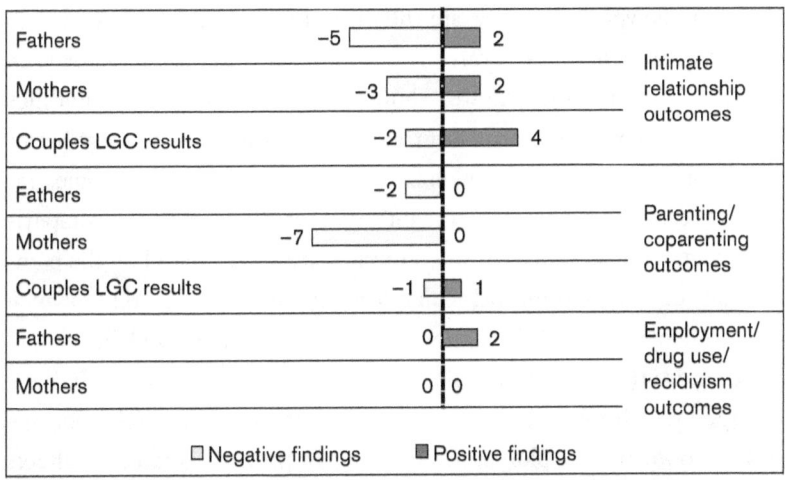

Figure 15. Treatment effects, New Jersey.

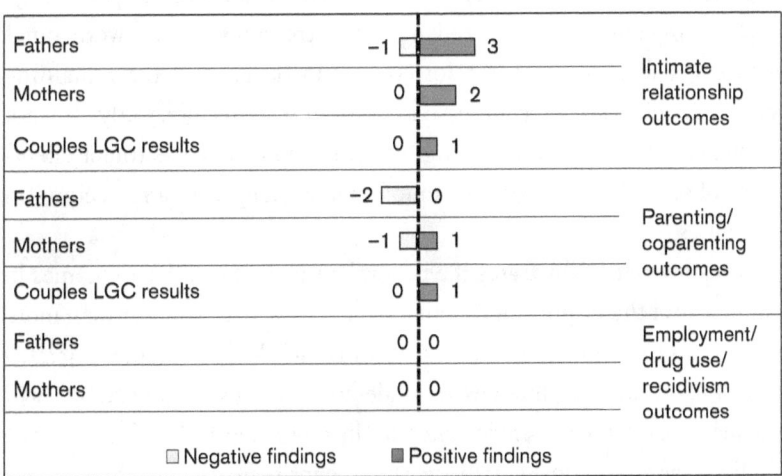

Figure 16. Treatment effects, New York.

(Indiana), however. To illustrate the overall pattern that emerged with quantitative techniques, figures 13–16 summarize the findings for each domain, by site. These figures show the number of positive findings (outcomes for which treatment group members did significantly better than comparison group members) and negative findings (outcomes for which treatment group members did significantly worse than comparison group members) in each site. Findings are shown based on the comparisons of weighted means, which were conducted separately for men and women, and on LGM models that were run at the couple level.

As figure 13 illustrates, a general pattern of positive effects in Indiana emerged with both analytic techniques. Of the 29 intimate-relationship-quality outcomes explored for Indiana, 15 positive treatment effects were found for men, 11 for women, and 7 for couples. In the remaining sites, effects were mixed, weak, and largely insignificant. Parenting and coparenting outcome patterns were similar. Among the 16 parenting/coparenting outcomes analyzed, 9 positive treatment effects were found for men, 5 for women, and 7 for couples in Indiana. In the remaining sites, participation in couples-based programming generally did not influence parenting/coparenting outcomes. Very few treatment effects were observed in any site for employment, drug use, and recidivism outcomes.

This overview illustrates the general pattern of positive outcomes in Indiana and the important fact that effects were observed for men more often than for women, or couples. To illustrate the benefits of using multiple quantitative techniques to understand program impact, we will compare results for a single outcome in more depth. We focus on the findings for an outcome variable within the intimate-relationship-quality domain: couple relationship bonding. We measured bonding as a score ranging from 0 to 9 based on three scale items about respondents' perceptions of the stability of the couple's relationship (e.g., "you believe you and your survey partner can handle whatever conflicts will arise in the future") and the extent to which the couple had fun together. Respondents' agreement with the items was measured on a Likert scale (strongly agree, agree, disagree, strongly disagree). As with other outcomes, the impact of couples-based programming on this outcome was assessed using both the comparison-of-weighted-means approach (to see if, on average, men and women who participated in the programs reported higher levels of bonding than men and women in the comparison group at 9, 18, and 34 months) and LGM (to see if, overall, treatment couples had more positive trajectories on this outcome than comparison couples over the entire follow-up period).

We concentrate on the Indiana findings because in the other sites, the intervention either did not affect bonding or had some negative effects, as was the case for men in Ohio at 9 and 18 months. In Indiana, the couples-based programming appeared to have had more of an impact for men (among whom we found positive treatment effects at all three follow-up periods) than women (among whom we found positive treatment effects only at 9 and 34 months). Women's assessments of bonding within the relationship were slightly lower than men's, and for both men and women, assessments of bonding tended to decline with each interview wave—but both men and women in the treatment group still had higher bonding scores at 34 months than those in the comparison group. Missing data were an issue with each interview wave, as we were not able to reach both members of each couple for interviews at every wave, and more men than women were interviewed at each time point.

The comparison-of-weighted-means approach suggested that couples-based programming promoted higher reports of bonding among individual men and women in Indiana, but it did not tell us whether treatment *couples,* on average, did better than comparison couples on this outcome. To answer that question, we used LGM to look at the average change over time for treatment couples and comparison couples, using available data from one or both members of the couple, and nesting the data for men and women within the same couple.

We found that, in Indiana, the treatment couples started off with higher levels of bonding at baseline and had a more positive trajectory over time. Therefore, the models confirm that the Indiana couples'

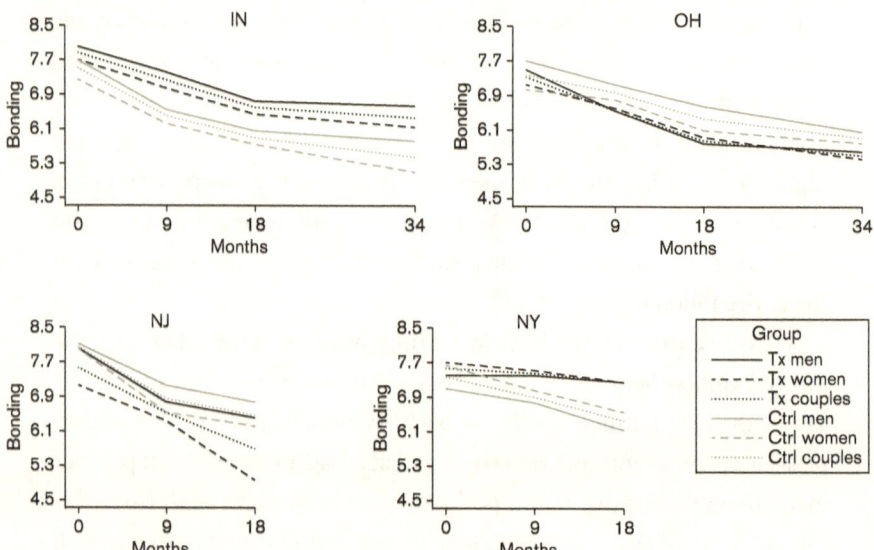

Figure 17. Trajectories for bonding based on latent growth curve models, by site and group. Image credit: Stephen Tueller.

retreats did produce couple-level effects on bonding scores, in addition to the individual-level effects discussed earlier for men and for women. No couple-level effects were found for bonding in other sites. Interestingly, however, the slopes generated by the models were *negative* for both treatment and comparison couples in Indiana and all other sites. This indicates that for both treatment and comparison couples, the couples' bonding levels deteriorated over time[3]—a finding consistent with the successively lower bonding scores at each wave observed in the comparisons of weighted means.

To illustrate this pattern visually, figure 17 shows the trajectories over time for the bonding outcome for the treatment and comparison men and women in each site, along with the couples' averages. As

---

3. This finding is consistent with the successively lower bonding scores at each wave observed in the comparisons-of-weighted-means tables (as shown in the Appendix).

evident from the graphs, the clear pattern for all groups in each site is deterioration over time. In Indiana, this deterioration is steeper for the comparison group than the treatment group. Therefore, the positive difference between the slopes of the treatment and comparison couples in Indiana reflects that the treatment group deteriorated less than the comparison group over time, not that they improved more.

Another interesting pattern shown in the Indiana graph is the lower bonding scores reported by women than men, regardless of whether the couple attended the retreats or not. For both the treatment and comparison groups, the slope for the couples' average lies between the slope for men (as individuals) and the slope for women (as individuals), with the women's scores being lower than the men's. The lower scores among the female members of the couples are consistent with what we found in the comparison of weighted means discussed above, where women tended to rate the couples' level of bonding lower than men did.

That we found disparate accounts between men and women of the couple's level of bonding is similar in some ways to the divergent reports of partner abuse within the relationship provided by men and women discussed in chapter 4. However, since the study assessed partner abuse in terms of a set of specific and objective behaviors, one might expect both members of a couple to provide concordant responses if the negative consequences of reporting such a stigmatized—and, in most cases, criminalized—behavior could be eliminated. In contrast, the bonding scores we developed are based on respondents' very subjective perceptions of how well the couple can handle future conflicts and how much fun the couple has together. There is no objective "truth" to an outcome such as bonding, which is based purely on an individual's perceptions. One would not expect such perceptions to be the same for both members of the same couple, as an individual's personal outlook, previous relationship history, and many other considerations can influence the lens with which they view the current relationship.

Taken together, these quantitative findings illustrate the distinct and complementary information generated by applying both sets of quantitative techniques in a couples-based study. The comparison of weighted means showed us point-in-time treatment effects in Indiana for men and women *as individuals*. The LGM analysis, which treated couples as the unit of analysis, found that the overall trajectories of treatment couples were significantly better than those of comparison couples, with treatment couples demonstrating less deterioration in bonding scores over time than comparison couples.

WHAT CAN WE LEARN FROM QUALITATIVE DATA TO HELP UNDERSTAND QUANTITATIVE FINDINGS?

Based on quantitative analysis, the couples-based programming had a positive impact on men, women, and couples in Indiana. But *how* did this happen? Data from our in-depth qualitative study, particularly interviews with treatment couples in Indiana, are helpful in generating an understanding of how positive treatment effects could have been achieved by a fairly low-dosage intervention. Participants in the Indiana site's weekend retreat shared several distinct perspectives on their program experiences. Men and women vividly remembered their participation in the retreat. Many participants described it at great length, animatedly recalling its substance (course topics and activities) and other details that made the experience feel special. One woman gave a detailed description of how it felt to participate in the weekend program, complete with her overnight stay at a hotel:

> They put us in this relationship program where it was really nice. And I got to go to the hotel by myself. It was a suite. It was very relaxing. And then in the morning time we would have to wake up and this bus would come and get us and they'll take us to the [prison]—where they was at—where the inmates was at . . . and when we get in the room, it would have on the table like [a table tent with the couple's initials] with a rose. And we got to sit there. We got to spend all day with them from like—I think it was like 6:30 or 7:00 in the morning, all the way until like seven o'clock that evening. We was together and

there was no shackles, no nothing. We got to sit side by side at this table. And we got—we was talking about relationships, and we played games, and they asked us little questions, and ... you get to give him a kiss and a hug, or the men gets to get up and give you a massage in front of the whole class and all this fun stuff... and then we ate lunch together. They got to eat some kind of good stuff versus jail food—it's fried and chips and all that.... It was really, really nice and helpful. The program really helped us out relationship-wise.

Notably, women's accounts of program participation contained details about how this experience differed from typical prison visits ("we got to spend all day with them"; "there was no shackles, no nothing"; "you get to give him a kiss and a hug"). Some women also related how they and their partners achieved new levels of intimacy and connectedness in this setting. Anisa describes how the effects of the retreat reverberated into her next prison visit with Andre:

We had, like, a breakthrough type of thing when we were on one of the visits after one of the classes. I think we kind of were arguing a little bit maybe about something, or whatever, and he just started bawling, crying. And I think I had, I had never seen him cry then. But yeah, he had a lot of frustration and talked about growing up and his family and his mom and dad and stuff. So, he had like a big, major breakthrough, where he got to let a lot of feelings and stuff out.

Experiences with applying the concepts learned in the retreat varied. Some participants described how they used the skills they gained from the course to improve their partner relationships both during and after the male partner's incarceration:

Part of [the retreat] was about are you loving the person in the way that they need to be loved? ... It was amazing how on the spot on we were with that exercise ... We've used those words here to say, "Here's what I need from you for the next three months, because I'm scared about this, right. I've made it bigger than it is." I think we're really good at that, partly from that course. So that's great.

Others found that, although they enjoyed the course, the content was difficult to apply in the context of postrelease challenges. One participant noted that "at the time it seemed like it helped" but that she and her partner had returned to old patterns of arguing after he was released. Another felt that the program offered meaningful skills, but that her partner's postrelease alcohol abuse made it impossible to use those skills in communicating with him:

> PARTICIPANT: I liked it. It was the fact that it was teaching you how to communicate with your partner. They gave us a packet of how to talk, how to settle through an argument if you had an argument, how to talk it out and if you say something to make sure the person repeats it and you get to understand what you're saying and what they're saying.
> INTERVIEWER: Did you get to use it in relationship to [your partner]?
> PARTICIPANT: I tried it, but it didn't work.
> INTERVIEWER: How come?
> PARTICIPANT: Because he was drunk. [Participant laughs.] But I did. He was drunk. Never wanted to talk while he was sober. When he was sober, he was quiet, and if he did open his mouth, he had an attitude because he wasn't drunk ... but I really enjoyed that class, I really did. That whole weekend was really nice. I did enjoy that.

Such insights about the difficulties of applying relationship skills learned during the retreats after the male partner's release make sense in light of what we describe in earlier chapters, where reentry often brings brutal new difficulties, even for couples who maintained close ties during incarceration. In particular, the qualitative findings discussed in chapter 3 showed that men and women consistently express that the postrelease period poses distinctly different challenges from the ones they experienced during incarceration.

The Indiana qualitative data suggest how memorable participation was to couples even several years later—a finding that supports the sustained impacts detected using both quantitative analytic techniques. It also highlights how aspects of the program that had seemed of relatively little consequence to the research team (a simple table decoration and the provision of non–"jail food," for example) were regarded as important by participants, even after much time had passed. For many couples, including Anisa and Andre, the relationship skills they learned that weekend did not necessarily mean "happily ever after" once the incarceration ended. But the program seemed to bolster the kinds of bonding, communication, and mutual commitment to children and family that helped couples to weather the incarceration and the transition from prison to home. For Anisa and Andre, those gains stayed with them as they weathered a transition in their romantic relationship as well.

CONSIDERATIONS FOR FUTURE RESEARCH AND PRACTICE
Policy and Practice Implications

That a couples' weekend retreat had such positive impacts across many relevant domains surprised us. Indeed, the Multi-site Family Study's impact evaluation is unique among family-strengthening intervention studies in demonstrating sustained effects of a *low-dosage* activity on partnership and parenting outcomes in a low-income, justice-involved population. Both of the quantitative analytic approaches we used to assess program impact showed positive treatment effects for the couples-based healthy-relationship retreats. Comparisons of weighted means between the treatment and comparison groups in Indiana showed a number of positive treatment effects on family relationships (including intimate relationship quality, parenting, and coparenting) at all three follow-up waves. LGM analyses revealed that, over time, treatment couples in this site had better trajectories than comparison couples for a range of relationship measures and some parenting and coparenting measures, as well.

The finding that couples-based healthy-relationship retreats provided by correctional facilities actually made a difference for those who participated is extremely promising, given the dire need to identify effective ways to support families during incarceration. As evident from earlier chapters, the families in our study received very few services to help them remain connected during incarceration, and they generally felt unsupported by correctional facilities in their efforts to stay in contact. Yet, preserving family contact (through phone calls, in-person visits, and other modes of communication) and demonstrating strong communication and conflict resolution skills played an important role in improving postrelease family functioning. Beyond "just" improving postrelease family relationships, in-prison contact was also associated with improvements in the reentry outcomes that matter most to individuals, families, and society, including employment and avoiding recidivism. The clear implication is that facilitating contact between incarcerated family members and their loved ones and providing skills-based education to improve communication and conflict resolution skills could have widespread societal benefits.

Our findings also make clear that providing formal supports during incarceration is not sufficient. Given that relationship dynamics can change from incarceration to postrelease, reentry-specific planning and support are needed. The many couples who struggled with applying the skills learned during incarceration to the often-tumultuous reentry period could have benefited from prerelease planning and postrelease follow-up. Further, as evident from the high prevalence of partner abuse among our study families (see chapter 4), addressing abuse is critical to *safe* reentry. Any couples-based relationship education program needs to conduct comprehensive screening for partner abuse, provide basic universal education on relationship safety, and create opportunities for couples to end relationships in a safe and supported manner.

For those seeking to develop relationship-strengthening programs for families affected by incarceration, the impact findings provide other important lessons for program design. Most importantly, future program efforts would benefit from careful attention to the context in which they are implemented. Although each of the four sites included in the impact study had a distinct program model, the implementation context of the Indiana program distinguished it from other approaches in several ways. First, the program was delivered exclusively to residents of special character- and faith-based housing units, who were potentially readier to receive this type of support and who, after the retreats, may have been more likely to sustain what they learned given the environment fostered in the housing units. Second, according to program administrators, there was a good fit between the content covered in the healthy-relationship seminar (e.g., improving communication, managing expectations, understanding the impact of past experiences) and other program components available to the character- and faith-based housing residents; the retreat's curriculum seemed to reinforce and be reinforced by the other programming (which fostered spiritual, moral, and character development, as well as life skills). Third, as the qualitative data show, very specific contextual aspects of the Indiana healthy-relationship retreat itself (e.g., female partners staying in a hotel, couples being treated to experiences like having a special meal together) were highly salient for participants. Consistent healthy-relationship program effects in Indiana suggest that programs are likely to be more effective when design and implementation decisions consider the total context in which the program will operate.

Research Implications

Our impact study also generated important lessons for future research and evaluation efforts. We used a unique analytic approach to conduct both comparisons-of-weighted-means analyses and LGM. This enabled us to use all available data and take into account the nesting of individuals within couples. We were able, in turn, to discern a picture of individuals' statuses at a given postrelease time point and of the couples' average trajectories over time. Previous evaluations, in contrast, have typically examined outcomes only at individual waves and have often excluded couples for whom interviews were missing at a specific wave. Through the LGM analysis, we demonstrated that couples can be used as a unit of analysis even when data are missing for one member of the couple (as is so often the case with couples-based studies). By measuring improvement or deterioration from different starting points, couples-based analysis can provide crucial new information for developing and evaluating family-strengthening programs.

Even though using two quantitative analytic approaches did introduce complexity in interpreting certain findings, the results from the two approaches were generally consistent. The overall pattern of positive treatment effects in Indiana (and largely nonsignificant findings in the other sites) became obvious in the results of both techniques. The findings for many individual outcomes, including the example of bonding on which this chapter focuses, were also generally the same with both techniques. Outcomes found to be significantly better for treatment couples relative to comparison couples in Indiana in the LGM models were also significant in both the male and female point-in-time models. However, because we generally found weaker effects for women than men, a few outcomes had significantly positive treatment effects in the male point-in-time models and the couples' LGM models, but not in the female point-in-time models. Therefore, one could argue that the main value of the couples-based LGM models was to provide a single assessment of the overall difference across treatment and comparison couples over the entire follow-up period, whereas the main value of the point-in-time models was to discern gender differences and differences at specific follow-up waves.

The interesting within-couple gender differences that emerged in the quantitative analyses certainly confirm the value in interviewing both members of a couple to understand the impact of couples-based programming on each. Programming may genuinely impact the members of a couple in different ways, having a bigger effect for one member (in our study, generally the male partner) than the other. In addition, the outcomes used to assess program impacts may have different meanings for both members of the same couple. Particularly when examining attitudinal or subjective outcomes, one would not necessarily look for agreement between both members of a couple, as each brings his or her own perspective to bear. Attitudes, perceptions, and feelings about the couple's relationship quality and family functioning are important outcomes of healthy-relationship programming—outcomes for which different effects might logically be found for individuals within a couple. However, as evident in chapter 4, members of a couple can—and often do—provide contradictory accounts on outcomes where agreement would be expected if respondents were comfortable answering openly—such as whether one member has physically abused the other (or even the couple's marital status, which we found to be a source of discrepant accounts among some couples). Within-couple discrepancies in reports of a behavioral outcome for which objective truth exists are true incongruencies and cannot be satisfactorily resolved using any analytic technique—which can be extremely frustrating for researchers. Yet collecting (or using) data from only one member of the couple does not resolve the discrepancies; it simply hides them. Ruling out the data as worthless is an equally undesirable option. Instead, we attempted to overcome the issue by staying focused on the big picture we were seeing in the quantitative accounts and using qualitative data wherever possible to deepen our understanding of the processes behind the quantitative outcomes.

Although we did not have extensive qualitative data specifically on the topic of the couples-based healthy-relationship programming in the sites (even in Indiana), the in-depth interviews that did cover this topic were extremely helpful in generating a much deeper understanding of how positive impacts were achieved in Indiana. For example, without the qualitative data, we would never have picked up on the importance of seemingly minor efforts of the program developers to make the program special to couples—such as decorating the tables and providing non-"jail food." These contextual aspects of the retreats turned out to be extremely salient to participants, even after an extended period of time.

In sum, this chapter illustrates the value of using multidimensional analyses to identify effective strategies for couples-based programming for families affected by incarceration. As shown throughout the earlier chapters, families affected by incarceration desperately need programs that help them maintain ties, learn better relationship (and parenting) skills, and offer other supports during the incarceration of a partner and after release. It is important that researchers support the further development and refinement of effective intervention strategies by applying the best available methods. To do that job well involves selecting methods that are equipped to effectively address the known constraints of evaluating couples-based programs. When several methods are appropriate and feasible, as they were in this study, applying more than one can help generate richer insights and inform future program design in unexpected ways. Interpreting the results generated by numerous statistical models can be a complicated undertaking. But the effort to identify predominant patterns and factors that may explain the processes underlying them yields a much deeper understanding of the ways families benefit (or not) from couples-based relationship programming.

CHAPTER SEVEN

On the Horizon

The Social Science of Incarceration and Family Life

> The contemporary criminal justice system creates a unique form of social exclusion that is rooted in the invisibility of America's inmates. Crime and criminals are the subject of much attention and ire in America's newsrooms and living rooms, yet inmates are effectively hidden from public view.
> Becky Pettit, *Invisible Men*, 2012

For decades, social scientists have studied low-income families and households as one discrete sphere, and "criminals" and prisons as another. The distinction between these spheres and the kinds of people understood to occupy them still manifests in many of our biggest and best-resourced studies—from the invisibility of incarcerated and formerly incarcerated people in general population surveys (Pettit 2012) to the failure to account fully for prisoners' family lives and households in national criminal justice statistics (Wakefield, Lee, and Wildeman 2016). This divided work continues even now that we know poor children of color are more likely than not to experience the incarceration of a parent (Wildeman 2009). It continues despite long-standing evidence that family relationships play a key role in shaping criminal justice system involvement (e.g., Laub, Nagin, and Sampson 1998). And it continues even though we know criminal justice systems profoundly shape family life in poor communities (e.g., Hairston 1988).

Why has research—with a few remarkable exceptions—continued to craft separate stories of family life and of criminal justice system involvement? In part, the reason is that the separate agencies that fund the disparate operations of criminal justice systems and human services systems at the federal and state levels also fund research related to these systems. Despite the presence of forward-thinking staff in all agencies in these separate systems, each system is accountable for achieving a different set of objectives or outcomes—which, not surprisingly, are typically the focus of the studies they fund.

Truly cross-sector work remains a challenge. But without coordinated multisector studies, even the most meticulous scientific accounts of criminal justice system involvement and of low-income families and communities will continue to replicate the "commonsense" understanding of our day: that "criminals" and "struggling parents" are two different groups of people, to be engaged by two different sets of government systems with different, and perhaps competing, goals. Putting the weight of scientific inquiry behind commonsense social categories is nothing new in social science. The tendency to do so can be exacerbated when societal systems and structures reproduce our false dichotomies: victim versus offender, for example; promising student versus juvenile delinquent; involved parent versus convicted felon. But the best social scientific work can also do the opposite: apply rigorous forms of observation to freshly understand social phenomena that are subject to widely held but ill-founded cultural assumptions. Our ability to realize this latter goal and move from assumption into insight, as this volume explores, depends to a great extent on the methods we apply.

The Multi-site Family Study, the first study of its kind in the history of American social science, was funded through an interagency partnership forged by federal staff intent on better serving families across the wide gaps they observed between criminal justice and human services systems. This study gathered rich data on family life and criminal justice system involvement from different-sex couples in which the male partner was incarcerated, and it followed these families through his release from prison. The study was unprecedented in placing equal emphasis on study participants' contacts with the criminal justice system and on their parenting and partner relationships, with an extensive focus on understanding how so many low-income families in America construct their family lives "in the shadow of the prison" (Comfort 2007). Further, the study applied more rigorous and in-depth forms of observation to these phenomena than previously had been possible in a single study: it collected data from both members of study couples; it followed up with them for several years, as they weathered the incarceration and attempted postrelease reunification; and it supplemented survey data with open-ended, qualitative interviews and administrative data (such as official correctional records) that we linked to participants' survey responses.

The integrated dataset this endeavor produced and the analyses it enabled opened a window into human life in the crosshairs of two forms of government intervention: systems charged with supporting poor families and systems charged with controlling "criminals." It illuminated the strain of navigating a singular existence across divided prison, home, and community settings; of managing contact with family members alongside contact with the criminal justice system; and of attempting to succeed in the roles of parent, partner, worker, and subject of state surveillance all at once (Kerrison 2018).

At a systems level, our findings suggest that the extractive and surveilling (rather than supportive) orientation of correctional and community supervision policies toward men's partner and parenting relationships is dually devastating. First, these practices—arrest procedures that traumatize children, assignment of prisoners or parolees to locations hundreds of miles from their home community, exorbitant telephone rates for calls from prisons, the shifting of criminal justice system costs and fees onto families—can strain or destroy the ties that serve as a lifeline for postprison reintegration. Second, in so doing, the same practices may also undermine the chances of programmatic or institutional "success." By neglecting or undermining the interconnectedness of criminal justice system involvement and family life, such policies may actually prevent criminal justice agencies from moving the needle on their most widely stated metric (avoidance of reincarceration) while also thwarting the efforts of human services systems to stabilize families, promote positive parenting, and lift women and children out of poverty.

At an individual level, our research suggests that correctional and prisoner reentry programs and policies that neglect or undermine family relationships also threaten the delicate fabric of identity and resolve that prior research (e.g., Visher and Courtney 2007) suggests may be critical to successful reentry. These quantities are at a premium for those facing grinding prison conditions and long odds in their postrelease efforts at job seeking and parole compliance. They are equally precious and fragile for the partners, spouses, and family members of incarcerated people, who battle grueling poverty and personal trauma to provide for the emotional and material needs of their incarcerated loved ones and their children.

As it is for many parents at the economic and social margins, parenting was deeply meaningful for Multi-site Family Study participants—particularly in the context of their blocked access to mainstream, goal attainment–based forms of significance that are contingent on gainful employment, safe housing, and personal freedom. Our findings indicate that embeddedness in (and reference to) domestic life and family relationships furnished structure and motive for daily living, even when performed in nondomestic or seemingly counterdomestic spaces like prisons. Family roles and responsibilities helped the parents in our study locate themselves in their own lives, map a sense of broader meaning onto their daily activities (even when heavily occupied with the compulsory), and reach beyond their systematically shortened horizons into the greater possibility they sensed for their children. For incarcerated men, parenting and couple relationships also seemed to offer a platform for experiencing and expressing vulnerability and feeling. When relatively intact, these relationships gave fathers the precious chance to enact a form of full humanity in the presence of (and in reference to) their partner and children, even against the immediate and ongoing backdrop of dehumanizing social and institutional interactions.

In that context, we also found that federal programs aiming to support family relationships during and after incarceration can make an important contribution when they acknowledge and affirm loving, healthy partnerships and parenting relationships as valuable in and of themselves. Particularly striking, the mixed-methods evaluation approach chapter 6 describes revealed that participants in the family-strengthening program that showed the most consistent pattern of positive effects remarked more on the gestures of value and "specialness" the program made toward their relationship than on its educational content. These humanizing and validating elements stood out clearly against both the background of carceral dehumanization and the monitoring-and-extraction orientation toward family relationships that participants perceived (and resisted) in their other interactions with official systems.

MOVING FORWARD: INTEGRATING DATA, BREAKING SILOS, REIMAGINING SYSTEMS

We live in an era when we have the strongest capacity ever known to gather, compare, and integrate data; and when the internet, social media platforms, and other online tools are cultivating a fluidity of thinking that transcends traditional boundaries. The kinds of research outcomes that interest criminal justice systems (and researchers) and human services systems (and researchers) may still be largely distinct: criminalized activity, arrest, incarceration, and parole compliance on one hand, and family stability, healthy parenting, and economic self-sufficiency on the other. Yet small, new threads are slowly interconnecting these realms: a scholar of criminal justice retweets a story of children visiting their parents in prison; a family welfare specialist gets to know what resources are available for people with conviction histories. For students and established social science researchers alike, endless opportunities exist to make ourselves useful as well—by advancing the state of current knowledge about how individuals and families navigate experiences and identities that, although segmented by socially constructed systems, are in fact part of the complex whole of human existence.

The more integrated forms of inquiry made possible in the Multisite Family Study highlighted that "success" or "failure" often arose for study participants at the same intersections that more tidily packaged research approaches had hidden. Training our focus on those intersections revealed the tremendous creative adaptation involved in lives lived across these disparate spheres. If we choose to continue reproducing the taxonomies we have inherited—if we continue the study of criminal justice and of family welfare in separate disciplines, in separate research projects, and from distinct theoretical perspectives—we will miss capturing the ingenious survival and success strategies that people artificially divided by those categories have developed. These system-crossing strategies, if we can find ways to make them more visible in our research, may also be the key to understanding how we can remake the parallel infrastructures that have necessitated them.

Much work beckons at this threshold. How do poor families manage to stay housed as they lose an income-contributing adult? Or as they regain a non-income-contributing adult who may be unwelcome in subsidized housing due to a conviction history? How do parents manage their children's survival, even as they face poor job markets for non-college-educated workers, conviction-history-related employment discrimination, and poverty wages in the jobs they do secure? How do adults and children maintain healthy, loving family relationships while navigating the immense, shared behavioral health challenges of incarceration and reentry? The empirical approaches discussed in this book (for example, the couples-based trajectory analysis described in chapter 6 and the multivariate logistic regression with holistic, composite outcome variables described in chapter 5) are well suited to exploring these questions with the right data sources.

The Multi-site Family Study data are now publicly available,[1] and (as of this writing) untapped for integrated research on many issues affecting families who have experienced a father's imprisonment. We urge their use by others. In addition, ongoing advances in federal interagency-data linking promise to open several new frontiers of inquiry in the coming years. The U.S. Census Bureau and Bureau of Justice Statistics are developing secure data-linking protocols to make it possible to connect information across many different correctional and human services datasets.[2] Eventually, these agencies expect federal staff and researchers to be able to connect data on all individuals admitted to or released from a state prison (as maintained in the National Corrections Reporting Program) with information on enrollment in veterans' benefits, Supplemental Security Income, Temporary Assistance for Needy Families, and Medicaid; decennial Census survey data; records of employment and unemployment; and engagement with public housing, rental assistance, and subsidized mortgage programs.

As the Multi-site Family Study findings suggest, low-income, justice-involved individuals and families face substantial obstacles to accessing the many different services and infrastructures these federal datasets track. Succeeding in any one of these areas often demands resources that can either be proffered or retracted (for example, through exclusions related to conviction history) in the others. Linked quantitative analysis could support much richer inquiries into how people with conviction histories and their families engage with the interrelated but sometimes contradictory forms of benefit and restriction with which government systems present them. Such work would enrich many fields and disciplines. For example, medical and public health researchers

1. For more information on the quantitative dataset prepared from the Multi-site Family Study on Incarceration, Parenting and Partnering and publicly archived at the Institute for Political and Social Research, see https://aspe.hhs.gov/system/files/pdf/257876/ICPSROnePager.pdf.

2. For more information on the U.S. Census Bureau's Data Linkage Infrastructure, housed in the Center for Administrative Record Research and Applications, see www.census.gov/library/working-papers/series/carra-wp.html.

might use newly linked data to better illuminate how family-member incarceration shapes trajectories of physical health and health care utilization among children and adults when a family member goes to or returns from prison. Economic researchers could more precisely assess how the (often heavy) child-support-system obligations that greet many poor, reentering fathers shape their participation in both the formal workforce and in family life, as well as the individual, family, and national economic impacts of their double bind.

These federal data sources also offer fertile ground for answering methodological questions related to the distinctions between the accounts of people's lives contained in government administrative records and the accounts people themselves provide when responding to surveys. The "official" records generated through people's contact with government agencies have long been treated as the standard of truth against which their own accounts might or might not measure up. Yet even in sectors of government for which accurate record collection and maintenance is the agency's primary charge (such as voting and elections), recent work offers reason to reconsider the presumption that official records are more accurate than individuals' survey reports (Berent, Krosnick, and Lupia 2016). Further, systems that aim to deliver a particular service to the public may not be equipped to unilaterally account for whether the help or information sought was actually delivered and received. As Multi-site Family Study participants' experiences demonstrate, families navigating an incarceration must attempt to meet a very high-stakes, time-sensitive set of demands that require successful interface with a complex set of government systems. Triangulating between government records of those system contacts and family members' own accounts of their need for and receipt of different services and benefits could highlight areas where families' and agencies' needs, understandings, and priorities align or diverge. The methods described in chapter 5 for integrating and comparing official reincarceration data from state departments of correction with study participants' self-reports of their reentry experiences would be of use in such endeavors.

Finally, the next generation of quantitative work in this area must begin moving past the limited categories our team and others in this space have used to characterize people moving and adapting across domestic, carceral, and public spheres. Incarcerated or released, married or divorced, working in the formal economy or not—categories like these prove quite limited in capturing the fluid, continually adapting, and sometimes "à la carte" forms of interpersonal and material resourcing in which Multi-site Family Study participants engaged. Applying the kinds of integrated, mixed-method analytic approaches described in chapters 2 and 3 with linked qualitative and quantitative data could help inform the development of future quantitative measures that fully materialize the diverse and fluid family roles and material survival strategies families require at these intersections.

When our efforts succeed, though, they can create as many uncertainties as they resolve. As research using the mixed-method and multiple-reporter methodological approaches presented in chapter 4 will continue to reveal, research participants make complicated decisions about whether, when, and how to share information about their lives. Individuals living in poverty and under justice system surveillance have had to construct often inconsistent stories of their lives for system consumption. When asked about their experiences by researchers, for example, they may produce narratives of need and instability, such as those elicited by human services program-eligibility assessments and charitable organization gatekeeping; narratives of self-sufficiency and rehabilitation, such as those demanded by judges and parole boards; or something else entirely. No matter how much data we have—and perhaps especially when we have an abundance of data—these accounts may not resolve into a singular or definitive story.

Researchers need to be prepared to embrace this complexity because the challenges those multiple stories present are worth surmounting. In their very multiplicity lies valuable information about the process of storytelling in social research. Scientists have a great temptation to lay claim to each new and improved form of the truth we believe our efforts to have generated. In seizing opportunities to address the many remaining gaps in knowledge of family life and criminal justice system involvement, however, the goal must not be to replace one authoritative understanding with another. Generating true insight in this complex and contested realm will demand a reconsideration of who is producing knowledge, why, and for whom. It behooves us to learn more about how study participants engaged in both criminal justice systems and in family life see researchers: As more eyes and ears of the surveilling state? As potential sources of desperately needed help? As emissaries of, or to, the powers that be? And how do these dynamics and perceptions fluctuate with a new generation of scholars (e.g., Contreras 2013; Rios 2011) who incorporate their own experiences of criminalization and systems-related hardships into their approaches to research?

Regardless of the data we have and the methods that appeal to us, it is time to train a spotlight on both the formal scholarship and the informal meaning-making of families affected by incarceration. It is worth asking questions about the uses they envision and intend for the stories they share and staying open to the fundamental methodological implications their answers might have. Knowing where we researchers figure in systems of government protection and punishment (and the spaces between them) can guide us in designing data collection and analytic methods that best serve the goals research participants bring to our shared endeavors. Such methods must, at a minimum, begin to materialize the kinds of creative integration these families manage in traversing widely disparate settings and often contradictory systems for survival.

Maybe it seems too much to hope that diligent research can help to guide the remaking of our public systems in a form that values and sustains all of us. We know enough to suspect, though, that we cannot effectively protect and preserve low-income families with one set of government services while deploying another, more resource- and contact-intensive infrastructure that removes, punishes, and economically hobbles their members. We also know that the knowledge produced by researchers can only aspire to approximate the skillfulness of those already working daily to integrate these disparate systems in their bodies, minds, and homes. What we do not yet know is this: What could we achieve if the resources now devoted to the competing tasks of punishment and protection were focused, instead, on the singular goal of lifting up the most vulnerable among us? If fathers and mothers whose own dreams have been crushed by the systems that we have now are still capable of hope, if they can see a future other than that one on the horizon for their children, so can we.

APPENDIX

METHODOLOGY

PART A: TECHNICAL DETAIL ON MULTI-SITE
FAMILY STUDY APPROACH

Multi-site Family Study Overview

The Multi-site Family Study was sponsored jointly by the Office of the Assistant Secretary for Planning and Evaluation and the Administration for Children and Families (ACF) in the U.S. Department of Health and Human Services and conducted by RTI International. It was funded to evaluate the impact of a set of ACF-funded demonstration programs to support healthy family relationships among incarcerated and reentering fathers, their partners, and children. The Multi-site Family Study followed almost 2,000 incarcerated and reentering fathers and their partners for up to three years, beginning during the male partner's incarceration and typically continuing through his reentry into the community. The study produced the field's richest longitudinal, couples-based dataset on family life and criminal justice system involvement.

Features of the Multi-site Family Study Dataset

The Multi-site Family Study dataset is available for public use through the Interuniversity Consortium for Political and Social Research (ICPSR). These data offer an unprecedented glimpse into the intersection of family life and criminal justice system involvement. They incorporate accounts from both members of study couples, which are linked at the case level. Data are longitudinal, including up to four interview waves with each couple that typically capture the family's experiences during the incarceration when they enrolled in the study as well as their experiences after the male partner's release. In-depth qualitative data on families' reentry experiences, collected around the time of the release from prison, are also linked dyadically and to the quantitative interview data at the case level. (Publication of a public-use file that includes the qualitative data was under way as of this writing under a separate grant from the National Institute of Justice.) As discussed in chapter 7, these features will support a wealth of future analyses to better understand the experiences of this large and vulnerable population. (For those interested in pursuing future research with these data, the dataset and detailed accompanying documentation are available at www.icpsr.umich.edu/icpsrweb/ICPSR/studies/36639.)

Study Population

Four demonstration programs were selected for the impact evaluation component of the Multi-site Family Study: the grantees were the Indiana Department of Correction, the RIDGE Project (Ohio), the New Jersey Department of Corrections, and the Osborne Association (New York). The impact sites were selected based on offering (1) sufficient program intensity and projected enrollment to support the evaluation, (2) couple-based relationship services, (3) a stable program design at the time of site selection, and (4) sufficiently strong evaluation design possibilities. A fifth site, the Council on Crime and Justice (Minnesota), was originally included in the impact study, but data collection was discontinued in this site due to low enrollment; although Minnesota cases were not included in analyses assessing the impact of demonstration programming (chapter 6), data from this site were included in the analyses conducted for chapters 2 through 5.

Each demonstration program evaluated by the Multi-site Family Study enrolled incarcerated men and their committed romantic or coparenting partner in couples-based services. At the time of the study, these programs served different-sex couples. The timing of program enrollment varied relative to the male partner's prison term: one site enrolled participants upon admission to prison, one site enrolled individuals nearing release, and the other three accepted participants at any point during incarceration. In each of the five sites, participants provided consent for the study around the time of their program enrollment. In addition to being incarcerated and in a self-reported intimate or coparenting relationship, to be eligible, men also had to be 18 or older, speak English, be physically and mentally capable of participating in an interview, and agree to provide contact information for their partners. Couples in which a restraining order was in place were considered ineligible, as were couples in which the female partner denied that an intimate or coparenting relationship existed when contacted for her baseline interview.

To assess the impact of the demonstration programs, the sample also included similar individuals (incarcerated men and their committed romantic or coparenting partner) who did not receive these services. The prison-based nature of the programs and the demonstration sites' relative freedom in designing their own approaches required the development of site-specific impact study designs. The evaluation used a matched-comparison group design in Indiana, New Jersey, and New York, and a wait-list design in Ohio. Members of the Multi-site Family Study comparison groups received "treatment as usual"; that is, they could participate (or not) in whatever services were available in the absence of the demonstration program. (Additional detail on the site-specific designs is provided in part B and chapter 6's notes.) The analyses presented in chapters 2–5 combined data across sites and for treatment and comparison groups and controlled for site and/or treatment group status where relevant; the chapter 6 analysis focused on comparing the experiences of treatment- versus comparison-group members in order to assess program impact.

Development and Content of Multi-site Family Study Quantitative Interviews

The Multi-site Family Study survey instrument was designed to build an understanding of family experiences across correctional and community settings and across a variety of family relationship statuses and definitions. Individual interview questions and scales were adapted for this purpose from related family-strengthening program evaluations (including Building Strong Families, Supporting Healthy Marriage, and Community Healthy Marriage Initiative evaluations) as well as prisoner reentry research (including the Multi-site Evaluation of the Serious and Violent Offender Reentry Initiative and the Returning Home study). A team of academic experts in relationship and family research with justice-involved populations provided feedback during the instrumentation process and throughout the ten-year study period.

The draft baseline instruments were pilot-tested with people incarcerated in jail and their partners in the Raleigh-Durham area. Following the pilot test, the instruments were revised and programmed for computer-assisted personal interviewing.

At each wave, the interview instruments included questions on background characteristics (e.g., demographics, attitudes, motivation, criminal history, relationship history), service provision (e.g., types of services received, delivery format, number and duration of sessions), relationship quality and stability, parenting and child well-being, employment and economic stability, and criminal behavior and substance use. Each of the two members of the couple was interviewed separately. The content of the instruments used at each wave and for men and women was virtually identical, with built-in skip and fill patterns based on the male partner's incarceration status. Couples in which the male partner had not been released from his baseline incarceration continued to be asked about the extent of in-prison contact and were skipped out of questions that were dependent on community exposure (e.g., coresidence, partner violence). Couples in which the male partner had been released from his baseline incarceration were asked detailed questions about the first twenty-four hours after release and additional questions dependent on having community exposure (e.g., coresidence, partner violence). The first postrelease interview for these couples asked about experiences since the male partner's release; subsequent interview(s) asked about experiences since the previous interview.

Multi-site Family Study Recruitment and Data Collection Procedures

Beginning in December 2008, treatment group couples were invited to complete baseline interviews at the time of their enrollment in the demonstration programs, and comparison couples were invited to complete them at the point they were identified for the study. On average, the baseline interview occurred two and a half years after the male partner had been admitted to prison. As part of the baseline male interview, interviewers identified a "focal child" about whom more in-depth questions on parent-child interactions and child well-being were asked. One child was selected from among the male participant's children, with priority given to children who were parented by both members of the study couple and who were closest in age to 8 years old; the latter criterion was intended to allow for meaningful measurement of changes in child well-being over time via parent reports. (Children were not interviewed for this study.) After completing each incarcerated man's baseline interview, we contacted his partner and interviewed those who consented to participate in the study.

All interviews were conducted in person by RTI field interviewers who were extensively trained on confidentiality procedures and human-subjects protection issues for vulnerable populations. Interviewers obtained clearance from each of the state correctional facilities in which baseline interviews were conducted. To maintain confidentiality, protocols were put in place to ensure the same interviewer did not interview both members of a given couple. Informed consent was obtained from respondents prior to each interview. In addition, an informed consent form for the release of administrative data was administered to each respondent. The interviews were conducted using computer-assisted personal interviewing.[1] For particularly sensitive topics (such as partner violence, relationship quality, criminal behavior, and substance abuse), audio computer-assisted self-interviewing was used. This technique reduces social desirability bias (i.e., the tendency to give an answer that will be approved of) by providing greater confidentiality to respondents, who are able to listen to or read questions and enter their responses directly into the computer, rather than verbalize them to an interviewer.

Each interview lasted about two hours. Incentives were provided for all community-based interviews, which included nearly all female interviews at each wave and follow-up interviews for men who had been released. Incentives increased over time, ending up at $75 per interview.[2] All interviews were conducted in private locations. For the female partner, the respondent's home was a frequent interview location. Incarcerated individuals (including all men in the study at baseline) were interviewed in a private room in their correctional facility, with correctional staff out of earshot.

---

1. The only exception was that a paper version of the instrument was used in all interviews conducted in New York State Department of Corrections facilities, which prohibited the use of laptops.

2. Originally, we paid $35 to nonincarcerated female respondents and $40 to nonincarcerated male respondents, who had not received an incentive at baseline. We then increased the incentive to $40 for both groups. However, after struggling to increase eighteen-month response rates in a few sites, we ultimately increased the incentive to $75. Respondents also received a $25 bonus if they completed three interviews and a $5 bonus if they called in after receiving their lead letter.

Follow-up Approach and Timing

Multi-site Family Study participants were recontacted for follow-up interviews 9 and 18 months after baseline. In the two largest sites (Indiana and Ohio), an additional 34-month follow-up interview was conducted. Because program models varied, study sample members were released at varying points during the follow-up period. Some analyses, such as those described in chapter 5, focused exclusively on couples in which the male partner was released from incarceration over the course of the study and participated in at least one postrelease interview; this included 1,017 men. Other analyses, such as those described in chapter 6, included all men (and survey partners), regardless of release status.

Follow-up interviews were conducted in the community for all participants who were not incarcerated at the time of the interview and in correctional facilities for those who were. The male follow-up interview was conducted wherever the male participant was at the time, which could have been in a correctional facility (for men who did not get released from the baseline incarceration during the follow-up period or who had gotten released but had been reincarcerated) or in the community. Whenever needed, the study team obtained additional clearances to allow interviewers to reach study participants who had been transferred to a different state prison or were detained in a local jail.

In addition, qualitative interviews were conducted with a subsample of 166 (including 54 couples) Multi-site Family Study participants. In an effort to learn more about reentry experiences, this sample was limited to couples in which the male partner was released from incarceration between May 2012 and December 2015. Due to logistical considerations, we also limited the sample to couples who lived within thirty minutes of one of eight metropolitan areas in Indiana, Ohio, and New York City (where a small number of interviews were conducted). For men in the qualitative subsample who had not yet been released from prison, an in-depth interview was conducted with both members of the couple shortly before the man's release and again shortly after his release. If the male partner had already been released from prison, the couple was interviewed once. Potentially eligible sample members were screened over the telephone, and interviews were scheduled with those who met eligibility criteria.

Qualitative interviews were conducted by members of our team who attended a full-day training specifically tailored to the study, covering topics such as how to maintain a private interview setting in a residential home or correctional facility, protocols for protecting intracouple confidentiality, and strategies for probing about contextual factors surrounding incarceration and reentry. As with the quantitative component, the two members of each couple were interviewed individually; for interviews conducted in the community, the participant's study partner was not permitted to be in the same building at the time of the interview to protect confidentiality. Interviews lasted approximately one and a half hours and used a semistructured guide. Interviewers also referred to a respondent profile that contained selected quantitative interview responses provided by the participant during the impact study interviews, such as the age of the focal child and basic indicators of family and incarceration experiences. These profiles were used to inform certain parts of the qualitative interview.

The quantitative field effort took place from December 2008 through April 2014, and qualitative interviews were conducted between 2014 and 2015. All data collection procedures were reviewed and approved by RTI's Institutional Review Board. Research approval was obtained from departments of corrections in participating states. The study was also certified by the federal Office for Human Research Protections.[3]

Response Rates and Resulting Sample

Of the 1,991 men who completed baseline interviews, a partner baseline interview was completed for 1,482.[4] This resulted in 1,482 eligible couples in which both partners completed a baseline interview. These were the couples on

---

3. The Office for Human Research Protections (OHRP) is located in the U.S. Department of Health and Human Services. It has responsibility for ensuring that HHS-funded research is conducted in an ethical manner and will not harm the participants. Prisoners are considered a vulnerable class of research participants and have protections that require specific approval by OHRP of any research protocol.

4. Among the 509 partners who did not complete a baseline interview, 197 could not be located based on the information provided by the incarcerated male partner; 118 refused the interview, either directly or through someone else; 117 were unavailable after repeated attempts; 15 were ineligible to be interviewed because they were under 18, did not speak English, or were physically or mentally impaired; 5 started their interviews but did not complete them; 14 had moved out of the study area, were institutionalized, or were in a facility that did not allow interviewer access; and 43 were not interviewed for other reasons.

whom the dyadic analyses, including those aimed at understanding couple relationship dynamics (chapter 3) and intimate partner violence (chapter 4), focused. These study couples were typically in their early 30s at the time of the baseline interview. Twenty-five percent were married, over 60 percent were in intimate relationships, and the remainder were in coparenting relationships. Over 80 percent of sample members had children under the age of 18. The study sample was racially and ethnically diverse; just over half of men and just under half of women were Black, about one-third were White, and slightly less than 10 percent were Hispanic/Latino. The average couple had been together for seven years and coparented two minor children together. One-third of men and one-quarter of women reported not having a GED or high school diploma. Men had extensive histories of involvement with the criminal justice system: more than half reported being incarcerated as juveniles, and they averaged 12 previous arrests and 6 adult incarcerations each. Although their female partners had far less criminal justice system involvement, nearly half reported having ever been arrested, with an average of 1.4 arrests.

An additional 509 eligible men in the full study sample completed the baseline interview themselves, but their partner did not. These men were generally included in analyses aimed at understanding reentering men's experiences with fatherhood (chapter 2) and other aspects of reentry (chapter 5), as well as in analyses of the impact of family-strengthening programming (chapter 6). Although the subsamples were very comparable in terms of basic demographic characteristics, histories of criminal justice system involvement, and preincarceration experiences, several differences between this additional group of men and those whose partner did complete a baseline interview bear mention. Men whose partner did not complete a baseline interview had been incarcerated for significantly longer, were more likely to characterize their relationship as coparenting (versus married or intimate), reported lower overall happiness with their relationship, had fewer children, had significantly less frequent in-person and telephone contact with their partner, and had less contact with their children during their incarceration than men whose partner did complete a baseline interview.

Overall response rates for Multi-site Family Study men were 81.7 percent at baseline and around 75 percent for the 9-, 18-, and 34-month follow-up interviews. Response rates for women were 75.7 percent at baseline and near or above 75 percent for each follow-up wave. Total numbers of completed interviews, as well as response rates, are shown by wave in table A-1. Response rates

TABLE A-1

Response Rates, by Wave, Sex, and Group

	Baseline	9 Month	18 Month	34 Month
MEN				
Treatment				
Interviews completed	1,156	877	829	589
Ineligible cases	261	20	46	23
Non-interviews	264	259	281	175
Response rate	81.4%	77.2%	74.7%	77.1%
Comparison				
Interviews completed	835	627	608	445
Ineligible cases	296	4	25	13
Noninterviews	182	204	202	129
Response rate	82.1%	75.5%	75.1%	77.5%
Total				
Interviews completed	1,991	1,504	1,437	1,034
Ineligible cases	557	24	71	36
Noninterviews	446	463	483	304
Response rate	81.7%	76.5%	74.8%	77.3%
WOMEN				
Treatment				
Interviews completed	894	805	810	603
Ineligible cases	13	95	124	69
Noninterviews	249	256	222	115
Response rate	78.2%	75.9%	78.5%	84.0%
Comparison				
Interviews completed	588	543	572	415
Ineligible cases	20	85	101	81
Non-interviews	227	207	162	91
Response rate	72.1%	72.4%	77.9%	82.0%
Total				
Interviews completed	1,482	1,348	1,382	1,018
Ineligible cases	33	180	225	150
Non-interviews	476	463	384	206
Response rate	75.7%	74.4%	78.3%	83.2%

reflect the number of completed interviews divided by the number of eligible cases fielded. Follow-up interviews were fielded for all eligible men who completed baseline and for their partner—regardless of whether the partner completed baseline.[5]

A small number of people classified as eligible for baseline were reclassified as ineligible for one or more follow-up interviews because they had died, become physically or mentally incapable of participating in the follow-up interview, had put a restraining order in place against their study partner, or moved outside the study area. Also, a small number of women were classified as ineligible who had been located for the first time at one of the follow-up waves and retrospectively reported that they had not been in an intimate or coparenting relationship with the male study participant at the time of his baseline interview.[6] The specific number of male and female cases that were eligible at baseline but reclassified as ineligible at one or more follow-up interviews for any of these reasons is listed in table A-1 (see "Ineligible cases"). The noninterviews shown are eligible cases that were not successfully interviewed. This was typically because the respondent could not be located, but also included instances of refusal and of difficulty accessing respondents who were in treatment facilities or new correctional facilities from which approval could not be obtained in time for the interview.

PART B: ADDITIONAL TECHNICAL NOTES
BY CHAPTER

Chapter 2

The analyses presented in chapter 2 examined parenting after prison and its relationship to postprison reintegration. This work examined change in men's parenting choices and behaviors over the course of incarceration and reentry, identified predictors of positive parenting after release from prison, and explored how men's family roles and relationships contributed to their reentry success more broadly. We applied a mixed-method approach that incorporated quantitative data from reentering fathers as well as qualitative data from

---

5. The only exception is that some women (approximately 110) were not fielded for follow-up (and were classified as ineligible) because we had insufficient evidence to conclude that they actually existed (i.e., the male partner was never able to provide updated contact information and they had not been located at a previous wave).

6. The male partner was retained in the study because of the substantial resources that had already been expended to conduct his previous interviews.

interviews with fathers and their partners around the time of release. This section provides more detail about that methodological approach, as well as some supplemental detail (for example, complete results from the multiple regression model and p-values from t-tests) not included in the chapter.

ANALYTIC SAMPLE

The quantitative analysis for chapter 2 focused on 772 men (out of a total of 1,991 male study participants) who had children and who were released from prison prior to one of the study follow-up interviews. Like those in the full study sample, most of the fathers in this analytic subsample reported being in nonmarried intimate relationships that were exclusive and long-term. Fathers were typically in their early to middle thirties and had an average of three children.

The qualitative analyses presented in chapter 2 incorporated data from a subsample of 62 reentering fathers and their partners who completed qualitative interviews. Table A-2 compares the characteristics of the qualitative and quantitative analytic subsamples in terms of demographic, family, and incarceration-related characteristics. Fathers in the qualitative subsample resembled those in the quantitative sample; evident differences in relationship duration and child age at baseline likely represent characteristics that made these men and their partners more likely to agree to participate in another interview about their coparenting or romantic relationship several years after the baseline survey.

NOTES ON ANALYTIC APPROACH

We used data from fathers' baseline and first postrelease interviews to compare three key dimensions of their relationships with their children before and after incarceration: father-child coresidence, father-child financial support, and frequency of father-child activities. For each dimension, we used matched-pairs t-tests to compare postrelease experiences with preincarceration experiences (as reported retrospectively during the baseline interview).

Next, we used multiple regression to identify factors that shaped each of the three dimensions of father-child relationships after release from prison. Predictors of father-child coresidence and fathers' financial support for their children after release were identified using multivariate logistic regression models. Based on prior research and guided by the results of a series of bivariate logistic regressions, we tested for the potential influence of the independent variables shown in figure A-1 on father-child coresidence and financial

TABLE A-2

Characteristics of Reentering Fathers Subsample

	Fathers in sample	
	Quantitative (n=772)	*Qualitative (n=33)*
Age		
Age at study enrollment (mean)	32.5 years	33.7 years
Relationship with survey partner		
Relationship status		
Married	22%	21%
In an intimate relationship	72%	76%
In a coparenting relationship only	6%	3%
In an exclusive relationship	85%	91%
Duration of relationship, if married/intimate (mean)	7.1 years	10.1 years
Parenting/coparenting characteristics		
Number of children (mean)	3.1	2.8
Number of coparents (mean)	2.8	3.1
Age of focal child (mean)	7.0 years	6.1 years
Coparent any children with study partner	87%	82%
Incarceration history		
Age at first arrest (mean)	16.3 years	17.4 years
Number of previous adult incarcerations (mean)	6.5	7.0
Duration of current incarceration (mean)	2.3 years	2.5 years

support after the father's release from prison. In addition, these models controlled for program site and the baseline measure of the outcome.[7]

Then, using the same set of independent variables as for the coresidence and financial support models, we ran additional multivariate models to identify predictors of parental warmth, self-reported relationship quality, and

---

[7]. Several other variables explored as potential independent variables were not significantly correlated with father-child relationship quality, including assistance received with staying in touch with children during incarceration, father's childhood parenting situation (involvement of biological father, living in a two-parent home), and gender of the focal child.

Independent variables (Preincarceration)	Dependent variables (Postrelease)
• Incarceration history[1] • Marital status[2] • Relationship happiness[3] • Conflict resolution[4] • Father-child contact during incarceration[5] • Parenting class participation[6] • Age of child	• Coresidence with child[7] • Financial support for child[8] • Warmth toward child[9] • Quality of father-child relationship[10] • Frequency of father-child activities[11]

[1] Number of adult incarcerations.
[2] Whether the father was legally married to the person he named as his committed romantic or coparenting partner.
[3] The father's rating of his relationship with the survey partner from 1 to 10 (with higher numbers indicating greater happiness).
[4] The father's self-reported conflict resolution habits and skills in his relationship with the survey partner, using a multi-item scale from 0 to 12 (with higher values indicating better conflict resolution habits and skills).
[5] A four-point scale reflecting the types of contact the father reported having with the focal child during his incarceration: in-person visits, telephone calls, father sending mail, and father receiving mail.
[6] A dichotomous variable indicating whether the father reported participating in any parenting classes during the baseline incarceration.
[7] A dichotomous variable indicating whether the father reported living with his focal child at his first postrelease interview.
[8] A dichotomous variable indicating whether the father reported providing any monetary support for his focal child at his first postrelease interview.
[9] A 12-point scale dichotomized at 0–9 versus 10–12, reflecting how often the father reported engaging in the following activities with the focal child since his release from incarceration: praising the child, hugging or showing physical affection with the child, communicating with the child about his/her interests, and telling the child that he loves him/her.
[10] A single item asking fathers to rate their current relationship with their focal child, dichotomized as "poor or fair" and "good or excellent."
[11] How many days per week fathers reported an activity with their focal child, such as eating meals, going shopping, helping with homework, or doing something fun with the child. Residential fathers who engaged in an activity 6–7 days/week were compared with those who engaged in an activity 0–5 days/week. Nonresidential fathers who engaged in an activity 1–7 days/week were compared with those who engaged in an activity 0 days/week.

Figure A-1. Understanding what promotes positive parenting after reentry from prison. Image credit: Terry Hall.

activity frequency. These models were run separately for residential and nonresidential fathers, because of the possibility that the relationship between the independent variables and the dependent variables (which primarily used frequency-based measures such as "How often did you … ") might differ according to a father's residential status.

To assess whether four distinct dimensions of fathers' family roles and experiences contributed to their overall reentry success, we carried out a multivariate logistic regression. The dependent variable was a dichotomous indicator of reentry success 4 to 12 months after release, comprising five variables. Independent variables were selected using bivariate regressions, and like variables were grouped into four composites. Details on the constructs each composite was designed to measure and how its various dimensions were operationalized in constructing the composite variable appear in table A-3.

The multiple regression model controlled for baseline versions of the components of the dependent variable representing reentry success, as well as the age of the focal child. Since some of the independent variables and controls had a high proportion of missing values, we also ran another version of the regression in which we excluded the control for focal child financial support (since it had a high rate of missing values) and converted missing values to zeroes for the composites' component variables that had a high rate of missing values.

In addition, we used qualitative data to understand how family roles and experiences figured in fathers' reentry plans and experiences. Qualitative interview data were transcribed and loaded into ATLAS.ti, a qualitative data analysis software package, for coding. A codebook was developed jointly by the analysis team, incorporating deductive codes based on the study research questions, as well as inductive codes to capture themes that emerged during the coding and data review process. Queries of coded data were run in ATLAS.ti to capture segments of text that focused on parenting and reentry. Analysts read the code reports for these queries, identified salient themes, and met to discuss how these themes informed each of the quantitative findings. Analytic memos were used to develop and expand themes. Key themes and the exemplary quotations associated with them were tracked in an Excel spreadsheet.

SUPPLEMENTAL DETAIL ON RESULTS

The differences between pre- and postincarceration parenting reported in chapter 2 were highly statistically significant. Fewer fathers lived with their focal child after release from prison (50 percent) compared to the 6 months before the incarceration (70 percent, $p<.001$). The proportion of fathers who provided financial support for their focal child was significantly lower at the first postrelease follow-up interview (75 percent) than before the incarceration (87 percent, $p<.001$). Frequency of father-child activities also tended to decline from preincarceration to postrelease ($p<.001$).

TABLE A-3

Identifying What Kinds of Family Experiences Contribute to Reentry Success

Construct (composite variable)	Dimensions (component variables)	Values
Reentry success	• Whether respondent had recidivated • Whether respondent financially supported his focal child • Whether respondent used illegal drugs (other than marijuana) • Whether respondent was employed and working • Whether respondent lived with his survey partner	Dichotomous
Father of origin	• Whether respondent reported that his biological father was "very involved" or "somewhat involved" in raising him • Whether respondent felt "extremely close" or "somewhat close" to his biological father while growing up • Whether respondent answered "no" to a question about whether his father/stepfather was ever arrested	Range from 0 to 3, with higher values indicating more positive experiences
Family support	• Whether respondent has a family member who will loan him money if he needs it • Whether respondent has a family member who will provide him a place to live if he needs it • Whether respondent has a family member who will help him with transportation to work or appointments if he needs it • Whether respondent disagreed or strongly disagreed that he is often criticized or put down by his family	Range from 0 to 4, with higher values indicating more support

TABLE A-3
(continued)

Construct (composite variable)	Dimensions (component variables)	Values
Parental roles and responsibilities	• Whether respondent lived with his child/stepchild during the 6 months prior to incarceration • Whether focal child lived with its mother during the father's incarceration (versus with other family members or foster care) • Whether respondent strongly agreed that fathers should spend as much time taking care of their children as mothers • Whether respondent and his survey partner made major decisions for focal child together • Whether respondent was concerned about his focal child's happiness during his incarceration	Range from 0 to 5, with higher values indicating more responsibilities
Parenting involvement during incarceration	• Whether respondent strongly agreed that keeping in touch with his children during incarceration was very important to him • Whether respondent agreed or strongly agreed that he was satisfied with the amount of help he received with staying in touch with his children during this incarceration • Whether respondent reported that he felt he was "an excellent parent" or "a very good parent" to his focal child • Whether respondent reported that his relationship with his focal child during incarceration was "excellent" or "good" • Whether respondent scored as having high parental warmth on the parental warmth scale • Whether respondent reported having contact with his focal child during his incarceration in at least three of the following four ways: phone calls, sending mail, receiving mail, and visits	Ranges from 0 to 6, with higher values indicating more involvement

In the set of multiple regression models examining predictors of father-child relationship quality, paternal warmth, and frequency of father-child activities after the release from prison, the original models (as presented in chapter 2) controlled for several aspects of fathers' relationships with their study partner: marital status, relationship happiness, and conflict resolution skills. When these variables were removed from the models, father-child contact during the incarceration became a statistically significant predictor of frequency of father-child activities after release ($p<.05$ for both residential and nonresidential fathers) and of self-reported father-child relationship quality after release ($p<.05$ for nonresidential fathers only).

As shown in table A-4 (and summarized briefly in chapter 2), we also ran a multiple regression model examining how fathers' family experiences influenced their reentry success. Of the five independent variables included in the model, only parent-child interaction during the incarceration was statistically significant ($p<.05$); more parent-child involvement and contact during incarceration was associated with a higher likelihood of reentry success. Of the four control variables included in the model, only the variable indicating whether the respondent was employed and working at any point in the 6 months prior to incarceration was statistically significant ($p<.01$); respondents who were employed and working in the 6 months prior to incarceration were more likely to be successful in the 4 to 12 months after release.

Model results were similar when we increased the number of observations from 274 to 454 by converting missing values to zeroes for the composites' component variables that had high missingness. Parent-child interaction during incarceration was still the only statistically significant independent variable ($p<.001$). Among the controls, whether the respondent was employed and working at any point in the 6 months prior to incarceration was still statistically significant ($p<.001$); additionally, the composite indicator of intimate or coparenting relationship quality at baseline was significant ($p = .01$), with higher relationship quality at baseline associated with a higher likelihood of reentry success. We further increased the number of observations from 454 to 503 by excluding the control for whether the respondent financially supported his focal child before his incarceration. Doing this caused two additional independent variables to become significant: family support ($p<.05$) and parenting roles and responsibilities ($p<.05$). Higher levels of family support and parenting roles and responsibilities remained predictive of reentry success, as in the other model.

TABLE A-4

Results from Multiple Regression Model to Identify Predictors of Reentry Success

	Odds ratio	Std. err.	P>|z|
Independent variables			
Father of origin composite (range from 0 to 3), with higher values indicating a more positive experience	1.005	0.140	0.969
Family support composite (range from 0 to 4), with higher values indicating more family support	1.214	0.265	0.373
Parenting roles and responsibilities composite (ranges from 0 to 5), with higher values indicating the respondent has more parenting roles and responsibilities	1.237	0.172	0.126
Parent-child interactions during incarceration composite (ranges from 0 to 6), with higher values indicating more fatherhood involvement and contact during incarceration	**1.266**	**0.128**	**0.020**
Controls			
Financially support focal child during 6 months prior to incarceration (yes/no)	2.501	1.657	0.166
Any drug use (excluding marijuana) 6 months prior to incarceration (yes/no)	0.735	0.211	0.282
Employed and working at any point in the 6 months prior to incarceration (yes/no)	**2.174**	**0.640**	**0.008**
Composite indicator of intimate or coparenting relationship quality at baseline (1 = successful, 0 = not successful)	2.151	0.988	0.095
Age of focal child	1.001	0.035	0.982
Constant	0.007	0.008	0.000

The model included 274 observations, and the Pseudo R-squared from the model was 0.0875.

Chapter 3

The analyses presented in chapter 3 aimed to understand how reentry affects couples' relationships and how partners experience the transition from incarceration to release. As in the chapter 2 analytic work, we applied a mixed-method approach, combining quantitative and qualitative data collected with both members of study couples around the time of the male partner's release from prison. This section provides more detail about our methodological approach, as well as some supplemental detail (for example, p-values from statistical tests) not included in the chapter.

ANALYTIC SAMPLE

The quantitative analyses reported in this chapter are based on data collected in study couples' baseline and first postrelease interviews, which were conducted an average of 5.6 months after the male partner's release from the baseline incarceration. Analyses focused on 641 couples in which (1) the male partner was released from prison prior to the 9-, 18-, or 34-month interview, (2) both members of the couple completed the baseline and first postrelease interviews, and (3) at least one member of the couple reported being romantically involved with the other partner (as opposed to coparenting only) at baseline.

Most of the couples in both the quantitative and qualitative subsamples reported being in nonmarried intimate relationships that were exclusive and long-term. The majority of men and women had minor children and coparented at least one child together. Men had fairly extensive histories of involvement with the criminal justice system, reporting an average of 6.5 (quantitative sample) and 7.0 (qualitative sample) previous incarcerations during adulthood. In qualitative interviews, couples often explained that they had weathered several cycles of incarceration and reentry during their relationship. Table A-5 summarizes the characteristics of the study couples for each sample at the baseline interview, which took place on average about 2.5 years after the male partner's admission to prison.

NOTES ON ANALYTIC APPROACH

Descriptive analyses were first conducted to determine how couples' relationship status and quality after the male partner's release from incarceration differed from levels prior to and during the incarceration. Differences in couples' relationship experiences across time points were assessed using matched-pairs t-tests. A multivariate logistic regression model was used to

TABLE A-5
Characteristics of Reentering Couples Subsample

	Quantitative sample, men (n=641)	Quantitative sample, women (n=641)	Qualitative sample, men (n=33)	Qualitative sample, women (n=29)
Relationship with survey partner				
Study couple in an exclusive relationship	87%	86%	91%	89%
Average duration of relationship	7.9	7.2	10.1	10.0
Parenting/coparenting characteristics				
Has children under 18	86%	82%	85%	86%
Study partners coparent any children together	76%	74%	82%	76%
(among parents) Average # of children	2.7	2.4	2.8	2.5
(among parents) Average # of coparents	2.9	1.9	3.1	2.0
Average age of focal child	7.0	7.1	6.1	7.2
Age				
Average age at study enrollment	34.0	32.7	33.7	33.9
Incarceration history				
Average age at first arrest	16.8	(not asked)	17.4	(not asked)
Average # of previous adult incarcerations	6.5	1.2	7.0	1.8
Average duration of current incarceration	2.5 years	(n/a)	2.5 years	(n/a)

investigate baseline factors that predicted whether both members of the couple reported being in an intimate relationship with one another at postrelease follow-up. Drawing on the literature and results of a set of bivariate logistic regressions, we examined the potential role of the following independent variables in influencing relationship status after the male partner's release from prison:

- Duration of relationship at baseline (average of male and female partners' reports)
- Happiness with relationship at baseline (rating from 1 to 10, average of male and female reports)
- Whether couple coparented at least one child together (whether coparenting was indicated in both partners' reports)
- Contact between partners during the incarceration (a four-point scale reflecting the types of contact the male partner reported having with the female partner during the incarceration: in-person visits, telephone calls, sending mail, and receiving mail)
- Whether the couple was married at baseline (as opposed to in a nonmarried intimate relationship)
- Communication skills at baseline (scale from 0 to 12)
- Fidelity attitudes and behaviors at baseline (scale from 0 to 18)
- Duration of male partner's baseline incarceration (male partner's report)
- Satisfaction with assistance staying in touch with partner during incarceration (male partner's report)

The model controlled for program site and whether the male partner had received relationship education classes prior to the baseline interview.

Qualitative data were used to elucidate findings from the descriptive quantitative analyses and multivariate model. Transcripts from 68 qualitative interviews with 62 participants were included. All audio files were transcribed verbatim and transcripts were uploaded into ATLAS.ti for data management. A codebook was created using deductive codes that were developed based on the study research questions; inductive codes were developed iteratively based on interviewer and analyst memos and biweekly coder meetings. Queries of coded data were run in ATLAS.ti using codes relating to partnership, reentry, and postrelease expectations. Analysts read the code reports for these queries, identified salient themes, and discussed in group meetings how these themes related to the quantitative findings. Analytic memos were used to develop and expand themes, and exemplary quotations associated with key themes were tracked in an Excel spreadsheet.

SUPPLEMENTAL DETAIL ON RESULTS

As shown in table A-6 (and summarized briefly in chapter 3), we ran a multiple regression model examining whether aspects of couples' relationship experiences during the male partner's incarceration influenced their likelihood of being romantically involved after his release.

Several other variables explored as potential independent variables were not significantly correlated with postrelease intimate relationship status. These included whether the participants were enrolled in the demonstration program (versus receiving treatment as usual), whether they received relationship counseling, whether they reported physical violence in the relationship before the incarceration, what support they received from extended family or friends, their substance use, and the male partner's peer influences.

Chapter 4

The analyses presented in chapter 4 examined intimate partner violence (IPV) among couples in which the male partner was involved with the criminal justice system, including overall IPV prevalence, differences in reports of abuse before and after incarceration, and differences in male and female partners' reports of abuse within the same couple. We analyzed data from qualitative interviews in which participants volunteered their experiences and perceptions related to IPV and applied a variety of statistical techniques (including descriptive statistics, t-tests, and cross-lagged autoregression) to dyadic quantitative data collected during and after the male partner's incarceration. This section provides more detail about the methods we applied, as well as some supplemental information (for example, complete results from the cross-lagged autoregression) not included in chapter 4.

ANALYTIC SAMPLE

The analyses presented in chapter 4 focused on couples in which the male partner was released from prison prior to the 9-, 18-, or 34-month interview and in which both partners completed the first postrelease interview (n = 666 couples). Table A-7 summarizes the characteristics of these couples at the time of their baseline interviews (which took place on average 2.6 years after the male partner's admission to prison). The average age of men in this sample was 34 at baseline, and the average age of women was 33. Men had fairly extensive criminal justice histories, with justice system involvement beginning on average at age 17.

TABLE A-6

Predictors of Being Married or Romantically Involved after Release (N=641)

Predictor	Coefficient	Std. error	95% confidence interval	
			Lower	Upper
Duration of relationship at baseline	1.0789***	0.0202	1.0400	1.1193
Happiness with relationship at baseline	1.2497***	0.0606	1.1365	1.3742
Couple coparents at least one child	1.4265	0.2950	0.9511	2.1394
Contact between partners during incarceration	1.5455**	0.2123	1.1807	2.0230
Couple was married at baseline	1.5100	0.3627	0.9430	2.4178
Couple's communication skills at baseline	1.0210	0.0629	0.9049	1.1520
Fidelity attitudes and behaviors at baseline	1.1337**	0.0484	1.0426	1.2328
Duration of male partner's baseline incarceration	0.9624	0.0297	0.9059	1.0225
Satisfaction with assistance staying in touch with partner during incarceration	0.8332	0.1623	0.5687	1.2205
Male partner received relationship education at baseline	1.0351	0.1991	0.7100	1.5092
Site OH	1.1972	0.2645	0.7764	1.8460
NY	1.3841	0.7532	0.4764	4.0214
NJ	1.9781*	0.609	1.082	3.618
MN	0.6820	0.3101	0.2798	1.6628
Constant	0.0057***	0.0050	0.0010	0.0317

***p<0.001, **p<.01, *p<.05

TABLE A-7

Characteristics of Analytic Sample for Intimate Partner Violence

	Men (N=666)	Women (N=666)
Age		
Average age at study enrollment	33.9 years	32.7 years
Income		
Median annual individual income at first postrelease follow-up[1]	$15,600	$15,180
Incarceration history		
Average age at first arrest	17.0 years	(not asked)
Average # of previous adult incarcerations	6.5	1.3
Average duration of current incarceration	2.6 years	(n/a)

[1] Individual annual income for men at the time of the first postrelease interview ranged from $180 to $84,000. For women, the range was $240 to $66,000.

At the time of the first postrelease interview, respondents reported a median annualized income of $15,600 for men and $15,180 for women. About half of men (54 percent) and women (45 percent) in this sample were Black, another 33 percent of men and 42 percent of women were White, and 7 percent of men and 6 percent of women were Hispanic/Latino. The quantitative analysis that examined agreement within couples on abuse in the relationship before the male partner's incarceration was able to include a larger sample of 1,108 couples in which both members of the study couple completed a baseline interview and answered questions about IPV.

NOTES ON ANALYTIC APPROACH

For the multiple regression models to identify predictors of a couple reporting no physical violence at reentry, independent variables were selected based on prior research and results of a series of bivariate logistic regressions. Variables included in the final models are shown in table A-8.

For each independent variable listed in the table, men's and women's reports of the variable were tested in separate models. In addition, the models controlled for whether the couple was in the treatment or comparison group and whether they reported any physical violence prior to the male partner's incar-

TABLE A-8
Variables Included in Models

Variable	Time point
Healthy relationship beliefs (scale from 0 to 21, with higher scores indicating healthier beliefs)	Postrelease
Conflict resolution skills (scale from 0 to 12, with higher scores indicating better conflict resolution skills)	Postrelease
Length of the couple's relationship	Baseline
Whether partner "rarely" or "never" becomes jealous or possessive	Postrelease
Male partner's "street time" (number of days elapsed between the male's release and the postrelease interview)	Postrelease
Attitude toward partner violence (single item: "It is sometimes OK for couples to get a little rough physically, like pushing or hitting")	Postrelease
Isolation behavior victimization (single item: "Partner tried to keep you from seeing or talking with your friends or family")	Postrelease
Financial control victimization (single item: "Partner tried to keep money from you, make you ask for money, or take money from you")	Postrelease
Attitude toward compromise (single item: "People involved with you have to learn how to do things your way")	Postrelease
Confidence in partner's fidelity (single item: "You know you can count on your partner to remain faithful to you")	Postrelease
Importance of own fidelity to partner (single item: "It is very important to you to be faithful to your partner")	Postrelease
Relationship happiness (rating from 1 to 10 for the "number that best describes your happiness with your relationship now")	Postrelease
Emotional support from extended family (scale from 0 to 18, with higher values indicate higher family support)	Postrelease
Employed (yes/no)	Postrelease
Symptoms of clinical depression (CESD-9 score of 9 or above)	Postrelease
Symptoms of post-traumatic stress disorder (index from 0 to 4, with higher scores indicating more PTSD symptoms)	Postrelease
Problem drinking (index from 0 to 5, with higher scores indicating more drinking problems)	Postrelease

ceration. An additional variable, postrelease relationship status, was originally included in the multivariate models based on the literature and on its significance in bivariate logistic regression. However, the influence of relationship status observed in the multivariate models reversed that observed in the bivariate regressions, suggesting a spurious association. For this reason, we excluded relationship status from the final multivariate models.

The cross-lagged autoregression presented in chapter 4 used all available waves of longitudinal data to estimate effects of IPV victimization reports and relationship status reports (e.g., whether romantically involved) on one another for each pair of adjacent time points available in the dataset. This analysis applied a time-invariant, autoregressive cross-lagged (ARCL) model. An ARCL model is used to determine causality in longitudinal data by allowing a variable to be regressed on itself and additional lagged explanatory variables at each time point, allowing us to determine the influence of each variable separately (e.g., Bollen and Curran 2004). It enabled us to examine whether the rate of physical violence victimization among men and women who were no longer romantically involved after the male partner's release from prison was more likely driven by dynamics of violence-instigated separation or by separation-instigated violence. The ARCL models estimated four effects: (1) the effect of reporting abuse victimization at the first time point on abuse victimization at the second time point (an autoregressive effect), (2) the effect of abuse at the first time point on relationship status at the second time point (a cross-lagged effect), (3) the effect of relationship status at the first time point on relationship status at the second time point (an autoregressive effect), and (4) the effect of relationship status at the first time point on abuse reports at the second time point (a cross-lagged effect). Missing data were handled with the pairwise present method (that is, including an observation if it had a value for the time point of interest, even if other values in the observation were missing).

SUPPLEMENTAL DETAIL ON RESULTS

As presented briefly in chapter 4, we used matched-pairs t-tests to assess agreement between the two members of each study couple regarding the presence of abuse in the relationship during the 6 months before the male partner's incarceration. The differences in men's and women's reports of abuse within couples were highly statistically significant. Men's reports of perpetration differed from women's reports of victimization for frequent physical violence ($p<.001$), severe physical or sexual violence ($p<.001$), and frequent controlling behavior ($p<.001$). Women's reports of perpetration differed from men's reports of victimization for frequent physical violence ($p<.01$) and severe physical or sexual violence ($p<.001$).

We also applied two-sample t-tests to identify what factors differentiated couples in which only the female partner disclosed severe violence from those in which only the male partner disclosed it (not presented in chapter 4). Women in these female-disclosure couples reported lower relationship happiness ($p<.01$), lower relationship commitment ($p<.01$), and poorer couple communication ($p<.001$) than women in male-disclosure couples. They also had higher PTSD scores ($p<.05$), were more likely to binge drink ($p<.001$), and were more likely to indicate they had problems with anger ($p<.001$) or with physically hurting or getting rough with a partner or family member ($p<.001$) when under the influence. Finally, they disapproved more strongly of physical violence in relationships ($p<.05$) and felt less safe in their relationship ($p<.001$).

The cross-lagged autoregression assessed whether reporting abuse at one wave made it more likely that a respondent would no longer be in a relationship with the study partner at the next wave, or vice versa. Men's reported abuse victimization at the first postrelease interview exerted a statistically significant causal influence on relationship status at the second postrelease interview. Men who reported victimization at the first postrelease interview were 1.4 times less likely to be in a romantic relationship with their study partner at the second postrelease interview ($p<.05$). No comparable effect was present for women, among whom we had somewhat less statistical power to detect one.[8] No other cross-lagged effects were statistically significant for men or women.

Chapter 5

The analyses presented in chapter 5 assessed the reentry success of more than 1,000 released men using both traditional metrics of success (avoidance of rearrest or reincarceration) and holistic measures including couple relationship,

---

8. There were more men than women in the analytic samples for the prerelease interview wave (574 men and 552 women) and for the first postrelease interview wave (632 men and 590 women). For the second postrelease interview wave, there were more women than men (418 women and 390 men).

TABLE A-9

Characteristics of Reentry Success Analytic Subsample (N=1,017)

Relationship with survey partner	
Relationship status	
Married	24%
In an intimate relationship	71%
In a coparenting relationship only	5%
Parenting/coparenting characteristics	
Average # of children	3.0
Average age of focal child	7.0 years
Age, education, and employment	
Age at study enrollment (mean)	33.7 years
Has at least a high school diploma or GED	68%
Employed prior to incarceration	58%
Incarceration history	
Age at first arrest (mean)	16.9 years
Number of previous adult incarcerations (mean)	6.3
Length of current incarceration (mean)	2.6 years

parenting, employment, and substance use outcomes. We applied descriptive statistics to assess the proportion of reentering men who achieved "success" on each outcomes measure and constructed multiple regression models to explore predictors of reentry success as variously defined. This section provides more detail about these methods, as well as some supplemental information on predictors of recidivism not included in chapter 5.

ANALYTIC SAMPLE

The analyses presented in chapter 5 focused on 1,017 men in the Multi-site Family Study sample who were released from incarceration at some point during the follow-up period and who participated in at least one postrelease interview. Characteristics of the analytic sample of reentering men are shown in table A-9. Most of the men reported being in unmarried intimate relationships with their survey partners. On average, the men had three children. Just over half of the reentry sample had been employed prior to incarceration and two-thirds had at least a high school diploma or GED. Men had fairly extensive criminal histories beginning around age 17.

NOTES ON ANALYTIC APPROACH

Because the Multi-site Family Study was not designed to be a reentry study, study sample members were released at varying points during the follow-up period. To understand the men's reentry experiences at standardized time periods relative to release, we classified each postrelease interview of a sample member as having taken place (a) less than 4 months after the male partner's release, (b) 4 to 12 months after release, (c) 12 to 24 months after release, or (d) more than 24 months after release. Therefore, a given sample member's reentry experiences could be reflected at one, two, or three of these time periods.[9] In addition to the self-reported interview data, we used administrative data from the state departments of correction (DOCs) in the five states. DOC data were obtained for more than 90 percent of the reentry sample (937 men). We developed indicators of reincarceration in a state prison within 12 and 24 months of release from these data.

Our first set of reentry success analyses used a common indicator of recidivism: lack of reincarceration in state prison. We used simple descriptive statistics to identify the proportion of sample members who were not reincarcerated in a state prison (based on administrative corrections data) within 12 and 24 months of release and the average time to first reincarceration. We used multivariate models to examine potential predictors of reincarceration, including service receipt (alcohol or drug treatment, employment services, education services, family and couple services), family contact during incarceration, demographic characteristics, criminal history and incarceration characteristics, and attitudes and personal characteristics (see table A-10).

Our next set of analyses explored reentry success at four postrelease points using a multidimensional definition of success based on self-reported data. These analyses examined five aspects of reentry success:

---

9. In other words, the analytic samples that were included in analyses exploring success at each of the four time periods differed slightly at each time period. In addition, because Indiana and Ohio were the only two sites where the 34-month interviews were conducted, the "more than 24 months after release" analyses are limited to men from these sites.

TABLE A-10

Independent Variables Included in Models

Independent variable	Description
Education services	Received any education services at any point before release
Employment services	Received any employment services at any point before release
Alcohol or drug treatment	Received any alcohol or drug treatment at any point before release
Family services	Received any family/couple services at any point before release, including parenting classes, couples' relationship education, family counseling, or batterer intervention classes
In-person contact	Amount of in-person contact with family during baseline incarceration (summary indicator of amount of in-person contact from survey partner, children, and other family members)
Age	Age at baseline
Race	Race (White vs. non-White)
Ethnicity	Hispanic (Hispanic vs. non-Hispanic)
Marital status	Married at baseline
Number of children	Number of children at baseline
Previous arrests	Number of previous arrests
Duration of incarceration	Years incarcerated (baseline incarceration)
Education	Has at least a high school diploma/GED at baseline
Employment	Employed prior to incarceration
Alcohol/drug problems	Fewer problems with alcohol/drug use prior to incarceration (a scale measuring how often respondents experienced nine problematic behaviors related to drug or alcohol use in the six months prior to incarceration)
Physical health	No physical health limitations at baseline (no serious health problem that limits the amount or kind of work they can do)
Mental health	Good mental health at baseline (self-reported current emotional or psychological health as excellent, very good, or good)

Learning problems	Fewer learning problems (a scale based on six survey questions that cover respondents' difficulty with and speed in doing math in their daily lives, reading a newspaper or magazine, and writing letters or filling out forms)
Locus of control	Higher locus of control (a single item measuring how often the respondent feels he is able to control the important things in his life)
Group assignment	Treatment vs. comparison group
Site	IN, OH, NJ, or NY

- No rearrest or reincarceration (no self-reported arrests, time spent in county jail, or incarcerations in prison during the reference period)[10]
- No illicit drug use (no self-reported use of illicit drugs other than marijuana during the reference period)
- Employment (self-report of any employment at the time of the interview)
- Intimate or coparenting relationship quality (composite indicator of quality of relationship with survey partner using four survey items that measured the frequency with which the couple avoided conflicts and resolved issues constructively[11])
- Financial support for children (limited to men who were fathers of a minor child; a self-reported indicator of whether fathers provided at least some financial support to the focal child during the reference period)

We used simple descriptive statistics to assess the proportion of men who were classified as successful in any of the areas at each of the four postrelease

---

10. The self-reported measure of avoidance of rearrest and reincarceration differs from the official reincarceration measure used in the first set of models in several ways. The official reincarceration measure reflects only new incarcerations in a state prison (it does not include administrative data on new arrests, which we were unable to obtain at either the federal or state level for four of the five states). In contrast, the self-reported measure includes new arrests, new incarcerations in a county jail, and new incarcerations in a state prison. Therefore, the self-reported measure is more inclusive of a broader range of dimensions of recidivism and, as such, the results of the two analyses may differ.

11. Men were classified as successful who answered "never," "rarely," or "sometimes" to two statements about the escalation of arguments ("Your arguments get very heated" and "Small issues suddenly become big arguments") and "often," "sometimes," or "rarely" to two statements about resolving issues constructively ("You are good at working out your differences with each other" and "You and your survey partner calmly discuss something").

follow-up periods, as well as the proportion who were successful across all five dimensions. We applied multiple regression to identify predictors of overall and domain-specific reentry success using the same set of independent variables included in the recidivism models (see table A-10).

SUPPLEMENTAL DETAIL ON RESULTS

In the models run to identify predictors of recidivism based on official records, we found that men who were older at the time of their first arrest and at study enrollment were more likely to be successful in this outcome at both time periods (that is, to not have been reincarcerated in state prison within 12 or 24 months of release, $p<.05$ for 12 months and $<.001$ for 24 months). In addition, those who had more in-person contact with family members during their original incarceration ($p<.05$) and less problematic alcohol or drug use prior to that incarceration ($p<.05$) were more likely to avoid reincarceration within 24 months of release. Men with more previous arrests were less likely to be successful in this outcome at both time periods ($p<.01$ at 12 months and $<.05$ at 24 months).

Chapter 6

Chapter 6 presented results from the Multi-site Family Study program evaluation. This work assessed the impact of a set of demonstration programs that were designed to support healthy couple relationships and parenting among incarcerated and reentering fathers and their partners. We employed two distinct analytic approaches. Comparisons of weighted means tested for statistically significant differences between treatment and comparison groups, while latent growth curve modeling (LGM) examined outcome trajectories over time for treatment group couples and for comparison group couples in each site. In addition to assessing impact through these quantitative techniques, we incorporated qualitative data to generate a deeper understanding of how participants experienced the demonstration programs. This section provides more information about impact site selection and sample design and more detailed results of the comparison of weighted means and LGM work.

ANALYTIC SAMPLE

Site selection and sample design. Twelve demonstration program grantees were funded by the federal Office of Family Assistance from 2006 through 2011 to support healthy relationships between incarcerated fathers, their partners, and children. Four of these sites were included in the impact study: the Indiana Department of Correction, the RIDGE Project (Ohio), the New Jersey Department of Corrections, and the Osborne Association (New York). The impact sites were selected based on having sufficient program intensity and projected enrollment to support the evaluation, providing couples-based relationship services, having a stable program design at the time of site selection, and offering sufficiently strong evaluation design possibilities.

Each site delivered a unique family-strengthening program. As described in chapter 6, the impact study assessed the effectiveness of each site's couples-based activities, which usually constituted only a portion of the federally funded activities that were implemented. The impact sites varied in terms of the population targeted for services, the service delivery approach, and the program component or components evaluated. The evaluation used a matched comparison group design in three sites. To identify matched comparisons, a screening form was administered to men who met basic eligibility criteria (e.g., fathers incarcerated in comparable correctional facilities or housing units who had participated in programming similar to the prerequisite programming for treatment-group men) but who were not offered the program (in the New Jersey and New York sites) or who could not participate in the program due to timing (in the Indiana site). The screening forms were used to identify men for the comparison group who self-reported being in a committed intimate relationship and who felt that they and their partner would like to participate in the demonstration programming if it were available to them. In Ohio, a wait-list design was used to identify fathers in a committed relationship who were incarcerated in prisons served by the program, attended a recruitment presentation about the program, completed an application for the program, and were screened as eligible by program staff but never started the first course in the program because they were transferred, released, or remained on the wait list before a new class was rolled out at their facility during their study participation period.

Resulting sample size and characteristics. Characteristics of impact sample members are shown in Tables A-11 (men) and A-12 (women). The impact analyses excluded the 83 men and 72 women recruited from a fifth study site in Minnesota, which closed follow-up data collection early due to low enrollment. The analytic samples also excluded a small number of men (n = 24) and women (n = 16) from the New York sample who were removed from the impact analyses during the propensity modeling process (described in chapter 6) to achieve better balance between treatment and comparison groups. The treatment and comparison members were well matched on most demographic

TABLE A-II

Demographic Characteristics of Male Impact Analysis Sample, by Site and Group (Weighted)

	IN		OH		NJ		NY	
	TREATMENT (N=272)	COMPARISON (N=387)	TREATMENT (N=462)	COMPARISON (N=166)	TREATMENT (N=133)	COMPARISON (N=82)	TREATMENT (N=118)	COMPARISON (N=48)
Age (mean years)	34.5	34.2	32.1	31.9	34.3	33.8	38.3	36.2
Relationship status								
Married	25%	24%	22%	18%	19%	16%	60%	45%
In an intimate relationship	72%	71%	69%	72%	74%	79%	36%	52%
In a coparenting relationship only	3%	5%	9%	10%	8%	4%	4%	4%
Has children under 18	81%	84%	93%	90%	91%	89%	68%	67%
Number of children (mean)	3.0	3.1	3.1	3.2	2.6	2.6	2.3	2.2
Average age of focal child (yrs)	8.5	8.1	8.0	7.6	8.1	7.4	10.1	8.0
Race/ethnicity								
White, non-Hispanic	45%	41%	23%	23%	11%	9%	10%	6%
Black, non-Hispanic	46%	47%	60%	62%	72%	74%	65%	60%
Other, non-Hispanic	2%	2%	2%	0%	3%	14%	1%	2%
Hispanic (all races)	4%	6%	9%	6%	13%	3%	21%	9%
Multiracial	3%	4%	6%	8%	2%	0%	4%	23%
Born outside of United States	1%	2%	1%	1%	7%	6%	12%	24%

Highest educational attainment								
Less than high school	28%	27%	39%	39%	40%	47%	21%	28%
GED	18%	23%	27%	29%	23%	24%	30%	31%
High school diploma	9%	9%	12%	8%	22%	20%	9%	4%
Vocational	5%	7%	1%	2%	2%	6%	1%	1%
Some college	21%	21%	16%	18%	11%	4%	20%	27%
Advanced degree	18%	14%	5%	4%	2%	0%	19%	8%
Ever repeated grade	38%	36%	53%	44%	46%	53%	40%	40%
Ever been suspended/expelled	76%	78%	88%	86%	81%	87%	67%	89%

TABLE A-12
Demographic Characteristics of Female Impact Analysis Sample, by Site and Group (Weighted)

	IN		OH		NJ		NY	
	TREATMENT (N=255)	COMPARISON (N=294)	TREATMENT (N=362)	COMPARISON (N=126)	TREATMENT (N=95)	COMPARISON (N=60)	TREATMENT (N=67)	COMPARISON (N=32)
Age (mean years)	32.7	32.8	30.6	30.8	34.2	33.3	38.0	36.9
Relationship status								
Married	23%	25%	22%	18%	23%	17%	65%	52%
In an intimate relationship	70%	59%	60%	61%	61%	74%	26%	38%
In a coparenting relationship only	8%	16%	18%	21%	16%	9%	9%	9%
Has children under 18	74%	78%	87%	91%	82%	87%	75%	57%
Number of children (mean)	2.4	2.4	2.5	2.6	2.1	2.2	2.6	2.0
Average age of children (yrs)	7.8	7.7	7.5	7.2	8.0	7.6	9.3	7.1
Race/ethnicity								
White, non-Hispanic	55%	53%	30%	32%	12%	16%	16%	28%
Black, non-Hispanic	36%	38%	55%	54%	72%	70%	56%	56%
Other, non-Hispanic	1%	1%	2%	0%	1%	1%	6%	2%
Hispanic (all races)	3%	4%	7%	7%	15%	12%	22%	13%
Multiracial	5%	3%	7%	6%	0%	2%	0%	2%
Born outside of United States	0%	1%	1%	1%	1%	3%	20%	20%

Highest educational attainment								
Less than high school	18%	29%	29%	20%	18%	27%	22%	31%
GED	11%	9%	7%	8%	5%	3%	8%	2%
High school diploma	23%	21%	19%	20%	28%	36%	14%	11%
Vocational	4%	6%	7%	8%	8%	4%	5%	8%
Some college	31%	27%	30%	30%	29%	21%	32%	29%
Advanced degree	13%	9%	9%	14%	12%	9%	18%	18%
Ever repeated grade	20%	24%	26%	27%	22%	25%	25%	9%
Ever been suspended/expelled	41%	47%	55%	49%	45%	48%	29%	31%

characteristics. Not surprisingly, given the specific populations targeted for programming and variation in the prisoner populations across the four states, some cross-site differences in sample characteristics were evident.

NOTES ON ANALYTIC APPROACH

The impact analysis examined outcomes in three domains: intimate relationship status and quality; parenting and coparenting; and employment, illicit drug use, and recidivism. Outcome selection focused on measures that could reasonably be expected to improve for the treatment group relative to the comparison group (based on the nature of the couples-based programming being evaluated) or that were amenable to change through improvements in other, more directly affected outcomes. Operationalizing both intimate relationship quality and parenting and coparenting quality in a multidimensional manner was a priority in the study, given the multitude of ways that program participation might have affected couples and the need to understand a number of aspects of family functioning.

The intimate relationship status and quality domain included 29 outcomes reflecting various aspects of relationship status, cohabitation, fidelity, communication skills, conflict resolution, bonding, partner violence (including victimization and perpetration of physical violence and controlling behavior), and frequency of contact during incarceration. Sixteen outcomes were explored in the parenting and coparenting domain, including parent-child relationship quality, joint decision-making about children, parental warmth, fulfillment of parenting responsibilities, cohabitation, financial support, and frequency of activities. Finally, the employment, illicit drug use, and recidivism domain included five outcomes: employment status, use of illicit drugs (excluding marijuana), self-reported rearrest (men only), self-reported reincarceration (men only) and reincarceration in state prison based on administrative data obtained from the state DOC (men only).

Propensity modeling was used to develop weights to minimize the possibility of selection bias (that is, the possibility that preexisting differences between treatment and comparison couples influenced outcomes separately from the treatment received), given the nonexperimental designs implemented and attrition bias (the likelihood that follow-up data for some respondents were not missing at random). Two statistical techniques were used to quantitatively assess the impact of couples-based programming on outcomes: comparisons of weighted means and LGM. The first approach, comparisons of weighted means, tested for statistically significant differences between treatment and comparison groups on the outcomes of interest. Comparisons were made for men and women in each site and at each follow-up wave. To determine whether the outcome differed significantly for treatment and comparison group members, we estimated weighted logistic regression models for the binary outcomes and weighted linear regression models for the nonbinary outcomes. For each outcome model, the baseline value of the outcome was included as a control. The estimated impact was calculated by subtracting the weighted mean for the comparison group from the weighted mean for the treatment group.

The second approach, LGM, compared how outcome trajectories of treatment group couples over time differed from outcome trajectories of comparison couples in each site. We used a recent extension of the growth model to dyadic data called the common fate growth model (Ledermann and Macho 2014, Whittaker, Beretvas, and Falbo 2014). This model allowed us to estimate whether each couple changed over time and whether the average couple-level change varied between the treatment and comparison groups. This facilitated a comparison of the trajectories of treatment couples with those of comparison couples to understand whether treatment couples improved more (or deteriorated less) than the comparison couples over time, beginning with baseline. This was a mixed-effects model (one that had both fixed effects and random effects) estimated under a structural equation modeling framework (to take into account that individual sample members were nested within couples and that repeated measures were nested within individuals).

Both the comparison-of-weighted-means approach and the couples-based LGM approach used the weights developed to adjust for selection and attrition bias, controlled for the baseline measure of each outcome, and used all available interview data, including data from men whose partner had not completed interviews. In addition, qualitative interview transcripts were analyzed to identify themes related to participants' experiences in the demonstration programs (see the Appendix content for chapters 2 and 3 for a description of this process).

SUPPLEMENTAL DETAIL ON RESULTS

Detailed results of the comparison of weighted means analyses for the outcome of bonding are shown in table A-13. These results allowed us to see if, on average, men and women who participated in the programs reported higher levels of bonding than men and women in the comparison group at 9, 18, and 34 months. As evident from the table, positive treatment effects for this outcome

TABLE A-13
Treatment and Comparison Means and Effect Sizes for Bonding, by Site, Sex, and Wave

Outcome	N			Mean			Impact	Effect Size
	Total	Treat	Comp	Treat	Comp	p-Value		
Indiana								
Male sample								
9-mo. follow-up	558	243	315	7.38	6.51	+++	0.87	0.37
18-mo. follow-up	532	236	296	6.70	6.05	+++	0.65	0.24
34-mo. follow-up	494	223	271	6.64	5.88	+++	0.76	0.28
Female sample								
9-mo. follow-up	500	243	257	7.03	6.224	+	0.81	0.3
18-mo. follow-up	481	227	254	6.491	5.698	n.s.	0.79	0.28
34-mo. follow-up	450	215	235	6.115	4.964	+++	1.15	0.38
Ohio								
Male sample								
9-mo. follow-up	469	350	119	6.55	7.11	−−−	−0.56	−0.3
18-mo. follow-up	450	322	128	5.77	6.57	−−−	−0.81	−0.32
34-mo. follow-up	440	323	117	5.48	6.00	n.s.	−0.52	−0.21
Female sample								
9-mo. follow-up	407	301	106	6.56	6.79	n.s.	−0.23	−0.09
18-mo. follow-up	414	308	106	5.86	6.03	n.s.	−0.17	−0.07
34-mo. follow-up	399	298	101	5.44	5.71	n.s.	−0.27	−0.09

New Jersey								
Male sample								
9-mo. follow-up	159	93	66	6.69	7.07	n.s.	−0.38	−0.18
18-mo. follow-up	152	89	63	6.27	6.59	n.s.	−0.32	−0.12
Female sample								
9-mo. follow-up	133	81	52	6.31	6.52	n.s.	−0.21	−0.09
18-mo. follow-up	139	84	55	5.12	6.37	n.s.	−1.25	−0.43
New York								
Male sample								
9-mo. follow-up	138	97	41	7.31	6.77	n.s.	0.53	0.21
18-mo. follow-up	130	96	34	7.22	5.99	n.s.	1.23	0.44
Female sample								
9-mo. follow-up	88	61	27	7.63	6.91	n.s.	0.72	0.32
18-mo. follow-up	88	60	28	7.03	6.22	n.s.	0.81	0.33

n.s. No statistically significant impact.

+++/++/+ Statistically significant positive impact at the .01/.05/.10 level.

−−−/−−/− Statistically significant negative impact at the .01/.05/.10 level.

TABLE A-14
Treatment and Comparison Differences in Bonding for Baseline (Intercept) and Change over Time (Slope) for Couples, by Site, Based on Latent Growth Curve Models

Site	N			Mean intercept				Mean slope			
	Total	Treat	Comp	Treat	Comp	p	Treat	T-C	Comp	p	Effect Size
Indiana	664	279	385	7.53	7.13	+++	−0.44	0.14	−0.58	++	0.089
Ohio	639	469	170	6.98	7.27	–	−0.52	−0.07	−0.45	n.s.	−0.037
New Jersey	285	160	125	7.28	7.5	n.s.	−1.01	−0.12	−0.89	n.s.	−0.034
New York	195	135	60	7.62	7.35	n.s.	−0.18	0.44	−0.62	n.s.	0.089

n.s. No statistically significant impact.
+++/++/+ Statistically significant positive impact at the .01/.05/.10 level.
−−−/−−/− Statistically significant negative impact at the .01/.05/.10 level.

were found only in Indiana; in the remaining sites, the intervention either did not affect bonding or had some negative effects (this was the case for men in Ohio at 9 and 18 months). In Indiana, the couples-based programming appeared to have had more of an impact for men as a group (where we found positive treatment effects at all three follow-up periods) than for women as a group (where we found positive treatment effects only at 9- and 34-month follow-up periods). Women's assessments of bonding within the relationship were slightly lower than men's and, for both men and women, assessments of bonding tended to decline with each interview wave (even though for both men and women, those in the treatment group had higher bonding scores at the 34-month interview than those in the comparison group). Also evident in the table is that missing data were an issue with each interview wave, with more men than women interviewed at each time point (i.e., both members of the couple were not reached for interviews at every wave).

The results of the LGM analysis for the bonding outcome are shown for each site in table A-14. The intercept indicated in the table reflects sample members' baseline reports of bonding, whereas the slope reflects change over time. As evident in the table, members of the comparison group in Indiana had poorer ratings of bonding at baseline than members of the treatment group ($p<.01$), and those ratings also declined more steeply over time ($p<.05$). This steeper descent suggests a treatment effect.

REFERENCES

Aaron, Lauren, and Danielle H. Dallaire. 2010. "Parental Incarceration and Multiple Risk Experiences: Effects on Family Dynamics and Children's Delinquency." *Journal of Youth and Adolescence* 39 (12):1471–1484.

Aiello, Brittnie L., and Jill. A. McCorkel. 2017. "'It Will Crush You Like a Bug': Maternal Incarceration, Secondary Prisonization, and Children's Visitation." *Punishment & Society* 20 (3):351–374. doi: 10.1177/1462474517697295.

Alper, Mariel, Matthew R. Durose, and Joshua Markman. 2018. *2018 Update on Prisoner Recidivism: A 9-Year Follow-up Period (2005–2014)*. Special Report NCJ 250975. Washington, DC: Bureau of Justice Statistics, Office of Justice Programs, U.S. Department of Justice.

Amato, Paul R., and Joan G. Gilbreth. 1999. "Nonresident Fathers and Children's Well-Being: A Meta-Analysis." *Journal of Marriage and the Family* 61 (3):557–573.

Arditti, Joyce A. 2003. "Locked Doors and Glass Walls: Family Visiting at a Local Jail." *Journal of Loss and Trauma* 8:115–138.

———. 2005. "Families and Incarceration: An Ecological Approach." *Families in Society: Journal of Contemporary Social Services* 86 (2):251–260.

———. 2012. *Parental Incarceration and the Family: Psychological and Social Effects of Imprisonment on Children, Parents, and Caregivers*. New York: NYU Press.

Arditti, Joyce A., Jennifer Lambert-Shute, and Karen Joest. 2003. "Saturday Morning at the Jail: Implications of Incarceration for Families and Children." *Family Relations* 52:194–205. doi: 10.1111/j.1741-3729.2003.00195.x.

Arditti, Joyce A., Sara A. Smock, and Tiffaney S. Parkman. 2005. "'It's Been Hard to Be a Father': A Qualitative Exploration of Incarcerated Fatherhood." *Fathering* 3 (3):267.

Armstrong, Tisha G., Gretchen Heideman, Kevin J. Corcoran, Bonnie Fisher, Krista L. Medina, and John Schafer. 2001. "Disagreement about the Occurrence of Male-to-Female Intimate Partner Violence: A Qualitative Study." *Family & Community Health* 24 (1):55–75.

Bahr, Stephen J., Lish Harris, James K. Fisher, and Anita H. Armstrong. 2010. "Successful Reentry : What Differentiates Successful and Unsuccessful Parolees?" *International Journal of Offender Therapy and Comparative Criminology* 54 (5):667–692.

Bales, William D., and Daniel P. Mears. 2008. "Inmate Social Ties and the Transition to Society: Does Visitation Reduce Recidivism?" *Journal of Research in Crime and Delinquency* 45 (3):287–321.

Barrick, Kelle, Pamela K. Lattimore, and Christy A. Visher. 2014. "Reentering Women: The Impact of Social Ties on Long-Term Recidivism." *Prison Journal* 94 (3):279–304.

Bartlett, Tess S., and Anna Eriksson. 2018. "How Fathers Construct and Perform Masculinity in a Liminal Prison Space." *Punishment & Society*. https://doi.org/10.1177/1462474518757092.

Beck, Allen J. 2006. "The Importance of Successful Reentry to Jail Population Growth." Jail Reentry Roundtable, Urban Institute, Washington, DC, June 27. https://www.urban.org/sites/default/files/beck.ppt.

Beckmeyer, Jonathon J., and Joyce A. Arditti. 2014. "Implications of In-Person Visits for Incarcerated Parents' Family Relationships and Parenting Experience." *Journal of Offender Rehabilitation* 53:129–151.

Berent, Matthew K., Jon A. Krosnick, and Arthur Lupia. 2016. "Measuring Voter Registration and Turnout in Surveys: Do Official Government Records Yield More Accurate Assessments?" *Public Opinion Quarterly* 80 (3):597–621. doi: 10.1093/poq/nfw021.

Berg, Mark T., and Beth M. Huebner. 2011. "Reentry and the Ties That Bind: An Examination of Social Ties, Employment, and Recidivism." *Justice Quarterly* 28 (2):382–410. doi: 10.1080/07418825.2010.498383.

Berger, Amanda, Jennifer Manlove, Elizabeth Wildsmith, and Nicole R. Steward-Streng. 2012. *Relationship Violence among Young Adult Couples*. Research Brief. Washington, DC: Child Trends. https://www.childtrends.org/wp-content/uploads/2012/06/Child_Trends-2012_06_01_RB_Couple Violence.pdf.

Bir, Anupa, Robert Lerman, Elise Corwin, Brian MacIlvain, Allison Beard, Kelly Richburg, and Kevin Smith. 2012. *Impacts of a Community Healthy Marriage Initiative.* OPRE Report #2012-34A. Washington, DC: Office of Planning, Research and Evaluation, Administration for Children and Families, U.S. Department of Health and Human Services. https://www.acf.hhs.gov/sites/default/files/opre/chmi_impactreport.pdf.

Black, Michele C., Kathleen C. Basile, Matthew J. Breiding, Sharon G. Smith, Mikel L. Walters, Melissa T. Merrick, Jieru Chen, and Mark R. Stevens. 2011. *The National Intimate Partner and Sexual Violence Survey (NISVS): 2010 Summary Report.* Atlanta, GA: National Center for Injury Prevention and Control, Centers for Disease Control and Prevention. https://www.cdc.gov/violenceprevention/pdf/nisvs_report2010-a.pdf.

Bobbitt, Mike, Robin Campbell, and Gloria L. Tate. 2006. *Safe Return: Working toward Preventing Domestic Violence When Men Return from Prison.* New York: Vera Institute of Justice. https://www.vera.org/publications/safe-return-working-toward-preventing-domestic-violence-when-men-return-from-prison.

———. 2011. "Safe Return: Working toward Preventing Domestic Violence When Men Return from Prison." *Federal Sentencing Reporter* 24 (1):57–61. doi: 10.1525/fsr.2011.24.1.57.

Bobbitt, Mike, and Marta Nelson. 2004. *The Front Line: Building Programs That Recognize Families' Role in Reentry.* Issues in Brief. New York: Vera Institute of Justice. https://www.prisonpolicy.org/scans/vera/249_476.pdf.

Bollen, Kenneth A., and Patrick J. Curran. 2004. "Autoregressive Latent Trajectory (Alt) Models: A Synthesis of Two Traditions." *Sociological Methods & Research* 32 (3):336–383. doi: 10.1177/0049124103260222.

Breiding, M.J., J. Chen, and M.C. Black. 2014. *Intimate Partner Violence in the United States—2010.* Atlanta, GA: National Center for Injury Prevention and Control, Centers for Disease Control and Prevention. https://www.cdc.gov/violenceprevention/pdf/cdc_nisvs_ipv_report_2013_v17_single_a.pdf.

Brown, Geoffrey L., Brent A. McBride, Nana Shin, and Kelly K. Bost. 2007. "Parenting Predictors of Father-Child Attachment Security: Interactive Effects of Father Involvement and Fathering Quality." *Fathering* 5 (3): 197–219. doi: 10.3149/fth.0503.197.

Brunton-Smith, Ian, and Daniel J. McCarthy. 2017. "The Effects of Prisoner Attachment to Family on Re-Entry Outcomes: A Longitudinal Assessment." *British Journal of Criminology* 57 (2):463–482.

Burnett, Ros. 2004. "To Reoffend or Not to Reoffend? The Ambivalence of Convicted Property Offenders." In *After Crime and Punishment: Pathways to*

Offender Reintegration, edited by Shadd Maruna and Russ Immarigeon. Cullompton, Devon: Willan.

Bushway, Shawn D. 2004. "Labor Market Effects of Permitting Employer Access to Criminal History Records." *Journal of Contemporary Criminal Justice* 20 (3):276–291. doi: 10.1177/1043986204266890.

Butts, Jeffrey A., and Vincent Schiraldi. 2018. *Recidivism Reconsidered: Preserving the Community Justice Mission of Community Corrections.* Papers from the Executive Session on Community Corrections. Cambridge, MA: Program in Criminal Justice Policy and Management, Harvard Kennedy School. https://www.hks.harvard.edu/sites/default/files/centers/wiener/programs/pcj/files/recidivism_reconsidered.pdf.

Caetano, Raul, Suhasini Ramisetty-Mikler, Patrice A. Caetano Vaeth, and T. Robert Harris. 2007. "Acculturation Stress, Drinking, and Intimate Partner Violence among Hispanic Couples in the U.S." *Journal of Interpersonal Violence* 22 (11):1431–1447. doi: 10.1177/0886260507305568.

Capaldi, Deborah M., Hyoun K. Kim, and Lee D. Owen. 2008. "Romantic Partners' Influence on Men's Likelihood of Arrest in Early Adulthood." *Criminology* 46 (2):267–299.

Carson, E. Ann. 2014. "Prisoners in 2013." *BJS Bulletin,* NCJ 247282, September 2014. Washington, DC: Bureau of Justice Statistics, Office of Justice Programs, U.S. Department of Justice. http://www.bjs.gov/content/pub/pdf/p13.pdf.

Carson, E. Ann, and Daniela Golinelli. *2013. Prisoners in 2012: Trends in Admissions and Releases, 1991–2012.* Prisoners Series, NCJ 243920. Washington, DC: Bureau of Justice Statistics, Office of Justice Statistics, U.S. Department of Justice. http://www.bjs.gov/index.cfm?ty=pbdetail&iid=4842.

Cattaneo, Lauren B., and Lisa A. Goodman. 2005. "Risk Factors for Reabuse in Intimate Partner Violence: A Cross-Disciplinary Critical Review." *Trauma Violence Abuse* 6 (2):141–175. doi: 10.1177/1524838005275088.

Center on Addiction and Substance Abuse. 2010. *Behind Bars II: Substance Abuse and America's Prison Population. Special Report.* New York: National Center on Addiction and Substance Abuse at Columbia University. https://www.centeronaddiction.org/addiction-research/reports/behind-bars-ii-substance-abuse-and-america%E2%80%99s-prison-population.

Cheng, Tyrone C., and Celia C. Lo. 2015. "Racial Disparities in Intimate Partner Violence and in Seeking Help with Mental Health." *Journal of Interpersonal Violence* 30 (18):3283–3307. doi: 10.1177/0886260514555011.

Christian, Johnna. 2005. "Riding the Bus: Barriers to Prison Visitation and Family Management Strategies." *Journal of Contemporary Criminal Justice* 21 (1):31–48.

Christian, Johnna, Jeff Mellow, and Shenique Thomas. 2006. "Social and Economic Implications of Family Connections to Prisoners." *Journal of Criminal Justice* 34 (4):443–452.

Christiansen, Shawn L., and Rob Palkovitz. 2001. "Why the 'Good Provider' Role Still Matters: Providing as a Form of Paternal Involvement." *Journal of Family Issues* 22 (1):84–106.

Cid, José, and Joel Martí. 2012. "Turning Points and Returning Points: Understanding the Role of Family Ties in the Process of Desistance." *European Journal of Criminology* 9 (6):603–620. doi: 10.1177/1477370812453102.

Comfort, Megan. 2003. "In the Tube at San Quentin: The 'Secondary Prisonization' of Women Visiting Inmates." *Journal of Contemporary Ethnography* 32 (1):77–107. doi: 10.1177/0891241602238939.

———. 2007. "Punishment beyond the Legal Offender." *Annual Review of Law and Social Science* 3:271–96.

———. 2008. *Doing Time Together: Love and Family in the Shadow of the Prison.* Chicago: University of Chicago Press.

Comfort, Megan, Olga Grinstead, Kathleen McCartney, Philippe Bourgois, and Kelly Knight. 2005. "'You Can't Do Nothing in This Damn Place!': Sex and Intimacy among Couples with an Incarcerated Male Partner." *Journal of Sex Research* 42 (1):3–12.

Comfort, Megan, Kate Krieger, Justin Landwehr, Tasseli McKay, Christine Lindquist, Rose Feinberg, Erin Kennedy, and Anupa Bir. 2018. "Partnerships after Prison: Couple Relationships during Reentry." *Journal of Offender Rehabilitation* 57 (2): 188–205.

Comfort, Megan, Tasseli McKay, Justin Landwehr, Erin Kennedy, Christine Lindquist, and Anupa Bir. 2016. "The Costs of Incarceration for Families of Prisoners." *International Review of the Red Cross* 98 (3):783–798. doi: 10.1017/S1816383117000704.

Comfort, Megan, Olga G. Reznick, Samantha E. Dilworth, Diane Binson, Lynae Darbes, and Torsten B. Neilands. 2014. "Sexual HIV Risk among Male Parolees and Their Female Partners: The Relate Project." *Journal of Health Disparities Research and Practice* 7 (6):42–69.

Condry, Rachel. 2007. *Families Shamed: The Consequences of Crime for Relatives of Serious Offenders.* Cullompton, Devon: Willan.

Conger, Rand D., Xiaojia Ge, Glen H. Elder, Frederick O. Lorenz, and Ronald L. Simons. 1994. "Economic Stress, Coercive Family Process, and Developmental Problems of Adolescents." *Child Development* 65 (2):541–561.

Contreras, Randol. 2013. *The Stickup Kids: Race, Drugs, Violence, and the American Dream.* Berkeley: University of California Press.

Cooke, Cheryl L. 2005. "Going Home: Formerly Incarcerated African American Men Return to Families and Communities." *Journal of Family Nursing* 11 (4):388–404. doi: 10.1177/1074840705281753.

Cooper, Hannah L. F., Claire D. Clark, Terrika Barham, Venita Embry, Bethany Caruso, and Megan Comfort. 2014. "'He Was the Story of My Drug Use Life': A Longitudinal Qualitative Study of the Impact of Partner Incarceration on Substance Misuse Patterns among African American Women." *Substance Use and Misuse* 49 (1–2):176–188.

Courtney, Mark E., Amy Dworsky, JoAnn S. Lee, and Melissa Raap. 2009. *Midwest Evaluation of the Adult Functioning of Former Foster Youth: Outcomes at Ages 23 and 24.* Chicago: Chapin Hall at the University of Chicago. https://rhyclearinghouse.acf.hhs.gov/sites/default/files/docs/18690-Midwest_Evaluation-Outcomes_at_Ages_23_and_24.pdf.

Cunradi, Carol B., Melina Bersamin, and Genevieve Ames. 2009. "Agreement on Intimate Partner Violence among a Sample of Blue-Collar Couples." *Journal of Interpersonal Violence* 24 (4):551–568. doi: 10.1177/0886260508317189.

Dallaire, Danielle H. 2007. "Incarcerated Mothers and Fathers: A Comparison of Risks for Children and Families." *Family Relations* 56 (5):440–453.

Datchi, Corinne C. 2017. "Masculinities, Fatherhood, and Desistance from Crime: Moderating and Mediating Processes Involved in Men's Criminal Conduct." *Journal of Men's Studies* 25 (1):44–69.

Davis, Ann. 1992. "Men's Imprisonment: The Financial Cost to Women and Children." In *Prisoners' Children: What Are the Issues?*, edited by Roger Shaw, 74–85. London: Routledge.

Demers, Jennifer M., Alexa P. Roberts, Sidney Bennett, and Victoria L. Banyard. 2017. "Victim Motivations for Disclosing Unwanted Sexual Experiences and Partner Abuse." *Affilia* 32 (3):327–343. doi: 10.1177/0886109917704936.

deVuono-Powell, Saneta, Chris Schweidler, Alicia Walters, and Azadeh Zohrabi. 2015. *Who Pays? The True Cost of Incarceration on Families.* Oakland, CA: Ella Baker Center, Forward Together, and Research Action Design. https://ellabakercenter.org/sites/default/files/downloads/who-pays.pdf.

Dunn, Elizabeth, and J. Gordon Arbuckle. 2002. *Children of Incarcerated Parents and Enhanced Visitation Programs: Impacts of the Living Interactive Family Education (LIFE) Program.* Columbia, MO: University of Missouri Extension. http://extension.missouri.edu/4hlife/documents/evaluation/reports/G2_lifereport8-02.pdf.

Dutton, Donald G., and Stephen D. Hart. 1992. "Risk Markers for Family Violence in a Federally Incarcerated Population." *International Journal of Law and Psychiatry* 15 (1):101–112.

Duwe, Grant, and Valerie Clark. 2013. "Blessed Be the Social Tie That Binds: The Effects of Prison Visitation on Offender Recidivism." *Criminal Justice Policy Review* 24 (3):271–296.

Eddy, J. Mark, Charles R. Martinez, and Bert Burraston. 2013. "VI. A Randomized Controlled Trial of a Parent Management Training Program for Incarcerated Parents: Proximal Impacts." *Monographs of the Society for Research in Child Development* 78 (3):75–93. doi: 10.1111/mono.12022.

Eddy, J. Mark, and Julie Poehlmann, eds. 2010. *Children of Incarcerated Parents: A Handbook for Researchers and Practitioners*. Washington, DC: Urban Institute Press.

Edin, Kathryn, and Maria Kefalas. 2011. *Promises I Can Keep: Why Poor Women Put Motherhood before Marriage*. Berkeley: University of California Press.

Edin, Kathryn, Timothy J. Nelson, and Rechelle Paranal. 2004. "Fatherhood and Incarceration as Potential Turning Points in the Criminal Careers of Unskilled Men." In *Imprisoning America: The Social Effects of Mass Incarceration*, edited by Mary Pattillo, David Weiman, and Bruce Western, 46–75. New York: Russell Sage Foundation.

Elder, Glen H., Jr., Tri Van Nguyen, and Avshalom Caspi. 1985. "Linking Family Hardship to Children's Lives." *Child Development*:361–375.

Federal Communications Commission. 2017. "Inmate Telephone Service." Last updated/reviewed September 8, 2017. https://www.fcc.gov/consumers/guides/inmate-telephone-service.

Fishman, Laura T. 1990. *Women at the Wall: A Study of Prisoners' Wives Doing Time on the Outside*. Albany: State University of New York Press.

Fowler, Cathrine, Chris Rossiter, Angela Dawson, Debra Jackson, and Tamara Power. 2017. "Becoming a 'Better' Father: Supporting the Needs of Incarcerated Fathers." *Prison Journal* 97 (6):692–712.

Freeland Braun, Margaret J. 2012. "Intimate Partner Violence during the Transition from Prison to the Community: An Ecological Analysis " PhD diss., Portland (OR) State University.

Freeman, Andrew, Julie A. Schumacher, and Scott Coffey. 2015. "Social Desirability and Partner Agreement of Men's Reporting of Intimate Partner Violence in Substance Abuse Treatment Settings." *Journal of Interpersonal Violence* 30 (4):565–79. doi: 10.1177/0886260514535263.

Geller, Amanda, Carey E. Cooper, Irwin Garfinkel, Ofira Schwartz-Soicher, and Ronald B. Mincy. 2012. "Beyond Absenteeism: Father Incarceration and Child Development." *Demography* 49 (1):49–76. doi: 10.1007/s13524-011-0081-9.

Geller, Amanda, Irwin Garfinkel, Carey E. Cooper, and Ronald B. Mincy. 2009. "Parental Incarceration and Child Well-Being: Implications for Urban Families." *Social Science Quarterly* 90 (5):1186–1202.

Geller, Amanda, Irwin Garfinkel, and Bruce Western. 2006. *The Effects of Incarceration on Employment and Wages: An Analysis of the Fragile Families Survey*, Working Paper 2006–01-FF. Princeton, NJ: Center for Research on Child Wellbeing, Woodrow Wilson School, Princeton University. https://pdfs.semanticscholar.org/a748/257cf094a1868ba70514c09098462f2c5dde.pdf.

———. 2011. "Paternal Incarceration and Support for Children in Fragile Families." *Demography* 48 (1):25–47. doi: 10.1007/s13524-010-0009-9.

Gill, Charlotte, and David B. Wilson. 2016. "Improving the Success of Reentry Programs." *Criminal Justice and Behavior* 44 (3):336–359. doi: 10.1177/0093854816682048.

Giordano, Peggy C., Stephen A. Cernkovich, and Jennifer L. Rudolph. 2002. "Gender, Crime, and Desistance: Toward a Theory of Cognitive Transformation." *American Journal of Sociology* 107 (4):990–1064.

Girshick, Lori B. 1996. *Soledad Women: Wives of Prisoners Speak Out*. Westport, CT: Praeger.

Glaze, Lauren E., and Laura M. Maruschak. 2010. *Parents in Prison and Their Minor Children*. BJS Special Report NCJ 222984. Washington, DC: Bureau of Justice Statistics, Office of Justice Programs, U.S. Department of Justice. https://www.bjs.gov/content/pub/pdf/pptmc.pdf.

Golden, Shelley D., Krista M. Perreira, and Christine P. Durrance. 2013. "Troubled Times, Troubled Relationships: How Economic Resources, Gender Beliefs, and Neighborhood Disadvantage Influence Intimate Partner Violence." *Journal of Interpersonal Violence* 28 (10):2134–2155. doi: 10.1177/0886260512471083.

Gordon, Liz, ed. 2018. *Contemporary Research and Analysis on the Children of Prisoners: Invisible Children*. Cambridge, UK: Cambridge Scholars Publishing.

Grinstead, Olga, Bonnie Faigeles, Carrie Bancroft, and Barry Zack. 2001. "The Financial Cost of Maintaining Relationships with Incarcerated African American Men: A Survey of Women Prison Visitors." *Journal of African-American Men* 6 (1):59–70.

Hagan, John, and Juleigh Petty Coleman. 2001. "Returning Captives of the American War on Drugs: Issues of Community and Family Reentry." *Crime & Delinquency* 47 (3):352–367.
Hairston, Creasie F. 1988. "Family Ties during Imprisonment: Do They Influence Future Criminal Activity?" *Federal Probation* 52 (1):48–52.
Hairston, Creasie F., and William Oliver. 2005. *Domestic Violence and Prisoner Reentry: Experiences of African American Women and Men*. New York: Vera Institute of Justice. https://www.vera.org/publications/domestic-violence-and-prisoner-reentry-experiences-of-african-american-women-and-men.
———. 2011. "Women's Experiences with Men's Incarceration and Reentry." In *Women and Girls in the Criminal Justice System*, edited by Russ Immarigeon. Kingston, NJ: Civic Research Institute.
Hairston, Creasie F., James Rollin, and Han-jin Jo. 2004. *Family Connections during Imprisonment and Prisoners' Community Reentry*. Research Brief: Children, Families, and the Criminal Justice System. Chicago: Jane Addams College of Social Work, University of Illinois at Chicago.
Hampton, Robert, William Oliver, and Lucia Magarian. 2003. "Domestic Violence in the African American Community: An Analysis of Social and Structural Factors." *Violence Against Women* 9 (5):533–557.
Haney, Craig. 2003. "The Psychological Impact of Incarceration: Implications for Postprison Adjustment." In *Prisoners Once Removed: The Impact of Incarceration and Reentry on Children, Families, and Communities*, edited by Jeremy Travis and Michelle Waul, 33–66. Washington, DC: Urban Institute.
Haney, Lynne. 2010. *Offending Women: Power, Punishment, and the Regulation of Desire*. Berkeley: University of California Press.
Harlow, Caroline W. 2003. *Education and Correctional Populations*. BJS Special Report NCJ 195670. Washington, DC: Bureau of Justice Statistics, Office of Justice Programs, U.S. Department of Justice. https://www.bjs.gov/content/pub/pdf/ecp.pdf.
Harris, Alexes. 2016. *A Pound of Flesh: Monetary Sanctions as Punishment for the Poor*. New York: Russell Sage Foundation.
Hayes, D., M. Butler, J. Devaney, and A. Percy. 2018. "Allowing Imprisoned Fathers to Parent: Maximising the Potential Benefits of Prison-based Parenting Programmes." *Child Care in Practice* 24 (2):181–197. https://doi.org/10.1080/13575279.2017.1420038.
Herman-Stahl, Mindy, Marni L. Kan, and Tasseli McKay. 2008. *Incarceration and the Family: A Review of Research and Promising Approaches for Serving Fathers*

and Families. Washington, DC: Assistant Secretary for Planning and Evaluation (ASPE), Administration for Children and Families/Office of Family Assistance, U.S. Department of Health and Human Services. https://aspe.hhs.gov/report/incarceration-and-family-review-research-and-promising-approaches-serving-fathers-and-families.

Herrera, Veronica M., Jacquelyn D. Wiersma, and H. Harrington Cleveland. 2010. "Romantic Partners' Contribution to the Continuity of Male and Female Delinquent and Violent Behavior." *Journal of Research on Adolescence* 21 (3):608–618.

Hofferth, Sandra L., Nicole D. Forry, and H. Elizabeth Peters. 2010. "Child Support, Father–Child Contact, and Preteens' Involvement with Nonresidential Fathers: Racial/Ethnic Differences." *Journal of Family and Economic Issues* 31 (1):14–32.

Holzer, Harry J., Steven Raphael, and Michael A. Stoll. 2004. "How Willing Are Employers to Hire Ex-Offenders." *Focus* 23 (2):40–43.

Hutton, Marie. 2016. "Visiting Time: A Tale of Two Prisons." *Probation Journal* 63 (3):347–361.

Jasinski, Jana L., and Glenda K. Kantor. 2001. "Pregnancy, Stress and Wife Assault: Ethnic Differences in Prevalence, Severity, and Onset in a National Sample." *Violence and Victims* 16 (3):219–232.

Johnson, Elizabeth I., and Jane Waldfogel. 2002. "Parental Incarceration: Recent Trends and Implications for Child Welfare." *Social Science Review* 76 (3):460–479.

———. 2004. "Children of Incarcerated Parents: Multiple Risks and Children's Living Arrangements." In *Imprisoning America: The Social Effects of Mass Incarceration*, edited by Mary Pattillo, David Weiman and Bruce Western, 97–131. New York: Russell Sage Foundation.

Johnson, Rucker. 2009. "Ever-Increasing Levels of Parental Incarceration and the Consequences for Children." In *Do Prisons Make Us Safer? The Benefits and Costs of the Prison Boom*, edited by Steven Raphael and Michael A. Stoll, 177–206. New York: Russell Sage Foundation.

Kaeble, Danielle, and Lauren E Glaze. 2016. Correctional Populations in the United States, 2015. Washington, DC: Bureau of Justice Statistics, Office of Justice Programs, U.S. Department of Justice.

Kang, Cecelia. 2017. "FCC Decides to Cap Prices of In-State Phone Calls by Prison Inmates." Interview by Michael Martin. *All Things Considered* (National Public Radio), June 18, 2017. https://www.npr.org/templates/transcript/transcript.php?storyId=533438857.

Karberg, Jennifer C., and Doris J. James. 2005. *Substance Dependence, Abuse, and Treatment of Jail Inmates, 2002.* BJS Special Report NCJ 209588. Washington, DC: Bureau of Justice Statistics, Office of Justice Programs, U.S. Department of Justice. https://www.bjs.gov/content/pub/pdf/sdatji02.pdf.

Kelly, Joan B., and Michael P. Johnson. 2008. "Differentiation among Types of Intimate Partner Violence: Research Update and Implications for Interventions." *Family Court Review* 46(3):476–499. doi:10.1111/j.1744-1617.2008.00215.x.

Kerrison, Erin M. 2018. "Risky Business, Risk Assessment, and Other Heteronormative Misnomers in Women's Community Corrections and Reentry Planning." *Punishment & Society* 20 (1):134–151.

Khan, Maria R., Lindy Behrend, Adaora A. Adimora, Sharon S. Weir, Caroline Tisdale, and David A. Wohl. 2011. "Dissolution of Primary Intimate Relationships During Incarceration and Associations with Post-Release STI/HIV Risk Behavior in a Southeastern City." *Sexually Transmitted Diseases* 38 (1):43–47. doi: 10.1097/OLQ.0b013e3181e969d0.

King, Valarie. 1994. "Nonresident Father Involvement and Child Well-Being: Can Dads Make a Difference?" *Journal of Family Issues* 15 (1):78–96.

Kreager, Derek A., Ross L. Matsueda, and Elena A. Erosheva. 2010. "Motherhood and Criminal Desistance in Disadvantaged Neighborhoods." *Criminology* 48 (1):221–258.

La Vigne, Nancy G., Rebecca. L. Naser, Lisa E. Brooks, and Jennifer L. Castro. 2005. "Examining the Effect of Incarceration and In-Prison Family Contact on Prisoners' Family Relationships." *Journal of Contemporary Criminal Justice* 21 (4):314–335. doi: 10.1177/1043986205281727.

Ladlow, Linzi, and Bren Neale. 2016. "Risk, Resource, Redemption? The Parenting and Custodial Experiences of Young Offender Fathers." *Social Policy and Society* 15 (1):113–127. doi: 10.1017/S1474746415000500.

Landreth, Garry L., and Alan F. Lobaugh. 1998. "Filial Therapy with Incarcerated Fathers: Effects on Parental Acceptance of Child, Parental Stress, and Child Adjustment." *Journal of Counseling & Development* 76 (2):157–165.

Larson, Reed W., Maryse H. Richards, Giovanni Moneta, Grayson Holmbeck, and Elena Duckett. 1996. "Changes in Adolescents' Daily Interactions with Their Families from Ages 10 to 18: Disengagement and Transformation." *Developmental Psychology* 32 (4):744–754. doi: 10.1037/0012-1649.32.4.744.

Lattimore, Pamela K., and Christy A. Visher. 2009. *The Multi-Site Evaluation of SVORI: Summary and Synthesis. The Multi-Site Evaluation of the Serious and Violent Offender Reentry Initiative.* Research Triangle Park, NC: RTI

International; Washington, DC: Urban Institute. https://www.ncjrs.gov/pdffiles1/nij/grants/230421.pdf.

Lattimore, Pamela K., Christy A. Visher, and Danielle M. Steffey. 2008. *Pre-Release Characteristics and Service Receipt among Adult Male Participants in the SVORI Multi-Site Evaluation*. Research Triangle Park, NC: RTI International; Washington, DC: Urban Institute.

Laub, John H., Daniel S. Nagin, and Robert J. Sampson. 1998. "Trajectories of Change in Criminal Offending: Good Marriages and the Desistance Process." *American Sociological Review* 63 (2):225–238.

Laursen, Brett, and W. Andrew Collins. 2004. "Parent-Child Communication during Adolescence." In *Routledge Handbook of Family Communication*, edited by Anita L. Vangelisti. Mahwah, NJ: Lawrence Erlbaum.

LeBel, Thomas P., Matt Richie, and Shadd Maruna. 2015. "Helping Others as a Response to Reconcile a Criminal Past: The Role of the Wounded Healer in Prisoner Reentry Programs." *Criminal Justice and Behavior* 42 (1):108–120.

LeBlanc, Adrian Nicole. 2003. *Random Family: Love, Drugs, Trouble, and Coming of Age in the Bronx*. New York: Scribner.

Ledermann, Thomas, and Siegfried Macho. 2014. "Analyzing Change at the Dyadic Level: The Common Fate Growth Model." *Journal of Family Psychology* 28 (2):204–213. doi: 10.1037/a0036051.

Lee, Hedwig, Tyler McCormick, Margaret T. Hicken, and Christopher Wildeman. 2015. "Racial Inequalities in Connectedness to Imprisoned Individuals in the United States." *Du Bois Review: Social Science Research on Race* 12 (2):269–282.

Leite, Randall, and Patrick McKenry. 2006. "A Role Theory Perspective on Patterns of Separated and Divorced African-American Nonresidential Father Involvement with Children." *Fathering* 4 (1):1.

Lindquist, Christine, Megan Comfort, Justin Landwehr, Rose Feinberg, Julie Cohen, Tasseli McKay, and Anupa Bir. 2016, March. *Change in Father-Child Relationships before, during, and after Incarceration*. Research Brief. Prepared for Office of the Assistant Secretary for Planning and Evaluation (ASPE), U.S. Department of Health and Human Services. https://aspe.hhs.gov/pdf-report/change-father-child-relationships-during-and-after-incarceration.

Lindquist, Christine, Tasseli McKay, Anupa Bir, and Danielle M. Steffey. 2015. *The Experiences of Families during a Father's Incarceration: Descriptive Findings from Baseline Data Collection for the Multi-site Family Study on Incarceration, Parenting and Partnering*. Washington, DC: Office of Planning, Research and Evaluation, Administration for Children and Families, U.S. Department of

Health and Human Services. https://aspe.hhs.gov/system/files/pdf/137556/MFS-IP%20BaselineReport.pdf.

Lindquist, Christine, Danielle Steffey, Stephen Tueller, Rose Feinberg, Tasseli McKay, and Anupa Bir. 2016, December. *Predictors of Reentry Success*. Research Brief. Prepared for Office of the Assistant Secretary for Planning and Evaluation (ASPE), U.S. Department of Health and Human Services. https://aspe.hhs.gov/system/files/pdf/255886/reentrysuccessbrief.pdf.

Lindquist, Christine, Danielle Steffey, Stephen Tueller, Tasseli McKay, Megan Comfort, and Anupa Bir. 2018. "The Multi-Site Family Study on Incarceration, Partnering and Parenting: Program Impacts." *Journal of Offender Rehabilitation* 57 (2):115–143.

Lipsey, Mark W., Nana A. Landenberger, and Sandra J. Wilson. 2007. "Effects of Cognitive-Behavioral Programs for Criminal Offenders." *Campbell Systematic Reviews* 2007:6. doi: 10.4073/csr.2007.6.

Lopoo, Leonard, and Bruce Western. 2005. "Incarceration and the Formation and Stability of Marital Unions." *Journal of Marriage and Family* 67 (3):721–734.

Lundquist, Erika, JoAnn Hsueh, Amy Lowenstein, Kristen Faucetta, Daniel Gubits, Charles Michalopoulos, and Virginia Knox. 2014. *A Family-Strengthening Program for Low-Income Families: Final Impacts from the Supporting Healthy Marriage Evaluation*. OPRE Report 2014-09A. Washington, DC: Office of Planning, Research and Evaluation, Administration for Children and Families, U.S. Department of Health and Human Services. https://www.mdrc.org/sites/default/files/shm2013_30_month_impact_reportrev2.pdf.

MacDonald, D., and D. Kelly. 1980. *Follow-up Survey of Post-Release Criminal Behavior of Participants in Family Reunion Program*. Albany: Department of Correctional Services, State of New York.

Maldonado, Solangel. 2006. "Recidivism and Paternal Engagement." *Family Law Quarterly* 40 (2):191–211.

Markson, Lucy, Friedrich Lösel, Karen Souza, and Caroline Lanskey. 2015. "Male Prisoners' Family Relationships and Resilience in Resettlement." *Criminology & Criminal Justice* 15 (4):423–441. doi: 10.1177/1748895814566287.

Massoglia, Michael, Brianna Remster, and Ryan D. King. 2011. "Stigma or Separation? Understanding the Incarceration-Divorce Relationship." *Social Forces* 90 (1):133–155. doi: 10.1093/sf/90.1.133.

McKay, Tasseli, Megan Comfort, Christine Lindquist, and Anupa Bir. 2016. "If Family Matters: Supporting Family Relationships during Incarceration and Reentry." *Criminology & Public Policy* 15 (2).

McKay, Tasseli, Rose Feinberg, Justin Landwehr, Julianne Payne, Megan Comfort, Christine Lindquist, Erin Kennedy, and Anupa Bir. 2018. "Always Having Hope": Father-Child Relationships at Reentry." *Journal of Offender Rehabilitation* 57 (2):162–187.

McKay, Tasseli, Justin Landwehr, Christine Lindquist, Rose Feinberg, Megan Comfort, Julia Cohen, and Anupa Bir. 2018. "Intimate Partner Violence in Couples Navigating Incarceration and Reentry." *Journal of Offender Rehabilitation* 57 (5):273–293.

McKay, Tasseli, Christine Lindquist, Justin Landwehr, Derek Ramirez, and Anupa Bir. 2018. "Postprison Relationship Dissolution and Intimate Partner Violence: Separation-Instigated Violence or Violence-Instigated Separation?" *Journal of Offender Rehabilitation* 57 (5):294–310.

Medina, Krista Lisdahl, John Schafer, Paula K. Shear, and Tisha Gangopadhyay Armstrong. 2004. "Memory Ability Is Associated with Disagreement about the Most Recent Conflict in Polysubstance Abusing Couples." *Journal of Family Violence* 19 (6):379–389. doi: 10.1007/s10896-004-0683-8.

Mele, Christopher, and Teresa A. Miller, eds. 2005. *Civil Penalties, Social Consequences*. New York: Routledge.

Miller, Keva M. 2006. "The Impact of Parental Incarceration on Children: An Emerging Need for Effective Interventions." *Child and Adolescent Social Work Journal* 23 (4):472–486. doi: 10.1007/s10560-006-0065-6.

Mills, Alice, and Helen Codd. 2008. "Prisoners' Families and Offender Management: Mobilizing Social Capital." *Probation Journal* 55 (1):9–24. doi: 10.1177/0264550507085675.

Minnesota Department of Corrections. 2011. *The Effects of Prison Visitation on Offender Recidivism*. St. Paul: Minnesota Department of Corrections.

Moran, Dominique. 2013. "Between Outside and Inside? Prison Visiting Rooms as Liminal Carceral Spaces." *GeoJournal* 78 (2):339–351.

Mowen, Thomas J., and Christy A. Visher. 2016. "Changing the Ties That Bind." *Criminology & Public Policy* 15 (2):503–528.

Mumola, Christopher J. 2000. *Incarcerated Parents and Their Children*. BJS Special Report NCJ 182335. Washington, DC: Bureau of Justice Statistics, Office of Justice Programs, U.S. Department of Justice. https://www.bjs.gov/content/pub/pdf/iptc.pdf.

———. 2006. "Parents under Correctional Supervision: National Statistics." Paper presented at Children of Parents in the Criminal Justice System: Children at Risk, National Institute on Drug Abuse (NIDA) research meeting, Bethesda, Maryland.

Murray, Joseph, David P. Farrington, and Ivana Sekol. 2012. "Children's Antisocial Behavior, Mental Health, Drug Use, and Educational Performance after Parental Incarceration: A Systematic Review and Meta-Analysis." *Psychological Bulletin* 138 (2):175–210. doi: 10.1037/a0026407.

Naser, Rebecca L., and Christy A. Visher. 2006. "Family Members' Experiences with Incarceration and Reentry." *Western Criminology Review* 7 (2):20–31.

Nelson, Marta, Perry Dees, and Charlotte Allen. 2011. *The First Month Out: Post-Incarceration Experiences in New York City*. New York: Vera Institute of Justice. https://www.researchgate.net/publication/238341461_The_First_Month_Out_Post-Incarceration_Experiences_in_New_York_City.

Norman, Julie A. 1995. "Children of Prisoners in Foster Care." In *Children of Incarcerated Parents*, edited by Katherine Gabel and Denise Johnston, 124–134. New York: Lexington Books.

Nurse, Anne M. 2002. *Fatherhood Arrested: Parenting from within the Juvenile Justice System*. Nashville: Vanderbilt University Press.

———. 2004. "Returning to Strangers: Newly Paroled Young Fathers and Their Children." In *Imprisoning America: The Social Effects of Mass Incarceration*, edited by Mary Pattillo, David Weiman and Bruce Western, 76–96. New York: Russell Sage Foundation.

Oliver, William, and Creasie F. Hairston. 2008. "Intimate Partner Violence during the Transition from Prison to the Community: Perspectives of Incarcerated African American Men." *Journal of Aggression, Maltreatment, and Trauma* 16 (3):258–276. doi: 10.1080/10926770801925577.

Pager, Devah. 2007. *Marked: Race, Crime, and Finding Work in an Era of Mass Incarceration*. Chicago: University of Chicago Press.

Parke, Ross D., and K. Alison Clarke-Stewart. 2003. "The Effects of Parental Incarceration on Children: Perspectives, Promises, and Policies." In *Prisoners Once Removed: The Impact of Incarceration and Reentry on Children, Families, and Communities*, edited by Jeremy Travis and Michelle Waul, 189–232. Washington, DC: Urban Institute.

Pearson, Frank S., Douglas S. Lipton, Charles M. Cleland, and Dorline S. Yee. 2002. "The Effects of Behavioral/Cognitive-Behavioral Programs on Recidivism." *Crime & Delinquency* 48 (3):476–496. doi: 10.1177/001112870204800306.

Pearson, Jessica. 2004. "Building Debt While Doing Time: Child Support and Incarceration." *Judges' Journal* 43 (1):5–12.

Pettit, Becky. 2012. *Invisible Men: Mass Incarceration and the Myth of Black Progress*. New York: Russell Sage Foundation.

Pew Charitable Trusts. 2010. *Collateral Costs: Incarceration's Effect on Economic Mobility*. Washington, DC: Pew Charitable Trusts. https://www.pewtrusts.org/~/media/legacy/uploadedfiles/pcs_assets/2010/collateralcosts1pdf.pdf.

Pleck, Joseph H., and Sandra L. Hofferth. 2008. "Mother Involvement as an Influence on Father Involvement with Early Adolescents." *Fathering* 6 (3):267–286. doi: 10.3149/fth.0603.267.

Poehlmann, Julie. 2005. "Incarcerated Mothers' Contact with Children, Perceived Family Relationships, and Depressive Symptoms." *Journal of Family Psychology* 19 (3):350–357. doi: 10.1037/0893-3200.19.3.350.

Poehlmann, Julie, Danielle Dallaire, Ann Booker Loper, and Leslie D. Shear. 2010. "Children's Contact with Their Incarcerated Parents: Research Findings and Recommendations." *American Psychologist* 65 (6):575–598.

Poortman, A. R. (2018). "Postdivorce Parent-Child Contact and Child Wellbeing: The Importance of Predivorce Parental Involvement." *Journal of Marriage and Family* 80 (3): 671–683. https://doi.org/10.1111/jomf.12474.

Pruitt Walker, Sheri. 2011. "The Effects of the Incarceration of Fathers on the Health and Wellbeing of Mothers and Children." PhD diss., University of Maryland.

Rebecca Project for Human Rights. 2010. *Mothers Behind Bars: A State-by-State Report Care and Analysis of Federal Policies on Conditions of Confinement for Pregnant and Parenting Women and the Effect on Their Children*. Washington, DC: National Women's Law Center. https://www.nwlc.org/sites/default/files/pdfs/mothersbehindbars2010.pdf.

Reichenheim, Michael E., Leite Moraes, Claudia, Souza Lopes, Claudia, and Gustavo Lobato. 2014. "The Role of Intimate Partner Violence and Other Health-Related Social Factors on Postpartum Common Mental Disorders: A Survey-Based Structural Equation Modeling Analysis." *BMC Public Health* 14 (1):427.

Renner, Lynette M., and Kristen S. Slack. 2006. "Intimate Partner Violence and Child Maltreatment: Understanding Intra- and Intergenerational Connections." *Child Abuse & Neglect* 30 (6):599–617. doi: 10.1016/j.chiabu.2005.12.005.

Renzetti, Claire M. 2009. *Economic Stress and Domestic Violence*. CRVAW Faculty Research Reports and Papers. Lexington: Center for Research on Violence Against Women, University of Kentucky UKnowledge. http://uknowledge.uky.edu/cgi/viewcontent.cgi?article=1000&context=crvaw_reports.

Rios, Victor M. 2011. *Punished: Policing the Lives of Black and Latino Boys*. New York: NYU Press.

Roberts, Dorothy. 2002. *Shattered Bonds: The Color of Child Welfare*. New York: Civitas Books.

Robertson, Kirsten, and Tamar Murachver. 2007. "Correlates of Partner Violence for Incarcerated Women and Men." *Journal of Interpersonal Violence* 22 (5):639–655. doi: 10.1177/0886260506298835.

Rodriguez, Nino. 2016. *If I Had Money: Black Fathers and Children, Child Support Debt, and Economic Insecurity in Mississippi*. Madison, WI: Center for Family Policy and Practice. https://cffpp.org/our_publication/if-i-had-money-black-fathers-and-children-child-support-debt-and-economic-security-in-mississippi/.

Rose, Dina R., and Todd R. Clear. 2003. "Incarceration, Reentry, and Social Capital: Social Networks in the Balance." In *Prisoners Once Removed: The Impact of Incarceration and Reentry on Children, Families, and Communities*, edited by Jeremy Travis and Michelle Waul, 313–341. Washington, DC: Urban Institute Press.

Roy, Kevin M., and Omari L. Dyson. 2005. "Gatekeeping in Context: Babymama Drama and the Involvement of Incarcerated Fathers." *Fathering* 3 (3):289–311.

Schafer, John, Raul Caetano, and Catherine L. Clark. 2002. "Agreement about Violence in U.S. Couples." *Journal of Interpersonal Violence* 17 (4):457–470. doi: 10.1177/0886260502017004007.

Schafer, John, Raul Caetano, and Carol B. Cunradi. 2004. "A Path Model of Risk Factors for Intimate Partner Violence among Couples in the United States." *Journal of Interpersonal Violence* 19 (2):127–142.

Schluter, Philip J., Max W. Abbott, and Maria E. Bellringer. 2008. "Problem Gambling Related to Intimate Partner Violence: Findings from the Pacific Islands Families Study." *International Gambling Studies* 8 (1):49–61. doi: 10.1080/14459790701870134.

Schnittker, Jason. 2014. "The Psychological Dimensions and the Social Consequences of Incarceration." *Annals of the American Academy of Political and Social Science* 651 (1):122–138.

Schwartz-Soicher, Ofira, Amanda Geller, and Irwin Garfinkel. 2011. "The Effect of Paternal Incarceration on Material Hardship." *Social Service Review* 85 (3):447–473.

Scott, Marvin B., and Stanford M. Lyman. 1968. "Accounts." *American Sociological Review* 33 (1):46–62. doi: 10.2307/2092239.

Seltzer, Judith A. 1991. "Relationships between Fathers and Children Who Live Apart: The Father's Role after Separation." *Journal of Marriage and the Family* 53 (1):79–101. doi: 10.2307/353135.

Sered, Susan Starr, and Maureen Norton-Hawk. 2014. *Can't Catch a Break: Gender, Jail, Drugs, and the Limits of Personal Responsibility.* Berkeley: University of California Press.

Shapiro, Carol, and Meryl Schwartz. 2001. "Coming Home: Building on Family Connections." *Corrections Management Quarterly* 5 (3):52–61.

Sharpe, Gilly. 2015. "Precarious Identities: 'Young' Motherhood, Desistance and Stigma." *Criminology & Criminal Justice* 15 (4):407–422.

Shearer, Cindy L., Ann C. Crouter, and Susan M. McHale. 2005. "Parents' Perceptions of Changes in Mother-Child and Father-Child Relationships During Adolescence." *Journal of Adolescent Research* 20 (6):662–684. doi: 10.1177/0743558405275086.

Shollenberger, Tracey L. 2009. *When Relatives Return: Interviews with Family Members of Returning Prisoners in Houston, Texas.* Washington, DC: Justice Policy Center, Urban Institute. https://www.urban.org/research/publication/when-relatives-return-interviews-family-members-returning-prisoners-houston-texas.

Shortt, Joann Wu, Deborah M. Capaldi, Hyoun K. Kim, and Lee D. Owen. 2006. "Relationship Separation for Young, at-Risk Couples: Prediction from Dyadic Aggression." *Journal of Family Psychology* 20 (4):624. doi: 10.1037/0893-3200.20.4.624.

Signorelli, Maria Salvina, Eleonora Arcidiacono, Giuseppina Musumeci, Santo Di Nuovo, and Eugenio Aguglia. 2014. "Detecting Domestic Violence: Italian Validation of Revised Conflict Tactics Scale (CTS-2)." *Journal of Family Violence* 29 (4):361–369.

Simons, Ronald L., and Ashley B. Barr. 2014. "Shifting Perspectives: Cognitive Changes Mediate the Impact of Romantic Relationships on Desistance from Crime." *Justice Quarterly* 31 (5):793–821. doi: 10.1080/07418825.2012.704388.

Slep, Amy M. Smith, Heather M. Foran, Richard E. Heyman, and Jeffery D. Snarr. 2010. "Unique Risk and Protective Factors for Partner Aggression in a Large-Scale Air Force Survey." *Journal of Community Health* 35 (4):375–383. doi: 10.1007/s10900-010-9264-3.

Smith, Peter Scharff. 2014. *When the Innocent Are Punished: The Children of Imprisoned Parents.* Palgrave Studies in Prisons and Penology, edited by Ben Crewe, Yvonne Jewkes and Thomas Ugelvik. Hampshire, UK: Palgrave Macmillan.

Smith, Sandra S. 2007. *Lone Pursuit: Distrust and Defensive Individualism among the Black Poor.* New York: Russell Sage Foundation.

Søgaard, Thomas Friis, Torsten Kolind, Birgitte Thylstrup, and Ross Deuchar. 2016. "Desistance and the Micro-Narrative Construction of Reformed Masculinities in a Danish Rehabilitation Centre." *Criminology & Criminal Justice* 16 (1):99–118.

Solomon, Amy L., Kelly D. Johnson, Jeremy Travis, and Elizabeth C. McBride. 2004. *From Prison to Work: The Employment Dimensions of Prisoner Reentry*. Research Report. Washington, DC: Justice Policy Center, Urban Institute. https://www.urban.org/sites/default/files/publication/58126/411097-From-Prison-to-Work.PDF.

Song, Hyojong, Youngki Woo, Heeuk D. Lee, and John K. Cochran. 2018. "The Dynamics of Intra-Family Relationships During Incarceration and the Implications for Children of Incarcerated Parents." *International Journal of Offender Therapy and Comparative Criminology* 62 (12):3775–3796. doi: 10.1177/0306624X18755481.

Spangaro, Jo, Jane Koziol-McLain, Anthony Zwi, Alison Rutherford, Mary-Anne Frail, and Jennifer Ruane. 2016. "Deciding to Tell: Qualitative Configurational Analysis of Decisions to Disclose Experience of Intimate Partner Violence in Antenatal Care." *Social Science & Medicine* 154:45–53. doi: 10.1016/j.socscimed.2016.02.032.

Steinberg, Laurence. 2001. "We Know Some Things: Parent–Adolescent Relationships in Retrospect and Prospect." *Journal of Research on Adolescence* 11 (1):1–19. doi: 10.1111/1532-7795.00001.

Stoll, Michael A., and Shawn D. Bushway. 2008. "The Effect of Criminal Background Checks on Hiring Ex-Offenders." *Criminology & Public Policy* 7 (3):371–404.

Straus, Murray A., and Emily M. Douglas. 2004. "A Short Form of the Revised Conflict Tactics Scales, and Typologies for Severity and Mutuality." *Violence and Victims* 19 (5): 507–520. doi:10.1891/vivi.19.5.507.63686.

Straus, Murray A., Sherry L. Hamby, Sue Boney-McCoy, and David B. Sugarman. 1996. "The Revised Conflict Tactics Scales (CTS2): Development and Preliminary Psychometric Data." *Journal of Family Issues* 17 (3):283–316. doi: 10.1177/019251396017003001.

Sugie, Naomi F. 2012. "Punishment and Welfare: Paternal Incarceration and Families' Receipt of Public Assistance." *Social Forces* 90 (4):1403–1427. doi: 10.1093/sf/sos055.

Swann, Christopher, and Michelle Sheran Sylvester. 2006. "The Foster Care Crisis: What Caused Caseloads to Grow?" *Demography* 43 (2):309–335.

Taanila, Anja, Elina Laitinen, Irma Moilanen, and Marjo-Ritta Jarvelin. 2004. "Effects of Family Interaction on the Child's Behavior in Single-Parent or Reconstructed Families." *Family Process* 41 (4):693–708. doi: 10.1111/j.1545-5300.2002.00693.x.

Taft, Casey T., Thema Bryant-Davis, Halley E. Woodward, Shaquita Tillman, and Sandra E. Torres. 2009. "Intimate Partner Violence against African American Women: An Examination of the Socio-Cultural Context." *Aggression and Violent Behavior* 14 (1):50–58.

Tonry, Michael. 2011. *Punishing Race: A Continuing American Dilemma*. New York: Oxford University Press.

Troy, Victoria, Kerri E. McPherson, Carol Emslie, and Elizabeth Gilchrist. 2018. "The Feasibility, Appropriateness, Meaningfulness, and Effectiveness of Parenting and Family Support Programs Delivered in the Criminal Justice System: A Systematic Review." *Journal of Child and Family Studies* 27 (6):1732–1747. doi: 10.1007/s10826-018-1034-3.

Turney, Kristin. 2014. "Stress Proliferation across Generations? Examining the Relationship between Parental Incarceration and Childhood Health." *Journal of Health and Social Behavior* 55 (3):302–319. doi: 10.1177/0022146514544173.

———. 2015. "Hopelessly Devoted? Relationship Quality during and after Incarceration." *Journal of Marriage and Family* 77 (2):480–495. doi: 10.1111/jomf.12174.

Turney, Kristin, Christopher Wildeman, and Jason Schnittker. 2012. "As Fathers and Felons: Explaining the Effects of Current and Recent Incarceration on Major Depression." *Journal of Health and Social Behavior* 53:465–481.

Visher, Christy A. 2011. "Incarcerated Fathers." *Criminal Justice Policy Review* 24 (1):9–26. doi: 10.1177/0887403411418105.

Visher, Christy A., Nicholas W. Bakken, and Whitney D. Gunter. 2013. "Fatherhood, Community Reintegration, and Successful Outcomes." *Journal of Offender Rehabilitation* 52 (7):451–469.

Visher, Christy A., and Shannon M.E. Courtney. 2007. *One Year Out: Experiences of Prisoners Returning to Cleveland*. Returning Home Policy Brief. Washington, DC: Urban Institute. https://www.urban.org/sites/default/files/publication/43021/311445-One-Year-Out-Experiences-of-Prisoners-Returning-to-Cleveland.PDF.

Visher, Christy A., Sara A. Debus-Sherrill, and Jennifer Yahner. 2011. "Employment after Prison: A Longitudinal Study of Former Prisoners." *Justice Quarterly* 28 (5):698–718.

Visher, Christy A., Vera Kachnowski, Nancy G. La Vigne, and Jeremy Travis. 2004. *Baltimore Prisoners' Experiences Returning Home.* Washington, DC: Urban Institute. http://webarchive.urban.org/UploadedPDF/310946_Baltimore-Prisoners.pdf.

Visher, Christy A., and Jeremy Travis. 2003. "Transitions from Prison to Community: Understanding Individual Pathways." *Annual Review of Sociology* 29:89–113.

Wadsworth, Martha E., and Bruce E. Compas. 2002. "Coping with Family Conflict and Economic Strain: The Adolescent Perspective." *Journal of Research on Adolescence* 12 (2):243–274.

Wakefield, Sara, Hedwig Lee, and Christopher Wildeman. 2016. "Tough on Crime, Tough on Families? Criminal Justice and Family Life in America." *Annals of the American Academy of Political and Social Science* 665 (1): 8–21.

Wakefield, Sara, and Christopher Wildeman. 2011. "Mass Imprisonment and Racial Disparities in Childhood Behavioral Problems." *Criminology & Public Policy* 10 (3):793–817.

———. 2013. *Children of the Prison Boom: Mass Incarceration and the Future of American Inequality.* New York: Oxford University Press.

Western, Bruce. 2006. *Punishment and Inequality in America.* New York: Russell Sage Foundation.

Western, Bruce, Jeffrey R. Kling, and David F. Weiman. 2001. "The Labor Market Consequences of Incarceration." *Crime & Delinquency* 47 (3):410–427.

Western, Bruce, and Becky Pettit. 2010. "Incarceration and Social Inequality." *Daedalus: The Journal of the American Academy of Arts & Sciences* 139 (3):8–19.

White, Helene Raskin, and Ping-Hsin Chen. 2002. "Problem Drinking and Intimate Partner Violence." *Journal of Studies on Alcohol* 63 (2):205–214.

White, Robert J., Edward W. Gondolf, Donald U. Robertson, Beverly J. Goodwin, and L. Eduardo Caraveo. 2002. "Extent and Characteristics of Woman Batterers among Federal Inmates." *International Journal of Offender Therapy and Comparative Criminology* 46 (4):412–426. doi: 10.1177/0306624X02464004.

Whittaker, Tiffany A., S. Natasha Beretvas, and Toni Falbo. 2014. "Dyadic Curve-of-Factors Model: An Introduction and Illustration of a Model for Longitudinal Nonexchangeable Dyadic Data." *Structural Equation Modeling* 21 (2):303–317. doi: 10.1080/10705511.2014.882695.

Wildeman, Christopher. 2009. "Paternal Imprisonment, the Prison Boom, and the Concentration of Childhood Disadvantage." *Demography* 46:265–280.

———. 2012. "Imprisonment and Infant Mortality." *Social Problems* 59 (2):228–257.

———. 2014. "Parental Incarceration, Child Homelessness, and the Invisible Consequences of Mass Imprisonment." *Annals of the American Academy of Political and Social Science* 651 (1):74–96. doi: 10.1177/0002716213502921.

Wildeman, Christopher, Anna R. Haskins, and Julie Poehlmann-Tynan, eds. 2017. *When Parents Are Incarcerated: Interdisciplinary Research and Interventions to Support Children.* Washington, DC: American Psychological Association.

Wildeman, Christopher, and Christopher Muller. 2012. "Mass Imprisonment and Inequality in Health and Family Life." *Annual Review of Law and Social Science* 8:11–30.

Wildeman, Christopher, Jason Schnittker, and Kristin Turney. 2012. "Despair by Association? The Mental Health of Mothers with Children by Recently Incarcerated Fathers." *American Sociological Review* 77 (2):216–243.

Wildeman, Christopher, and Bruce Western. 2010. "Incarceration in Fragile Families." *Future of Children* 20 (2):157–177.

Wilson, David B., Leana A. Bouffard, and Doris L. MacKenzie. 2005. "A Quantitative Review of Structured, Group-Oriented, Cognitive-Behavioral Programs for Offenders." *Criminal Justice and Behavior* 32 (2):172–204. doi: 10.1177/0093854804272889.

Women's Prison Association. 2009. *Mothers, Infants and Imprisonment: A National Look at Prison Nurseries and Community-Based Alternatives.* New York: Institute on Women and Criminal Justice. https://www.wpaonline.org/wpaassets/Mothers_Infants_and_Imprisonment_2009.pdf.

Wood, Robert G., Quinn Moore, Andrew Clarkwest, Alexandra Killewald, and Shannon Monahan. 2012. *The Long-Term Effects of Building Strong Families: A Relationship Skills Education Program for Unmarried Parents.* OPRE Report 2012-28A. Washington, DC: Office of Planning, Research and Evaluation, Administration for Children and Families, U.S. Department of Health and Human Services. https://www.acf.hhs.gov/sites/default/files/opre/bsf_36_mo_impact_report.pdf.

Yeung, W. Jean, John F. Sandberg, Pamela E. Davis-Kean, and Sandra L. Hofferth. 2001. "Children's Time with Fathers in Intact Families." *Journal of Marriage and Family* 63 (1):136–154. doi: 10.1111/j.1741-3737.2001.00136.x.

Zlotnick, Caron, Dawn M. Johnson, and Robert Kohn. 2006. "Intimate Partner Violence and Long-Term Psychosocial Functioning in a National Sample of American Women." *Journal of Interpersonal Violence* 21 (2):262–75. doi: 10.1177/0886260505282564.

INDEX

Page references including *box*, *fig.*, and *table* refer to boxes, figures, and tables, respectively.

abusive couple relationship. *See* intimate partner violence
Administration for Children and Families (ACF), 16–17, 141
age of incarcerated men, and recidivism, 96, 97
ATLAS.ti database, 25, 154, 161
audio computer-assisted self-interviewing technique, 145, 161

Building Strong Families, 16, 143
Bureau of Justice Statistics, 7–8, 92, 135

Center for Urban Families, 42
children: and couple relationship longevity, post-imprisonment, 56; father's coresidence with, post-incarceration, 22–31, 25 *fig*, 26 *fig*, 30 *fig*; focal children, defined, 17, 18, 41, 144–45; in foster care system, 6, 11, 89, 156; psychosocial development of, 12. *See also* father-child relationship
Columbia University, 92–93

Community Healthy Marriage Initiative, 16, 143
confidentiality about intimate partner violence: study procedures, 67–68 *box*; survivors' reluctance to report violence, 64–69, 82–84, 86–87
contact during incarceration. *See* visitation/communication during incarceration
controlling behavior, defined, 68 *box*
Council on Crime and Justice (Minnesota), 142
couple relationship, 44–62; and coresidence in intimate relationships, 48–50, 49 *fig.*, 90; evaluating individuals vs. couples for, 111–12; exclusivity during and after imprisonment, 52–55, 53 *fig.*; future research on, 57–61; and impact of reentry on family life, 44–45, 62; legal marriage among incarcerated men vs. general population, 47; measuring relationship behaviors, 45–47;

couple relationship *(continued)*
  methodology, technical notes, 159–62, 160 *table;* overview, 14; predictors of staying together, 55–57, 163–64 *table;* reentry success and positive family functioning, 93–94, 96–101, 97 *fig.,* 98–99 *table;* relationship happiness in, 48, 49 *fig.,* 58; and sample of study participants, 61–62; social science research approach to, 132–33; status/quality before, during, and after imprisonment, 47–52, 48 *fig.,* 49 *fig. See also* family-strengthening programs; intimate partner violence
criminal activity, avoidance of. *See* desistance

demographic information. *See* Multi-site Family Study on Incarceration, Parenting, and Partnering
desistance: couple relationship and effect on, 46; and postrelease involvement with children, 32, 36; and reentry success, 92, 94, 105
domestic violence. *See* intimate partner violence

economic hardship: and intimate partner violence, 70–71; loss of income to family, during incarceration, 8–9; and relationship longevity, post-imprisonment, 56; and unpaid child support, 6–7; of visitation/communication during incarceration, 9–10
education level, and reentry success, 97, 103–6
employment: and couple relationship, 51–52; finding, for reentry success, 92–93, 96–101, 97 *fig.,* 98–99 *table*
exclusivity, of couple relationship, 52–55, 53 *fig.,* 58

family-strengthening programs, 107–28; "point-in-time" impact of programming, 112, 120, 126; bonding score differences between program sites, 117–19, 118 *fig.;* evaluation issues of, 110–12; example, 108–9; future policy and practice implications, 123–28; methodology, technical notes, 172–83, 174–77 *tables,* 180–82 *tables;* mixed-methods approach, for individual- and couple-level analyses, 112–20, 114 *fig.,* 115 *fig.,* 118 *fig.;* mixed-methods approach, value of, 107–8, 125–28, 133; overview, 15; qualitative data for understanding quantitative data, 120–23, 127; social science research approach to, 133
father-child relationship, 20–43; compartmentalization of family and incarceration, 1–4; future research about, 38–43; and high-quality vs. high frequency contact, 23–24; hopefulness for father derived from, 20–22, 33–35, 37–38, 40–43; improving research about reentry and, 35–38; methodology, technical notes, 150–58, 152 *table,* 153 *fig.,* 155–56 *table,* 158 *table;* mother's role in, 7, 22, 26–31, 37; overview, 14; parenting and reentry success, 31–35; parenting education for, 39–40; post-incarceration coresidence with children, 22–31, 25 *fig.,* 26 *fig.,* 30 *fig.;* reentry success and positive family functioning, 93–94, 96–101, 97 *fig.,* 98–99 *table,* 103–4; social science research approach to, 132; and unpaid child support, 6–7
Federal Communications Commission (FCC), on telephone rates from prisons, 10, 39, 42
fidelity. *See* exclusivity, of couple relationship
financial support by fathers: and father's coresidence with children,

post-incarceration, 22–31, 25 *fig.*, 26 *fig.*; and reentry success, 94, 96–101, 97 *fig.*, 98–99 *table*; and unpaid child support, 6–7
foster care system, 6, 11, 89, 156
Fragile Families and Child Wellbeing study, 3

gender differences, within-couple: abuse reporting discrepancies, 77–84, 111–12, 119; bonding score differences between family-strengthening programs, 117–19, 118 *fig.*; exclusivity in couple relationship, 53–54; in family-strengthening programs, 120–23, 126–27

Healthy Marriage and Responsible Fatherhood initiative (Administration for Children and Families), 16–17
healthy-relationship retreats. *See* family-strengthening programs

incarcerated women: children of, 11; and exclusivity in couple relationship, 53–54; postrelease parenting involvement and desistance, 32, 36; research on, 5
incarceration statistics: annual reentry from prison and jail, 63; and communities of color, 8; of parents and children of parents, 2–3, 11–12; reincarceration as measure of reentry success, 91–92, 95–97, 101–2. *See also* Multi-site Family Study on Incarceration, Parenting, and Partnering
Indiana Department of Correction (family-strengthening program): overview of program, 15, 107–9, 113; program design and participant selection, 124–25; qualitative data about contextual aspects, 121–23, 127; sample characteristics, 142–43;
treatment effects, 114–20, 114 *fig*. *See also* family-strengthening programs
instrumentation process, overview, 143–44
Interuniversity Consortium for Political and Social Research (ICPSR), 141–42
interviewing techniques: audio computer-assisted self-interviewing technique, 145, 161; confidentiality issues, 64–69, 67–68 *box*, 82–84, 86–87; qualitative research process, 146–47
intimate partner violence, 63–87; abuse before vs. after incarceration, 73–74, 74 *fig.*; abuse prevention programming before impending incarceration, 85; comparing abuse reports from both partners, 74–77; and exclusion criteria, 71n3; future research for, 84–87; interviewing techniques and confidentiality procedures, 67–68 *box*; methodology, technical notes, 162–67, 163–65 *tables*; overview, 14; and partners/spouses as "front line" of reentry, 63; prevalence of abuse, 69–72, 72 *fig*, 84; risk factors for abuse victimization or perpetration, 70; survivors' reluctance to report violence, 64–69, 82–84; within-couple abuse reporting discrepancies, 77–84, 111–12, 119. *See also* family-strengthening programs

justice-involved men. *See* couple relationship; family-strengthening programs; father-child relationship; intimate partner violence; reentry success
justice-involved women. *See* incarcerated women

mental health: children's psychosocial development, 12; and reentry success, 10–12, 100

methodology. *See* Multi-site Family Study on Incarceration, Parenting, and Partnering
Multi-site Evaluation of the Serious and Violent Offender Reentry Initiative, 93, 143
Multi-site Family Study on Incarceration, Parenting, and Partnering, 141–83; couple relationship, technical notes, 159–62, 160 *table*; data availability to public, 135; data collection for, 17–19, 18 *fig.*, 144–45; dataset features, 141–42; family-strengthening programs, technical notes, 172–83, 174–77 *tables*, 180–82 *tables*; father-child relationship, technical notes, 150–58, 152 *table*, 153 *fig.*, 155–56 *table*, 158 *table*; focal children, defined, 17, 18, 41, 144–45; follow-up approach and timing, 146–47; on impact of reentry on family life, 44–45, 62; incentives for participants, 145, 145n2; intimate partner violence, technical notes, 162–67, 163–65 *tables*; as multidimensional approach, 12–14, 130–31; origin of, 16–17; quantitative interviews, development and content of, 143–44; reentry success, technical notes, 167–72, 168 *table*, 170–71 *table*; response rates and sample size of, 4, 17–18, 61–62, 147–50, 149 *table*; sample characteristics, 142–43; sponsors of, 16–17, 141; weighted means and latent growth curve modeling (LGM), compared, 112–20, 114 *fig*, 115 *fig*, 118 *fig*, 123, 125–26, 172–83, 180–82 *tables*. *See also* couple relationship; family-strengthening programs; father-child relationship; intimate partner violence; reentry success

National Center on Addiction and Substance Abuse, Columbia University, 92–93

National Corrections Reporting Program, 135
National Institute of Justice, 142
National Intimate Partner and Sexual Violence Survey, 69n2
National Longitudinal Study of Adolescent to Adult Health, 3
New Jersey Department of Corrections (family-strengthening program): overview of program, 107, 113; sample characteristics, 142–43; treatment effects, 114 *fig*. *See also* family-strengthening programs

Office for Human Research Protections (OHRP, U.S. Department of Health and Human Services), 147n3
Osborne Association (New York, family-strengthening program): overview of program, 107, 113; sample characteristics, 142–43; treatment effects, 114 *fig.*

parenting. *See* father-child relationship
partners of incarcerated men. *See* couple relationship; family-strengthening programs; intimate partner violence
physical health, and reentry success, 100, 103
physical violence, defined, 68 *box*, 69n2
poverty. *See* economic hardship
probation/parole monitoring: intimate partner violence and worries of, 83; reentry success and support services during, 91. *See also* support services

qualitative research: on family-strengthening programs, 120–23, 127; on father-child relationship, 36–38, 41–43; for measuring couple relationship behaviors, 45–47, 60–61; qualitative interview process, 146–47. *See also* Multi-site Family Study on Incarceration, Parenting, and Partnering

race, and predictors of reentry success, 100

recidivism, avoiding, 91–92, 95–97, 101–2. *See also* reentry success

reentry success, 88–106; avoiding recidivism as measure of success, 91–92, 95–97, 101–2; case management needs, 84–85; coresidence with children, post-incarceration, 22–31, 25 *fig.*, 26 *fig.*, 30 *fig.*; defining "success," 91–95; example of challenges, 89–91; future research for, 101–6; intimate partner violence, preincarceration vs. postincarceration, 78; methodology, technical notes, 167–72, 168 *table*, 170–71 *table*; multidimensional approach, for measuring, 95–101, 97 *fig.*, 98–99 *table*; multidimensional approach, value of, 88–89, 106, 136; overview, 15; partners/spouses as "front line" of reentry, 63; predictors of, 158 *table*; social science research approach to, 132. *See also* desistance; family-strengthening programs

relationship dissolution: and intimate partner violence, 79–82; predictors of staying together, 55–57; prevalence of, due to incarceration, 9. *See also* couple relationship; family-strengthening programs

reporting discrepancy, about abuse: disagreement between partners about abuse, 74–78; and relationship dissolution, 79–82; and reports of abstinence from abuse, 78–79; and willingness to disclose abuse, 82–84

research methods. *See* Multi-site Family Study on Incarceration, Parenting, and Partnering

Revised Conflict Tactics Scale (CTS2), 67–68 *box*

RIDGE Project (Ohio, family-strengthening program): overview of program, 107, 113; sample characteristics, 142–43; treatment effects, 114 *fig. See also* family-strengthening programs

romantic relationship. *See* couple relationship; family-strengthening programs

RTI International, 141, 145, 147

separation-instigated violence, 79–82

skills training. *See* family-strengthening programs

social science of incarceration and family, 129–39; complex needs of, 137–39; federal data sources for, 135–36; future of quantitative research, 137; on individual level, 132–33; mixed-methods approach, value of, 107–8, 125–28, 133; Multi-site Family Study, as interagency collaboration, 130–31; Multi-site Family Study, data availability of, 135; multidimensional research on family and criminal behavior, 1–4, 6–7, 129–30; online tools for, 133–34; overview, 15–16; on systems level, 131–32. *See also* Multi-site Family Study on Incarceration, Parenting, and Partnering

spouses of incarcerated men. *See* couple relationship; family-strengthening programs; intimate partner violence

state prisons: departments of corrections (DOC) data, 169; National Corrections Reporting Program on, 135; reincarceration statistics, 95–96, 101–2. *See also* Indiana Department of Correction (family-strengthening program); New Jersey Department of Corrections (family-strengthening program) substance abuse: and family-strengthening program, 122; postrelease parenting involvement and desistance, 32, 36; and reentry success, 10, 92–93, 96–101, 97 *fig.*, 98–99 *table*, 105–6

Supporting Healthy Marriage, 16, 143

support services: and couple relationship, 59; and policy for supporting reentering men's parenting, 38–43; for reentry success, 88, 91, 102–6; safety needs and intimate partner violence, 84–85. *See also* family-strengthening programs

survey instrument development, overview, 143–44

trust issues: distrust of justice system, 70; of fathers, by mothers of their children, 29; of fathers, by their children, 27–28. *See also* family-strengthening programs

U.S. Census Bureau, 135

U.S. Department of Health and Human Services, 17, 141, 147n3

visitation/communication during incarceration: and couple relationship post-imprisonment, 50–51, 56, 59; distance and cost of, 9–10; and father-child relationship, post-incarceration, 30, 35–36, 39; FCC on telephone rates from prisons, 10, 39, 42; and intimate partner violence, 70–71; for reentry success, 88, 89, 100, 104; and support for maintaining family ties, 110–11. *See also* family-strengthening programs

women partners of incarcerated men. *See* couple relationship; family-strengthening programs; intimate partner violence

women, incarcerated. *See* incarcerated women

www.ingramcontent.com/pod-product-compliance
Lightning Source LLC
Chambersburg PA
CBHW020815230426
43666CB00007B/1014